ANDREW DEMPSTER has over 4(mountains. He is nearing com_ Munros and has climbed all th has written the first guidebook t ....on, he has compiled a list of Hughs – Scott... hills below 2,000 feet and has published the first volume of a guide to these summits. He has also walked and climbed in such varied locations as the Alps, the Pyrenees, the Himalaya, Africa, Iceland, Greenland and the USA. He is a retired mathematics teacher, currently living in rural Perthshire with his wife, Heather.

By the same author:

Classic Mountain Scrambles in Scotland, Mainstream 1992; new edition Luath Press 2016

The Munro Phenomenon, Mainstream 1995

The Grahams: A Guide to Scotland's 2,000ft Peaks, Mainstream 1997

Skye 360, Walking the Coastline of Skye, Luath Press 2003

100 Classic Coastal Walks in Scotland, Mainstream 2011

The Hughs: The Best Wee Hills Under 2,000ft, Volume 1, Luath Press 2015

The Munros

A History

ANDREW DEMPSTER

Luath Press Limited

EDINBURGH

www.luath.co.uk

First published 2021

ISBN: 978-1-910022-58-0

Printed and bound by
Clays Ltd., Bungay

Typeset in 10.5 point Sabon by
Main Point Books, Edinburgh

Contents

Introduction   9

Munro Timeline   13

Chapter 1   Veterans and Visionaries   19

            Early map-makers William Roy and
            Thomas Colby; early tourists and baggers;
            early lists: Matthew Forster Heddle
            and Sir Hugh Munro

Chapter 2   Munroist Ministers   54

            The Rev AE Robertson and the Rev ARG Burn

Chapter 3   Fire And Freedom   84

            Early Munroists, the 1930s working-class
            outdoor revolution, the Craigallion fire

Chapter 4   Topography and Topology   94

            Formation of the Scottish mountains;
            Munros and Tops analysis with heights

Chapter 5   Boomers and Baggers   118

            The post-war revolution, influences, books,
            media, magazines

Chapter 6   Rounds and Records   138

            Continuous Munro rounds, fell-running,
            other records

Chapter 7   The Why, the Wry and the Whimsical   180

            Reasons, risks, musings

Chapter 8   Below and Beyond   204

            Post-Munro activities, hill lists,
            The Munro Society

Chapter 9   Memorable Munros   232

            Profiles of some memorable Munros

Chapter 10 Wildness and Well-Being   273

            Conservation, land use, access, rewilding,
            well-being

Bibliography   293
Acknowledgements   295
Endnotes   296

Dedicated to all Munro baggers, past, present and future.

Introduction

WHEN MY BOOK *The Munro Phenomenon* (the natural precursor to this book) was published by Mainstream in 1995, over a thousand people were known to have climbed all 282 Munros. Today the tally is around 7,000, and rising rapidly. It is reckoned that at least 200 people a year 'compleat' a full round of the Munros.

The Munro Phenomenon was essentially a history of 'Munro-bagging' and an analysis of the rationale behind the growing popularity of this addictive pursuit. In the 25-plus years since the book's release, advancing years, hindsight, experience and wisdom have led me to re-evaluate the book's content, aims and conclusions. In addition, the formation of The Munro Society in 2002, the passing of the centenary of Sir Hugh Munro's death in 2019 and the COVID-19 hiatus of 2020 and beyond have given cause to stop and reflect. Several people have indeed commented that *The Munro Phenomenon* is long due a reprint – updated to include more modern trends, new records and different viewpoints.

This book attempts to tackle this challenge, but rather than simply reproduce *The Munro Phenomenon* with additional updated material, I have effectively started from scratch and written a book which I believe to be more relevant and focused on the issues and influences of today. Of course, history never changes... or does it? The name Matthew Heddle may not ring any bells, but it turns out that this 19th century 'mineralogist and mountaineer' was a key player in the subsequent creation of Hugh Munro's famous Tables. Indeed, following Heddle's death, Hugh Munro himself paid tribute to him, writing that

'Professor Heddle had climbed far more Scottish mountains than any man who has yet lived'. Quite how this influential character has fallen through the net is a mystery, but this book has attempted to raise Heddle from the trough of obscurity and restore his reputation to its rightful place in Munro history. (See chapter 1: Veterans and Visionaries.)

Moving to the present day, one phenomenal Munro exploit in 2020 deserves a mention in this introduction: namely, Donnie Campbell's staggering accomplishment of a complete round of the Munros in just under 32 days. In *The Munro Phenomenon*, I commented that doing 'the Munros in a month' could be considered to have 'ultimate challenge' status – now, a super-charged fell-runner has come within a hair's breadth of realising this dizzying goal. Munro legend Hamish Brown (the first person to perform a continuous round of the Munros) once commented that

> when someone does the Munros in a month, I will
> shake my head, and his hand.[1]

I still shake my head in disbelief at Donnie's incredible feat. You can read more about it in chapter 6: Rounds and Records.

One other 'undone' challenge posed in *The Munro Phenomenon* was a continuous round of all the Munros and Tops. The 'Tops' are an additional class of subsidiary summits which are not classified as full Munros, despite being over 3,000 feet (see chapter 4). Only a year after the release of the book, celebrated long-distance walker and backpacker Chris Townsend took up the challenge with relish, compleating the round in 118 days – again, see chapter 6 for more details.

On reading the last two paragraphs, some could be forgiven for thinking that Munros are only for super-fit, driven, highly motivated individuals. Think again, however. The vast majority of the seven thousand 'compleaters' mentioned at the start of this introduction are just ordinary, sane folk of all ages and occupations. Doctors and decorators, teachers and preachers, lawyers and labourers and even television presenters and politicians have all been smitten with the healthy addiction of a recreational activity which has now morphed into a gloriously rampant phenomenon.

This book has been written for all those Munroists and aspiring Munroists, but also for 'armchair' Munro-baggers who may have no intention of hauling themselves up a 3,000-foot peak, but nevertheless are curious about this growing craze. Indeed, if the book encourages just a few to swap their armchair for the more healthy delights of Munro climbing, then it will have been worth writing.

Munro Timeline

1590   The first recorded ascent of a Munro (Stuchd an Lochain) by Colin Campbell of Glen Lyon.

1791   Formation of the Ordnance Survey.

1819   Completion of the Scottish map survey by Thomas Colby.

1856   Sir Hugh Munro is born.

1882   Robert Hall's list of Scottish mountains is published.

1889   The Scottish Mountaineering Club is formed.

1891   The first edition of Munro's Tables appears in the *SMC Journal*.

1894   Hugh Munro is elected president of the SMC.

1901   The Rev AE Robertson becomes the first person to climb all the Munros (the first Munroist).

1919   Sir Hugh Munro dies aged 63.

1921   The SMC publishes its *General Guide* with Hugh Munro's revised and updated list of 3,000-foot mountains.

1923   The Rev A Burn becomes the second Munroist and the first person to also compleat all the Tops. (For an explanation of the spelling, please see chapter 2)

1929   JA Parker becomes the first person to compleat all the Munros *and* 3,000-foot peaks in England, Wales and Ireland (Furth).

1947   Mrs J Hirst becomes the first woman to compleat all the Munros (and Tops).
Mr and Mrs J Hirst also become the first married couple to compleat.

1949   WM Docharty becomes the first person to compleat all the Munros, Tops and Furth – known as the Grand Slam.

1960   Anne Littlejohn becomes the first woman to compleat the Grand Slam.

1964   Philip Tranter becomes the first person to compleat a second round of the Munros and climbs a record 19 Munros in 24 hours.

1965   WA Poucher's *The Scottish Peaks* is published.

1967   The first attempt at a continuous traverse of all the Munros by the Ripley brothers. 230 Munros are climbed.

1974   The first successful continuous, self-propelled traverse of all the Munros by Hamish Brown in 112 days.

1978   *Hamish's Mountain Walk* is published by Gollancz. Charlie Ramsay climbs 24 Munros in 24 hours (Ramsay's Round).

1981   Publication of new edition of *Munro's Tables* with the controversial Donaldson/Brown revisions.

1982   Kathy Murgatroyd makes the first continuous round of the Munros by a woman and the second continuous round, taking 134 days.

1984   George Keeping accomplishes the first continuous round of the Munros and English and Welsh 3,000 foot peaks in 165 days (entirely on foot).

1984–5 The first continuous winter round of the Munros in 83 days by Martin Moran (vehicle assisted).

1985   The SMC guide, *The Munros*, is published.

1985–6 The first continuous round of the Munros and Corbetts is made, within 13 months, by Craig Caldwell.

1986   Irvine Butterfield's *The High Mountains* is published.
        Ashley Cooper makes the first continuous round of the Munros and Furth.

1987   Martin Stone extends Ramsay's Round and climbs 26 Munros in 24 hours.

1988   Mark Elsegood compleats the Munros in 66 days with vehicular support.
        Jon Broxap climbs 28 Munros in 24 hours in the Shiel/Affric area.

1989   Paul Tattersall makes the first continuous round of the Munros while on or carrying a mountain bike.

1990   Hugh Symonds achieves the fastest continuous traverse of the Munros and Furth in 97 days; also including the fastest purely self-propelled (entirely

on foot and without ferries) round of the Munros in 67 days.
A team of seven fell runners complete the Munros by relay in under 13 days.
Stuart Clements and Kate Weyman become the first couple to accomplish a continuous round of the Munros.

1991   *The Munro Show* appears on Scottish Television.
Munro Tables centenary dinner held in the Roxburghe Hotel, Edinburgh.
Adrian Belton climbs 28 Munros in 24 hours in the Lochaber area, extending Ramsay's Round.

1992   Andrew Johnstone and Rory Gibson compleat the Munros in 51 days.

1993   A team of seven fell runners complete the Munros by relay in 11 days and 20 hours.

1994   Mike Cudahy compleats the Munros in 66 days and 7 hours entirely on foot, but using ferries.

1995   *The Munro Phenomenon* by Andrew Dempster is published and *Burn on the Hill* by Elizabeth Allan are published.
Andrew Allum begins his record round of all British peaks over 2,000 feet.

1996   Chris Townsend becomes the first person to accomplish a continuous round of the Munros and Tops.

1997   Publication of new edition of *Munro's Tables* (SMC) with 284 Munros. (Two later deleted, being under 3,000 feet.)

1999 *The Munroist's Companion* (SMC) by Robin N Campbell is published and *The Magic of the Munros* by Irvine Butterfield are published.

2000 Charlie Campbell compleats the Munros in 48 days.

2002 The Munro Society is formed by Iain Robertson and others.

2003 The Scottish Land Reform Act is introduced.

2005–6 Steven Perry completes the second continuous winter round of the Munros (without a vehicle) in 121 days.

2006 Walkhighlands website set up by Paul and Helen Webster.

2010 Stephen Pyke compleats the Munros in 39 days. Gerry McPartlin becomes the oldest continuous Munroist at age 66, taking 88 days.

2015 *Matthew Forster Heddle, Mineralogist and Mountaineer* by Hamish H Johnston is published.

2017 Jim Mann climbs 30 Munros in under 24 hours in the Cairngorms area.

2019–20 In 97 days, Kevin Woods compleats the third continuous winter Munro round using a vehicle.

2020 Donnie Campbell compleats the Munros in 32 days.
Sasha Chepelin climbs 32 Munros in under 24 hours in the Cairngorms area.

2021 The new large format SMC guide to the Munros is published.
Members of the Carnethy Hill Running Club of Edinburgh achieve the first recorded ascent of all the Munros in a day.

Veterans and Visionaries

ON THE LEVEL bealach below the high point of the Beinn a' Ghlò ridge in Perthshire, the wind shrieks like a banshee as it funnels furiously through the gap in the ridge. A lone figure is crouched over a wooden-shafted alpenstock, steadying himself in the frenzied maelstrom. The abominable cold impels him to persevere upwards, dragging his heavy hobnail boots through deep powder snow to another wind scoured bealach 500 feet above.

The figure then turns to face north-east with the merciless wind now thankfully behind him. The manic, turbulent gusts are now whipping up snow

in spiral columns several hundred feet high, penetrating everything, filling pockets and drifting between waistcoat and shirt, where it melted and then froze into a solid wedge of ice.[1]

The wind has partially stripped the final section of summit ridge of snow to reveal lethal, verglassed, angular rocks on which he attempts to gain purchase. Wild eddies of spindrift momentarily conceal maddening pockets of deep snow, into which he clumsily staggers, cursing under his breath.

After what seems like an eternity, his smarting eyes spot a substantial pile of heavily iced rocks, which he aims for like a man possessed. On reaching the cairn, with his back still to the buffeting wind, he lays down his long ice-axe and then removes his woollen mittens, stuffing them under his tweed jacket.

His hands, already cold, reach into a jacket pocket and pull out a round container. Fumbling desperately, he opens the lid, removes a pocket aneroid and proceeds to perform various height measurements, despite the frenzied flapping of his Inverness cape, which he continually pulls round him for extra warmth.

Leaden clouds are now scudding across the sky to reveal acres of blue above sculptured waves of white peaks in all directions. Thankfully, he has already recorded details of the views on a lower summit:

Views good – Cairngorms and Ben Alder groups, the Glencoe hills, Schiehallion (which does not show to advantage from here), Ben Lawers looking well, with Stobinian over his left shoulder, Ben Chonzie, the Fifeshire Lomonds and Sidlaws showing well, with the smoke of Dundee behind. The special feature, however, is the fine view of the higher peaks of Beinn a' Ghlò.[2]

The highest peak of Beinn a' Ghlò, on which he now stands, is a freezing and furious cauldron from which he knows he must immediately descend. His hands, now red and numb with cold, struggle to replace the aneroid back in its container and the container back to ice-lined pocket. He forces his Balmoral bonnet more firmly onto his head and briefly touches his beard, now a frozen mass of tiny icicles, as are his moustache and eyebrows. Before replacing his mitts, he pulls a solid ice-caked chunk of tablet from a pocket and forces it into his mouth, slowly releasing its sweetness and energy to his flagging form. Finally, he reaches into an inside pocket for a hip-flask. His fingers are useless, unfeeling appendages, but he manages to unscrew the flask and swig back a mouthful of the amber nectar within.

In seconds he replaces the flask, dons his mitts and grabs his axe to begin the steep descent to Glen Loch. On his journey through deep, drifting snow, he mercifully escapes the worst of the wind, but the relief is short-lived: blood returns to his hands, producing painful hot-aches. Over two hours later he reaches the lonely outpost of Daldhu and the start of the last seven miles through Gleann Fearnach to his nightly destination at the estate house of Dirnanean.

In the fastly fading light of the Scottish winter, he finally reaches shelter, where his hosts

> had to scrape me down with a knife to get the frozen snow off me before I could enter the house.[3]

He goes on to remark that 'in all my winter experience I never suffered so severely from cold'.

During that winter's day of 22 January 1891, Hugh Munro had completed a 20-mile mountain traverse from Blair Atholl to Dirnanean. An hour later, a thawed out, bathed and freshly dressed Munro sat before a roaring log fire with dram in hand, awaiting dinner. He would certainly deserve it.

Leaving aside the obvious fitness, fortitude and sheer determination of someone tackling the above expedition, which even in summer would be considered a long and challenging route, two observations stand out. Firstly, that the route *was* attempted in winter, and secondly, that a return to his point of departure at Blair Atholl was declined in favour of a new nightly destination.

Concerning the first point, Munro, a member of the Scottish Mountaineering Club (SMC), had previously intimated in the *SMC Journal* that he was looking for companions to join him in hill forays during the months of January, February and March, being 'much engaged' later in the year. It is also apparent that he relished winter climbing, and his series of articles entitled 'Winter Ascents' in early editions of the *SMC Journal* are proof of his finer appreciation of the Scottish peaks when under a mantle of snow and ice. He acknowledges that

> it cannot be denied that some few disadvantages attend

winter and early Spring climbing, but I am sure that all who have tried it will agree that the pleasure derived is more than ample compensation.[4]

I would surmise that such ample compensation would struggle to exert itself on his Beinn a' Ghlò traverse of 1891!

Concerning the second point, Munro had a passion for long cross-country routes through remote areas, often lasting several days. These were the days before motor transport dictated one's return to their starting place. Undoubtedly, the advent of the motor-car opened up large areas of the Highlands to the general public, but contrarily became a 'millstone' for those wishing to indulge in long through-routes.

After many other such skirmishes in the Scottish hills, in September of that year, Hugh Munro released his famous 'Tables of Heights over 3,000 feet', blissfully unaware that in doing so, his very name would soon become synonymous with Scottish mountains over 3,000 feet and that he was destined to become a legendary figure in Scottish Mountaineering.

Hugh Munro was undoubtedly the visionary in the formation of 'the Tables', but to fully understand the man and his mountains we must step back a century or more and examine briefly the various strands and influences which ultimately led to their publication.

In 1791, exactly a hundred years before the launch of Munro's Tables, the Ordnance Survey (OS) was founded. The existence of reliable and accurate mapping had an obvious, crucial bearing on this list. Almost half a century before this, at the time of the 1745 Jacobite Rebellion, there were no reliable maps of the Highlands in existence. Their absence at the time makes Charles Edward Stuart's five-month wander through the Highlands as a prime fugitive, with £30,000 on his head, a truly monumental feat. During his 22-week flight through the heather, he traversed many Munros and discovered a bewildering variety of hideouts in the high and lonely places.

He probably skulked past more summits than we are aware

of today and was at times so near to the enemy's campfires that he and his helpers could hear the soldiers' conversations. By the time he escaped to France in September 1746, the Prince must have been a thoroughly seasoned mountaineer, weather beaten, midge-ridden, skeletal, exhausted and a shadow of his former self. The iconic image of the 'Bonnie Prince' with kilt, blue doublet, powdered wig and starched lace ruffles is perhaps a poor reflection of the 'real' Prince. In a sense, Charles Stuart could be considered the first hill gangrel in Scotland, despite his wanderings lacking any recreational nature. The first *recorded* ascent of a Munro, however, had already been made by 'Mad' Colin Campbell of Glenlyon, around 1590, when he climbed Stuchd an Lochain in Glen Lyon.

In the wake of the 'Forty-Five' and the Culloden blood-bath, 'Butcher' Cumberland's Deputy Quartermaster, General Watson, decided that a map of the Highlands was essential. A specialist detachment was posted to Fort Augustus in 1747 to spend the next eight years on the Survey. One particular man stood out as largely responsible for the final product, a 21-year-old engineer named William Roy, whose competence and quest for perfection ensured his well-earned promotion to Surveyor-General of Coasts in Great Britain in 1765. Roy had always championed the formal establishment of a National Survey for the whole of Great Britain, and it is largely due to his vision that the Ordnance Survey was founded in 1791, a year after he died.

One final observation concerning Roy and mountain heights and topography was his visit to Schiehallion in 1774, when the Astronomer Royal, the Rev Nevil Maskelyne, succeeded in estimating the mass of the Earth by observing the gravitational attraction of the mountain on plumb lines. Roy spent an extra three days making geometrical and barometrical observations on neighbouring mountains and subsequently produced a paper entitled 'Rules for Measuring Heights with a Barometer'. At the same time, Dr Charles Hutton, an eminent geologist, came up with the ingenious notion of contour lines, which was to revolutionise cartography. Spot heights are all very well, but only show... well, height. Contour lines give a clear indication of the topography of mountains and general landscape, which we all take for granted today. Their general usage, however, did not come about until the mid-1800s.

Following the inauguration of the Ordnance Survey, the ambitious plan was the eventual production of a series of one-inch to the mile maps for the whole of Great Britain. Hot off the press and the first to appear was the map of Kent, published in New Year 1801. The first decade of the 19th century saw the heights of some 300 hills in England and Wales calculated with reasonable accuracy and the completion of the English series of maps.

The surveying principle of triangulation, using trigonometry, formed the basis of Ordnance Survey map-making, creating a three-dimensional interlocking network of triangles across the country. The latitude, longitude and height of two specific points could be used to determine the same for a third point, using a theodolite to measure the various angles. The 'points' in question are Triangulation Points or 'Trig Points', of which more modern versions can be found on many Munro summits.

By 1810, the triangulation was finally pushing on into Scotland, with all the extra challenges of terrain, weather and wildness that this would entail, and by 1819, the Survey was finally completed.

As a wee aside, a remark made by well-known outdoor guru Cameron McNeish in his fascinating biography *There's Always the Hills* stands out in my mind. His loathing of mathematics is most apparent, when in maths classes he would

gaze across the city to the blue outline of the Campsie Fells... and daydream, much to the annoyance of my teachers.[5]

(Totally understandable!) But the remark in question:

To this day I'm not sure what purpose algebra and trigonometry plays in the great scheme of things[6]

strikes me as rather ironic. The very maps which he no doubt uses to plan and 'daydream' were created using trigonometry and triangulation. Being an ex-mathematics teacher, I felt impelled to raise this, yet I will forgive him just this once... but don't let it happen again!

In 1810, the Rev George Skene DD made some phenomenally accurate barometric height measurements in the Cairngorms, being only four feet out with the height of Ben Macdui. After sending his son to climb Ben Nevis with his barometer, Ben Macdui lost the pride of place it had held until then as Britain's highest mountain. There was even an idea bandied about to build a burial vault 100 feet high on Ben Macdui's summit to reinstate its prior glory, a plan which fortunately failed to materialise.

As William Roy had been the prime instigator of the post-Forty-five map of Scotland, the Ordnance Survey of Scotland also had its own prime motivator, the colourful Thomas Colby, who became Director General in 1820. Like Roy, Colby possessed almost inexhaustible patience and a dogged determination to see the job through.

In the summer of 1819, Colby led a party covering the eastern side of Inverness-shire, Ross-shire, Caithness and Orkney Mainland, walking 513 miles in 22 days – an average of more than 23 miles a day. With only one rest day, Colby then led a fresh party west and north-west covering 586 miles in another 22 days – an average of more than 26 miles a day. Considering the roughness of the terrain, the weight of food and equipment, the often-abysmal weather and the time spent observing and measuring, these itineraries are truly mind-boggling. Colby possessed a fitness, toughness and a resolute indomitability that left others far behind. His men, too, who endured endless days carrying massive loads through wild, pathless country, should not be forgotten.

It was therefore highly fitting that the completion of the great Scottish Survey was marked by a celebration. All involved in this remarkable endeavour were treated to a mammoth feast, the chief dish being an enormous plum pudding weighing nearly a hundred pounds. The pudding was suspended by a cord from a wooden beam and boiled for a whole day in a copper pot. Colby, his staff and his men, after wolfing down the 'excellent' pudding, drank a toast: 'SUCCESS TO THE TRIG!'

Alongside all the manic map-making enterprises of the 18th and 19th centuries, another group of intrepid explorers were winding their way to the Scottish Highlands. As what could be described as the first Highland tourists, people like Thomas Pennant, Samuel Johnson and James Boswell, Dorothy Wordsworth, Sir Walter Scott and countless others began to see natural landscape not just as something to be tamed and measured, but to be appreciated for its inherent beauty. Sir Walter Scott introduced a whole new generation of visitors to the Highlands, and in particular, the Trossachs, an area for which he had a particular affinity.

It is also well-documented that a fair proportion of these pioneering travellers climbed mountains for pure enjoyment. One of the earliest of these was a young man named William Burrell who embarked on a Scottish tour from London in July 1758. Whilst staying at Luss on Loch Lomond, he related:

> On the opposite side (of Loch Lomond) stands a
> mountain of the same name of a prodigious height,
> overshadowing all the neighbouring rocks; the way to
> it is very irksome and in some places so steep that we
> were obliged to crawl on hands and knees. From the
> beginning of the ascent to the summit is five English
> miles; in several parts we sunk up to our knees in mire;
> we were fortunate enough to have a fine day.[7]

A quarter of a millennium later, Burrell would have witnessed hordes of hillwalkers hauling themselves up the well-trodden trade route to the summit. What on earth would he have thought? Being within a stone's throw of Glasgow and Scotland's southernmost Munro, Ben Lomond is well-visited and is the most common first Munro to be ascended.

However, not all travellers at this time were enamoured by mountainous scenery, and Johnson and Boswell described one mountain as 'a considerable protuberance'. Others perceived mountains as fearsome, menacing places, usually emphasising the gloomy, ominous and melancholic aspects of the dark cliffs and crags.

For some, it was not just the mountains that provoked fear and menace, but the spartan nature of overnight accommodation. Thomas Pennant, when in Sutherland, was unfortunate in encountering 'a gigantic and awful landlady; a spouse fit for Fin-Mac-Cuil himself' (I've met some of these as well). Johnson and Boswell at Glenelg were forced to supply their own hay on which to sleep in their greatcoats. A certain John MacCulloch (1773–1835) describes the wretchedness of breakfast in a 'vile pot-house' in Taynuilt. So miserably sluggish was the serving of musty bread, paste-like toast, tepid tea and 'damp and melancholy sugar' that the clouds were well down on Ben Cruachan, despite early morning sunshine. Yet 'a delicious herring, hot from the fire' provided temporary cheer.

MacCulloch was planning an ascent of Ben Cruachan and indeed ascended many other Scottish peaks, mostly between 1811 and 1821. He could lay claim to being Scotland's first peak-bagger, but his bold assertion that 'I have ascended almost every principal mountain in Scotland' must be taken with more than a pinch of salt. Despite his sub-standard breakfast in Taynuilt and the lowering clouds, he claimed Ben Cruachan's summit, one of around twenty he completed in Scotland – not quite every principal mountain. However, a look at his list of conquests reveals that he had made ascents of such notable summits as Ben Nevis, Ben Lawers, Schiehallion, An Teallach, Ben Lomond, The Cobbler, Ben Ledi, Ben More on Mull, Goat Fell (Arran), Alisa Craig and Dun Caan (Raasay), to name around half. By 'principal' mountains, he was referring to the ones which he regarded as having presence or attitude and therefore were worth climbing.

One notable failure however, was the 'iconic, unassailable

'pillar' of Suilven in the far north. In 1820 he wrote:

> To almost all but the shepherds, Suil Veinn is
> inaccessible; one of our sailors, well used to climbing,
> reached the summit with difficulty, and had much more
> in descending.[8]

His success (or lack of it) on Skye was equally abysmal, and he came to the conclusion that the main Cuillin ridge was totally out of bounds for mere mortals:

> The upper peaks are mere rocks, and with acclivities
> so steep and so smooth, as to render all access
> impossible.[9]

I would not doubt that even today, a few hillwalkers would totally agree with this assertion!

MacCulloch's trips to Scotland between 1811 and 1821 were not purely for recreational purposes; he had been appointed the post of geologist to the Trigonometrical Survey during these years, despite having studied medicine at Edinburgh University. Of course, at this time, having a scientific background in any discipline was essentially sufficient to become proficient in another. He was in fact later commissioned to produce a geological map of Scotland. However, MacCulloch is probably best remembered for his four-volume *Highlands and Western Islands of Scotland*, published in 1824, both a guide and a personal account of his explorations and mountaineering ascents. Of the various tourist guides which were starting to appear around this time, MacCulloch's is generally viewed as being superior.

One publication with obvious associations to Munro's Tables was *Scottish Tourist* (1825) by W Rhind, which contained the first table of 'Mountains in Scotland'. Although the list is longer than MacCulloch's 'principal mountains', it is essentially a potpourri of hills of all heights with no obvious criterion for inclusion other than the author's preference. Though many of the given heights are relatively accurate, others are ludicrously adrift, with an Orkney hill given a height of nearly 4,000 feet. Meall Fuar-mhonaidh on Loch Ness side attains Munro status despite it being a Graham (under 2,500 feet), and Buachaille Etive Mòr shrinks to 2,500 feet. The inclusion of Alisa Craig and Calton Hill are also interesting, as the latter could in no way be considered a mountain.

Whilst the likes of map-makers Roy and Colby and early mountain climbers such as MacCulloch had distinct, but chronologically more distant links to the eventual creation of Munro's Tables, there remains one individual who played a largely uncelebrated but substantial part in their formation – Matthew Forster Heddle. Heddle remained in relative obscurity until his great-great grandson, Hamish H Johnston, wrote his biography, published in 2015, entitled *Matthew Forster Heddle: Mineralogist and Mountaineer*. Quite how this 'unsung hero' failed to find his way into Munroist culture and literature is something of a mystery, but hopefully, Johnston's book and this account will go some way in addressing this serious imbalance.

Heddle was born in Orkney in 1828 and descended from Estate-owners. He enjoyed a comfortable home life and from a young age displayed a natural inclination towards the collection, classification and preservation of botanical specimens, shells, rocks and minerals. Curiously, Hugh Munro himself possessed exactly the same collecting tendencies as a youngster. The wild, natural coastline of Orkney and the surrounding sea were both a magnet for Heddle's inquiring and intrepid nature, and as well as wandering 'amongst the dangerous precipices and lofty sea-cliffs of his native islands', he would also 'traverse the wild seas' alone in a small boat.

From the age of nine, Heddle attended Edinburgh Academy and Merchiston Castle, where he excelled in academia. His mother had died when he was only four years of age, and his father tragically died just a decade later. However, Heddle still returned to his beloved Orkney during the long summer holidays to enjoy outdoor adventures in the company of his brothers.

Heddle went on to study medicine at Edinburgh University, where the curriculum also included natural history. Under the watchful eye of eminent mineralogist Professor Robert Jameson, Heddle wrote a chemical-mineralogical thesis relating mineralogical elements to possible medical treatments, a vision far ahead of its time. Following his graduation in 1851, he became a doctor in Edinburgh's Grassmarket area, which at the time was the worst part of the city for poverty and disease. Despite more British medical graduates training in Scotland than in England at the time and Edinburgh's citizens enjoying the highest quality of medical care anywhere in the world, the dismal, squalid nature of his surroundings and his low salary made Heddle

> look forward to the time when he might escape from
> the duties of a profession which was evidently so
> uncongenial to his natural tastes and inclination.[10]

Heddle retained his sanity by pursuing a parallel career in his true passions of geology and mineralogy, becoming president of the Edinburgh Geological Society aged only 23. It was largely because of Heddle that the National Museum of Scotland came into being following his successful championing for a Natural History Museum. His desire to leave medicine was finally realised in 1858 when he took up a position as chemistry lecturer at St Andrew's University, eventually graduating to Professor of Chemistry in 1862. At a time when universities were an all-male environment, Heddle defended women's education and in the year of his Professor-ship took on Elizabeth Garrett as a student in his class, only for the university to invalidate her matriculation. Not to be outdone, Garrett took private lessons from Heddle and eventually became Britain's first female doctor. Heddle also married in 1858 and went on to produce a healthy ten offspring!

The academic year at St Andrews allowed an extremely generous six months holiday, giving Heddle full opportunity to pursue his linked passions of mineralogy, geology and the exploration of the Scottish Highlands and Islands, usually accompanied by his great friend Patrick Dudgeon. During this fruitful and fulfilling period of his life, Heddle published a profusion of papers, many seminal, and in 1876 he cofounded the Mineralogical Society of Great Britain and Ireland, becoming its second president.

Despite Heddle's life and career flourishing at this time, a series of setbacks tested his resolve and endurance. University finances were becoming critical and Heddle himself was running low on cash, as well as developing health problems. Following a short stint in South Africa as adviser to a gold-mining company, he retired from the university on the grounds of ill health, but was granted Emeritus status. He continued to write papers until the last year of his life in 1897. His classic work, the two volumes of *The Mineralogy of Scotland*, were published posthumously in 1901.

The late 1870s and 1880s were Heddle's most prolific time in the Scottish mountains, and in 1879 he told his friend Archibald Geikie that

> I have not been and am not at all well; my heart is troubling me much – there is nothing puts it right like the mountain air, and Billy the 3rd.[11]

(The latter was a favourite geological hammer!) The benefits of the mountains for his physical health, however, were overshadowed by their benefits for his mental health. His sheer pleasure of being among hills was wholly apparent, both in his conversations and written accounts, commenting that

> every geologist must be more or less of an artist; he is none the worse if he be a little of a poet also.[12]

His poetic sensibilities are beautifully illustrated when he describes the hills of his beloved Sutherland as

Hills of all fashions and forms and tints – mountains
which rear their heads like waves which are curling
aloft to break, and have been petrified in the poise.[13]

'Stac Polly is a porcupine in a condition of extreme irascibility', he wrote, while 'its weathered pinnacles project against the sky in a wondrously felicitous similitude of human forms'.

Heddle's preferred type of walk were long, demanding, multi-day cross-country treks, when he could immerse himself completely in the landscape, gathering geological evidence as he went. His knapsack would grow heavier from accumulation of geological specimens, but this certainly did not deter him from climbing hills en route. He records having climbed 80 peaks during the course of his Sutherland fieldwork, in such areas as Torridon, Assynt and Coigach. It is evident that the more of these expeditions Heddle undertook, the more he enjoyed the hills for themselves, with rock and boulder hunting almost getting in the way. He also surmised that boulders found at high levels were most likely to have been there indefinitely, so he generally stuck to mountain ridges and tops, in contrast to previous rock searchers who had stayed low in the glens.

In addition to Archibald Geikie, several other companions regularly joined Heddle on his numerous exploits – namely, the Rev William Peyton, Colin Phillip and John Harvie-Brown. With the latter, Heddle spent several summers in the mid-1880s, island-hopping and generally enjoying a social life of drinks, jokes, songs and female appreciation. However, it was Peyton and Phillip who joined Heddle on many of his cross-country jaunts. Phillip was a proficient landscape artist, a keen mountaineer and one of the original members of the Scottish Mountaineering Club when it was founded in 1889.

During 1882, the Rev Peyton joined Heddle on a mammoth expedition which initially included the likes of Glen Dochart,

Glen Lyon, Creag Meagaidh and eventually Glen Shiel, where they based themselves at the Cluanie Inn. This inn has been a honeypot for hillwalkers for nearly two centuries and has recently been updated and extended. It was the next part of the trip, however, that had been a long-held hankering for Heddle.

Between Glen Shiel and Glen Carron to the north lies a vast tract of wild, mountainous country, containing nearly 40 Munros and where no roads penetrate. Three great east-west glens cut deep into this wilderness; Glen Affric, Glen Cannich and Glen Strathfarrar. The bulk of the area is covered presently by one of my favourite Ordnance Survey Landranger sheets (Sheet 25), and many an hour has been spent drooling and dreaming with a dram over possible future forays into this wonderful area. Having previously completed two multi-day traverses of the region – one north to south with a crowd of school kids and one south to north on a trans-Scotland walk – I have a deep affinity for this spectacular area.

What Heddle had termed 'the great traverse' was a route of some 45 miles from the Cluanie Inn northwards to Strathcarron and taking four days, staying in the homes of shepherds and keepers. Today, 'shepherds and keepers' would be replaced by bothies or tents. The other main difference between then and now are the enlargements of both Loch Mullardoch (Glen Cannich) in 1951 and Loch Monar (Glen Strathfarrar) in 1962 as part of post-war hydro-electric schemes. Both lochs have now drowned out parts of Heddle's route and the cottages where they stayed. Looking at the grotesquely enlarged versions of these lochs today, with their ugly 'tide-lines' and massive concrete dams, there is a feeling that both a unique Highland lifestyle and the peaceful innocence of two beautiful Highland glens have vanished forever.[14]

An article by Heddle describing his 'great traverse', 'South West Ross', appeared in the *Scottish Mountaineering Club Journal* posthumously in 1898 and was one of only two full accounts from his own pen, despite having undertaken countless other long expeditions in the Highlands. Several years after his traverse and other visits to the area, a geologist named Lionel Hinxman, a founding member of the SMC, annoyed Heddle when he claimed that the district was 'as yet unexplored'. Heddle's verbal reaction cited that

> I have been at the top of every 3,000 foot peak of the district named… and hardly think that the district can be said to be as yet unexplored.[15]

Indeed, Hugh Munro himself was a great admirer of Heddle and wrote of 'South West Ross':

> this article was written by one who not only had an intimate acquaintance with the country, but was also able to add much, out of his own knowledge, to existing maps.[16]

Although Heddle had not joined the SMC when it was founded, his vast knowledge, achievements and expertise were soon recognised by the powers that be, and he was made an Honorary Member of the Club by Hugh Munro in 1893. It was a decade earlier that Munro and Heddle first met by chance on the box seat of the mail coach from Kingussie to Fort William on 15 October 1883, where Heddle was going to attend the opening of the Ben Nevis Observatory the following day. Munro's first impressions of Heddle were highly favourable, and he remarked:

> What an agreeable travelling companion he was! What a fund of information, and how pleasantly he told it![17]

By the early 1890s, several people were known to be pursuing the 3,000-foot peaks in Scotland, namely Heddle, Phillip, Joseph Scott, Peyton and Munro. For a time, Heddle was way ahead of his rivals, remarking to his friend Geikie, in April, 1891, that 'I have now done 350 of the 409 3,000ers, Peyton 270 – Phillip 260, others nowhere'.

His competitive nature is obvious in this remark, but it is interesting that Munro himself is not mentioned, or perhaps implicitly included in the 'others nowhere'. In fact, Munro had only climbed 27 Tops when he joined the SMC in 1889. Early in 1891, in a talk to the St Andrews Literary and Philosophical Society, Heddle remarked that

> there were 409 hills in Scotland above 3,000 feet high of which I have been at the top of 350.[18]

These musings would appear to indicate that Heddle was in possession of a self-made, 409-peak list of 3,000-foot Scottish mountains, but unfortunately, that list has never been discovered.

Other than the highly subjective pseudo-lists of Scottish mountains, such as that of W Rhind in *Scottish Tourist* (1825), mentioned earlier, and a later 'authoritative Baddeley's Guide', listing only 31 hills (which never claimed to be a complete listing!), only one relatively serious attempt at cataloguing Scotland's hills had yet been undertaken. In 1882, Robert Hall's *The Highland Sportsman and Tourist* listed 236 heights of 3,000 feet or more, plus nearly 2,000 lower hills, each including county and district. However, this publication was clearly aimed at the 'hunting, shooting, fishing' fraternity and included little or no information on possible routes.

Both Heddle and Munro were unlikely to have been influenced by Hall's list and indeed were probably unaware of its existence. By this time, the Ordnance Survey had completed its comprehensive and detailed large scale (six inches to the mile) field survey of Scotland (1877), forming the basis for the one-inch series, with the 3,000-foot Tops appearing on 30 one-inch sheets. Both would have gleaned the bulk of their height and route information from these maps, as well as from many of the six-inch sheets.

By the early 1890s, Heddle's increasingly ill health was restricting many activities, but he stubbornly refused to allow it to hamper his hillwalking, regarding the exercise as something to be embraced at all costs. No doubt, he was thinking of his mental health as well. Rheumatism, lumbago and other assorted problems soon took their toll, however, and on an outing to Balquhidder in 1894, he remarked:

> walked 4 miles and climbed 1,100 feet – but was very tired. I think 3 miles is about my measure and I am not pulling up much.[19]

Heddle was 'only' 66 (the age I am as I write these words!), and it makes one wonder what he could have achieved had his health been in better shape. The first Munroist (one who has climbed every Munro)? It could well have been a possibility.

Since Heddle had climbed 350 three-thousanders, many more than Munro's list of 283 separate mountains, it would initially appear that in all likelihood, Heddle could easily have already climbed all the Munros. However, it is known that there were three Munros in Wester Ross that he definitely had not ascended, probably due partly to access problems and partly to his deteriorating health. A recent discovery of a set of Heddle's own maps by Hamish Johnston actually showed that Heddle had not ascended 110 Munro summits, indicating that many of his ascents were of subsidiary Tops rather than distinct mountains – Heddle did not distinguish between the two. Ironically, by 1897, the year of Heddle's death, the first Munroist, Rev AE Robertson, had only climbed 100 Munros; it would be another four years before he finished them. That the field was therefore wide open to Heddle, had circumstances been different, is a frustratingly difficult pill to swallow.

Following Heddle's death, Hugh Munro published a tribute to him, saluting his incredible achievements:

> There can be little doubt that Professor Heddle had climbed far more Scottish mountains than any man who has yet lived… no district was unknown to him, and scarcely any high mountain unclimbed by him, and

wherever he went there went not merely the trained geologist, but the truest lover and keenest observer of nature, and above all the Scottish mountains... It is indeed a privilege... to have known Professor Forster Heddle.[20]

Amen to that.

We now delve into the life of Hugh Munro, to learn a little of his character, passions, skills and aspirations, leading ultimately to the famous Tables, which would eventually result in his name needing no explanation in households across the country.

Hugh Thomas Munro was born in London in 1856, the eldest of nine children and the son of Sir Campbell Munro of Lindertis, a large, 3,000-acre estate, three miles south of Kirriemuir on the southern edge of the Eastern Grampians. During his childhood, he spent some of his time in London and the rest in the old family house of Drumleys at Lindertis, which would form the base of many of Munro's mountain sojourns.

As a youngster, his great delight was in collecting things, such as fossils, shells, eggs and butterflies, categorising and classifying them with extraordinary attention to detail. This 'collecting and organising' tendency continued into adulthood and goes far in explaining his consequent suitability for collecting and classifying Scotland's 3,000-foot summits.

At the age of 17, he went to Stuttgart to learn German and during this time developed a passion for walking and climbing in the Alps, which was soon to transfer to the Scottish peaks. He also showed a great love of travelling, thriving on change and variety, which ultimately stood him in good stead for his job as a professional courier, carrying foreign dispatches for diplomats.

He became Private Secretary to Sir George Colley, Governor of Natal, and in 1880, his stint in South Africa, where he enjoyed the social life and magnificent natural world of the Cape, was good convalescence following a bad attack of pleurisy. On the outbreak of the Basuto War, Munro volunteered for active service and endured much hardship and danger, carrying dispatches through deepest enemy territory. Following the end of the war and George Colley's death, Munro returned home, living principally at Lindertis, managing the property and gaining more experience in his beloved hills.

Politics played an active part in his life from this time, and in 1885 he stood as parliamentary Tory candidate for Kirkcaldy Burghs, but at that time Scotland was entirely Radical; a Conservative candidate had no chance of success. He enjoyed the fight, but would have hated the life in London as an MP. He continued to dabble in politics on a local level, organising meetings, hosting speakers at his home, and generally acting as a key player in the political life of Forfarshire, his local seat.

He married in 1892, a year after the publication of the 'Tables', which perhaps indicates the priorities ordering his mind at the time! Unfortunately, his wife died just ten years later, but during her life he shared his travelling bug and they enjoyed many trips together to such diverse destinations as the West Indies, Switzerland, Spain and Morocco. When his daughters were old enough, they too accompanied him on many delightful tours, culminating in a five-month round-the-world trip with his eldest daughter that included the likes of the Grand Canyon, Yosemite, Honolulu, Japan, China and Singapore.

Munro was also a notable musician, enjoying Wagner and showing much skill on the flute. He was a fine dancer and light on his feet, not partly helped by his fairly small and slight frame. In fact, his old friend and neighbour, George Ramsay, first president of the SMC, remarked that he was 'devoted to music' and 'as keen a dancer as a climber'. Being a warm-hearted host, he was a fine talker and story-teller, both in a social and formal sense. There was an occasion when Munro and another talkative companion had been out on the hills together, and on their return, both complained they had been silent all day, as neither could get a word in edgeways! He was, however, also a good listener and always gave opposing views fair consideration – unlike many of today's hard-headed zealots.

Munro was an original member of the SMC at its conception in 1889, and his knowledge, skills and experience saw him duly elected as president from 1894 to 1897, a post which he coveted and relished. In his obituary, William Douglas wrote:

> His joy at being elected president was intense. He even, in the exuberance of his delight, went the length of saying that he held the honour In higher esteem than he would have done had he been made Prime Minister of Great Britain.[21]

Despite Munro's upper class background and Conservative leanings, his first act upon taking on the role of President was to propose a motion that the Committee

> should adjudicate solely upon a candidate's qualifications (to join the SMC) and not upon his social status.[22]

That the motion was subsequently defeated says more about the SMC than Hugh Munro. By all accounts, Munro showed no indication that he preferred any particular class of men (or women!) to accompany him on the hill. However, being a landowner himself, he took an uncompromising position in relation to exclusion rights and did everything to avoid wandering on what he considered to be private land. This inevitably contributed to the rather compliant policies of the SMC concerning land access. His severe stance on this issue even resulted in his making many expeditions in total darkness to avoid being seen. An account of one significant such expedition is given later in this chapter.

As mentioned previously, Munro had only climbed 27 Tops upon joining the SMC at the end of 1889. However, Joseph Stott, the first editor of the *SMC Journal*, soon commissioned Munro to produce the Tables when it became pivotal to have a definitive list of 3,000-foot mountains. The SMC were fully aware that there must be at least 300 such summits, 'some perhaps never ascended', and they saw Munro's cataloguing, classifying and climbing abilities as essential attributes for the job. The stimulus that this assignment gave to Munro was manifestly obvious, and by the end of 1890 he was manically engrossed in major mountain excursions. In the course of only four winter months, he completed nearly 20, mostly multi-day expeditions in the hills – including the Beinn a' Ghlò outing described at the beginning of this chapter.

The fact that these were winter trips and largely solo may give the impression that Munro was reckless and foolhardy. However, he firmly believed that there was nothing dangerous about climbing alone, and there is no doubt that it occurred frequently amongst the early pioneers. Munro clearly enjoyed climbing alone, despite himself being a notably social and gregarious creature in other spheres of his life.

However, his solo winter exploits did not go entirely without incident. The last day of a marathon four-day sortie to the Cairngorms in February 1890 saw his skills and resolve tested to their limits. By today's standards, the sheer distances walked and climbed by Munro in the depths of winter are a testament to his incredible fitness, determination and tenacity.

He had left Lindertis on 6 February 1890 and 'crossed the Braes of Angus to Braemar' in glorious weather. It is not clear what route he took, but even by the obvious walking route via Glen Clova and Jock's Road, the total distance would have been over 30 miles. Even in summer, this is an extremely long day. The following day he was 'disappointed to find the clouds hanging low on the hills' so decided to skip any hill ascents and

> dawdled away some time in a cottage by the Linn of Dee, and some more at Derry Lodge.[23]

This lodge lies ten miles from Braemar and is today, sadly, boarded up and not in use. A partial clearance in the weather tempted him to think of a possible ascent of Cairntoul or Braeriach, but prudence and lack of time, together with a hankering to see the Lairig Ghru, (the main pass through the Cairngorms) saw him wandering through Glen Luibeg before swinging north to the Lairig where

the walking on this occasion was much facilitated, as
the glen in its upper and rougher parts was full of hard,
frozen snow, as smooth and as good to walk on as a
turnpike road.[24]

After a half-hour rest at the Wells of Dee (now 3.00pm), he
continued on through the narrowing jaws of the pass, where he
describes the sun setting 'in a soft pink haze, graduating through
many tints of yellow to an ethereal blue'. Finally, three and a half
hours later, after a long, dark trek through the Rothiemurchus
Forest, in starlight, he reached Aviemore Station, where he
caught a train to Kingussie – another 30-mile day!

The next day, Munro took the train to Kincraig Station and
at 8.30am set off while

a hard white frost and an intensely cold morning made
a quick walk of three or four miles up Glen Feshie
agreeable.[25]

He then struck off on the good path by the Allt Ruadh and reached
the top of Sgoran Dubh (now Sgòrr Dubh Mòr) by noon. Heading
south over Sgòr Gaoith, he followed the crest of the Gleann Einich
cliffs before making a long cross-country trek across the Moine
Mor (Great Moss) and a final ascent to Cairn Toul. The time was
now 2.45pm. He then proceeded to follow the ridge past Sgòr an
Lochain Uaine to Braeriach, where he spent ten minutes taking
in the fine view and identifying dozens of summits. At 4.30pm,
he left Braeriach and descended by the arête to the east of Loch
Coire an Lochain, to eventually reach the road in Gleann Einich
and Lynwilg Inn by 9.00pm... a 12-and-a-half hour day and yet
another 30-mile marathon.

On the final day, his luck was to change; things went adrift
from the beginning. A latish 8.45am start 'was regretted before
the day was over'. On failing to locate a bridge over the Morlich,
he stripped to ford it, after having to break the ice at the edges.
His subsequent agreeable walk through the Rothiemurchus

Forest was soon dampened by troublesome deep heather, tracks leading nowhere, hot sun and a total lack of cooling wind – yes, this is still February! By the time he reached Cairngorm's summit (2.40pm), ominous low cloud was already creeping up the glens and rolling across the top of Braeriach.

The combined circumstances of deteriorating weather and lateness of day would seem to suggest a return to base, but Munro decided to continue round the summit plateau to Ben Macdui, still nearly four miles distant. He 'was soon in dense mist, which froze to one's hair, clothes and beard'. The constant necessity of consulting map, compass and aneroid had wasted precious time, and it was 4.30 before he reached Ben Macdui's featureless summit.

His plan from here was to descend the relatively easy slopes to Loch Etchachan, nestling in a corrie a mile to the north-east. However, a miscalculation took him further north than intended, where

> I found myself at 5.00pm... on the top of the precipices
> overhanging Loch Avon... dangerous cliffs all round,
> the cold so intense that one could scarcely have lived
> an hour without moving. It was long after sunset,
> and the chances of getting out of difficulties before it
> became quite dark seemed slight.[26]

Munro had no flask and very little food. To put it bluntly, his situation was desperate.

Many lesser mortals, by this stage, would have panicked and become another grim hillwalking statistic. In our modern age, others would have used the lifeline of the mobile phone and mountain rescue – and stayed where they were. For Munro, this was not an option. He had to keep moving. Dashing up a steep, hard snow slope, with no time to cut steps (no crampons then!), he had to haul himself up with the point of his axe. After crossing an intervening spur, he then descended once again, hoping for easier ground. Instead, he found himself in a worse situation than before, amongst steeper and higher cliffs. His worst nightmare was fast becoming a reality. He momentarily considered descending a dangerously steep gully of hard snow and ice, but soon saw sense and again retreated upwards with the help of his ice-axe. Then, bearing left, an easy snow descent led to a stream bed and eventually

> deeply thankful to find myself at 5.45 on a dark night early in February, 3,100 feet above the sea, on the shores of the frozen Loch Etchachan.[27]

Finally, a descent to Glen Derry and eight miles of further walking in the dark took him to Derry Lodge at 8.30, 'where I was hospitably entertained by Fraser, the head stalker and his wife'.

Despite this decidedly potentially dangerous situation, Munro continued to profess his claim that 'solitary winter climbing, with proper precautions, is perfectly safe'. This claim is, not surprisingly, a contentious issue; certainly in today's climate of health and safety, many modern climbers and walkers would disagree with him.

The above account is a synopsis of an article in the *SMC Journal* entitled 'Winter Ascents in the Cairngorms' and is just one of 80 entries written by Munro over a period of about 20 years. The bulk of these are multi-day trips, which he revelled in, both in winter and summer. The majority of the outings were undertaken after his publication of the Tables in 1891. Other than pure enjoyment, his main motivation on a practical level was to climb all the hills on his list to check and clarify anomalies in height measurements. While the original list was 'definitive', there have been five distinct versions of the Tables. These versions contain differences not necessarily related to height, but also to topography and the distinction between Munros and Tops. A detailed discussion on this is given in chapter 4.

Despite the existence of the one- and six-inch maps, many

topographical details described in Munro's articles were not shown on these sheets, particularly in parts of the far north-west of Scotland, where it would be another 80 years before the Ordnance Survey managed to provide accurate and reliable mapping. One such part was the great wilderness area lying between Loch Maree and Loch Broom, now known as the Fisherfield Forest. The term 'forest' for many upland areas in Scotland is a throwback to earlier eras when natural forest covered the land, but sadly, little of this remains. The area contains a complex web of summits of all heights, including the Munro of Slioch and the two comprising the celebrated An Teallach massif. However, it is the cluster of inaccessible Munros in the centre of the region which have proved to be the most problematic for map-makers.

For a while it was commonly regarded that there were six Munros in this cluster, popularly known as the 'Fisherfield Six' by the Munro-bagging fraternity. However, four of the six have heights very close to 3,000 feet, and their Munro status has consequently wavered throughout the years. In fact one – Beinn a' Chlaidheimh – was demoted from Munro status as recently as 2011, resulting in the more alliterative 'Fisherfield Five'. Chapter 4 gives more details on these changes.

One of the five, A' Mhaighdean (the maiden), is generally regarded as the most remote Munro. Hugh Munro himself did not climb it until Easter Sunday, 1900, which, according to his account

was certainly not a tempting day for the hills – the worst of a very wet week.[28]

So Easter weather then was much as now! In his article 'A' Mhaighdean', Munro remarks that

Its very name is probably only known to a few of our members, whilst fewer still have climbed it. Even the Ordnance Surveyors do not seem to have mapped the district with their usual care, for while the six-inch map gives no height to the Maiden, the one-inch map only gives a 2,750-foot contour.[29]

In the first edition of the Tables nine years prior, Munro had commented in a footnote that Dr Heddle and Mr Colin Phillip both made the height over 3,100 feet, 'which is probably nearly correct.'

Following Heddle's and Phillip's lead, Munro and two companions, HGS Lawson and WN Ling, began at Kinlochewe 'in a pretty persistent downpour' to walk to the head of Lochan Fada, lying just to the south of the Fisherfield Five. In his article, Munro remarks:

> For many years I have desired to make this ascent, because of its remoteness, because of its commanding position in the centre of a most beautiful and interesting district, and last but not least, to determine as far as may be, its true height.[30]

These feelings have undoubtedly been echoed by hillwalkers throughout the years (myself included), and I rank the view westwards from the summit of A' Mhaighdean on a clear day as the epitome of all that is best about Highland grandeur.

A clear day however, was not Munro's fortune, and on arriving at Lochan Fada

> the hills were shrouded in mist and the rain had turned by this time into sleet.[31]

Luckily, by the time they had trudged along the trackless north shore of Lochan Fada to the south-east flank of the mountain, the mist had cleared and the sun was out. Heavy and drifting snow accompanied them to the summit, where they relished the incredible view and, of course, took aneroid readings. A descent to the loch was made in a speedy 35 minutes, where they discovered unanimously from three aneroid readings that the mountain was 2,060 feet above the loch. Knowing that the loch's elevation was 1,000 feet, they concluded that the height of A' Mhaighdean was 3,060 feet.

Current Tables list the height as 967 metres or 3,172 feet, though the contours on the os Landranger 19 still indicate a height less than this! Incidentally, the old one-inch maps used by Munro had contour spacings of 250 feet, and even these could not be totally relied upon. Two neighbouring peaks are worth mentioning here, as they both illustrate the ongoing confusion over heights of mountains in this area. The first, Ruadh Stac Mòr, lies less than a mile north-west of A' Mhaighdean and was only discovered to be a Munro in 1974, when its height was found to be a mere 11 feet above the magic 3,000-foot line. The second, Beinn Tarsuinn, was checked by aneroid measurements in 1929 by Corbett and Inglis and found to be 3,077 feet, yet it was still just a footnote in the Tables in 1953. In fact, Hamish Brown recalls doing a 1,000-foot rock climb in the immediate area, which was shown on the Landranger 19 map as 'rough pasture'. Everyone seemed to know that Beinn Tarsuinn was a Munro except the os.

Until the advent of motor-car travel in the early 1900s, Munro was a regular user of the West Highland railway and also sea-going craft, which plied the many sea-lochs off the west coast. One particular jaunt in February 1889 saw him sail from Mallaig to Inverie in the remote Knoydart peninsula, where the local laird put him up in the lodge. This little hamlet is still as remote now as it was then, and only accessible by boat or a very long walk.

The day after he sailed, Munro completed the walk over the high pass known as Mam Barrisdale to the fiord-like Loch Hourn, where he stayed at Skiary in a grimy hut offering only oatmeal and bad whisky! The following day, he walked to Loch Quoich Lodge, today submerged under the enlarged Loch Quoich, another tragic casualty of hydro-electrification. There, he lunched with the Factor and was kindly given a lift to Fort Augustus and nightly accommodation. The following day he took the Loch Ness Steamer to Drumnadrochit and continued west on foot to Glen Cannich with an overnight stop at Guisachan, near Tomich. Then followed an incredibly long day traversing the Mam Sodhail ridge of six Munros, north of Glen Affric. This is one of the longest continuous ridge walks in the Highlands (over 11 miles), which for February, was astounding. He then descended via the Glomach Falls, to the Shiel Inn on Loch Duich, to complete a gruelling 30 mile-plus day.

Lesser mortals would have rested the following day, but Munro decided on a short stroll along the Five Sisters ridge! Finally, on his last day, he crossed the Mam Ratagan pass and climbed Beinn Sgritheall, before descending to Glenelg, where the steamer *Clansman* took him to Glasgow, followed by the sleeper train to London.

When the motor-car began to make its presence felt in the early 1900s, Munro immediately saw its potential and commented:

> Without doubt, the motor-car offers possibilities, and brings within the scope of a day or two's expedition, regions which formerly, even with the help of a bicycle, would have taken thrice as long.[32]

One such region, which formed the basis of an article entitled 'Tomdoun', in Volume 12 of the *SMC Journal*, was the mountainous area east of Knoydart and south of Loch Quoich. The heart of the region is a long, almost unbroken ridge of five Munros, stretching from the iconic pyramid of Sgùrr na Cìche at the head of Loch Nevis to Gairich in the north-east. At this time there was no drivable road along the north shore of Loch Arkaig, and the end of this road today is a popular access point for the four western-most Munros mentioned above. Sourlies Bothy at the head of Loch Nevis is another excellent base and, not surprisingly, one of the most popular bothies in Scotland.

However, in Munro's time, the best access was from the

Kinloch Hourn road to the north and typically from the legendary Tomdoun Hotel, where Munro based himself for several days in the summer of 1912. Sadly, this grand, Highland hostelry closed recently, though I was lucky enough to stay there before its demise. Its Victorian decor, traditional feel and out-of-the-way situation were obviously too extreme for the modern tourist.

It is fascinating to read Munro's comments on the road conditions during his drive from Lindertis to Tomdoun:

> The road from Blair Atholl to Dalwhinnie we found surprisingly good. The rough stones which covered it about a year ago had, to a large extent, been removed.[33]

The road along Loch Laggan he described as 'scandalously bad' and between Spean Bridge and Invergarry as 'moderate'. He continues:

> Above Invergarry the road is stony, narrow and twisty and requires careful driving. Beyond Tomdoun it is considerably worse, and between Bunchaolie and Kinlochquoich it is very bad.[34]

Yet with the car, Munro and his companion, J Rennie, 'left home at 12.30 and were at Tomdoun in comfortable time for dinner'. This would suggest a time of around seven hours, which even with today's A9 and faster cars would not be too long of a journey, considering the extra volume of traffic today.

Munro went on to enjoy four excellent hill days from his Tomdoun base, the longest involving the ridge mentioned above, though only as far as Sgùrr Mòr, from a Sgùrr na Cìche start (four Munros). The fifth Munro, Gairich, lies some distance beyond an obvious break in the ridge and then, as today, is normally ascended separately from the eastern end of Loch Quoich. It is ironic that due to the enlargement of the loch, access to these four Munros from the north today is harder than it was then. Other than using a kayak to cross the loch, there is simply no easy way to gain this ridge; a southerly or westerly approach is the standard option. The double irony is that despite this inaccessibility, these hills see more visitors in a single summer season today than in probably the whole of Hugh Munro's lifetime.

Munro was 56 on this Tomdoun trip; he would only live seven more years. His quest to climb all the hills from his Tables was as strong as ever, and five years later, in 1917, he was within a hair's breadth of completing his mission. He commented:

> I still aspire to stand on the summit of the only three
> Tops in Scotland exceeding 3,000 feet in height which
> I have not yet climbed. Raeburn, Collie, Garden and
> others, however, must combine to haul me up on a rope;
> otherwise the ascents will not be made.[35]

This last comment was not referring to any lack of ability or even advancing years, but rather to his rheumatism, which had also affected Matthew Heddle in his later life. In fact, the condition had been recurrent throughout most of his life, which seems unbelievable, considering his gargantuan days on the hill.

So what three Tops had he still to ascend? It is known that upon his death in 1919, Munro had failed to complete his list, but some accounts assert that he had three summits left, while others say he had only two. The 'official' historical record stated that Munro had climbed all the Tops except the Inaccessible Pinnacle on Skye and Càrn Cloich-Mhuilinn in the Cairngorms. These two, together with a third summit, Càrn an Fhìdhleir, at the head of Glen Feshie, made up the three which Munro referenced in 1917.

At this point it should be mentioned that Munro's 1891 Tables listed 538 summits over 3,000 feet, of which he regarded 283 as separate, distinct mountains and 255 as lesser, subsidiary 'Tops'. Confusingly, the term 'Tops' can also refer to the combined list of all 538 summits. In this book, 'Munro' refers to 'distinct mountain' and 'Top' refers to 'subsidiary Top'. The question of how Munro decided which summits were 'Munros' and which were 'Tops' is discussed at some length in chapter 4.

It was obvious that Hugh Munro was aiming to climb all 538 summits on his list and not just the distinct mountains, so it is worth looking at the status of the three aforementioned summits, as ascertained by Munro in 1891. Full 'Munro' status was given to Càrn an Fhìdhleir and Càrn Cloich-Mhuilinn, while the Inaccessible Pinnacle was warranted 'Top' status. Today, the first remains a Munro, while the other two have reversed their statuses. It is understandable that the 'In Pin' should now be a Munro, as it is higher than the parent summit of Sgùrr Dearg; why Munro himself let it pass as a Top is discussed in chapter 4.

Munro was saving Càrn Cloich-Mhuilinn as his last summit, and some have remarked that its subsequent demotion to Top status would have appalled him. However, as the last summit on his list, I don't think Munro would have been bothered with whether it was a Munro or Top.

Concerning the other two summits, an assortment of theories have been put forward as to why Munro had not climbed them. Firstly, the Inaccessible Pinnacle is commonly regarded as the 'hardest' Munro and the only one requiring a modicum of rock climbing ability to reach its airy summit. For many 'baggers', it is their last Munro. In the early days of the SMC, there was a friendly rivalry between so-called 'Salvationists' and 'Ultramontanes', the first group being essentially hillwalkers who climbed hills by their easiest routes and engaged in rock work only if absolutely necessary; while the second group, essentially rock climbers, searched out difficult routes for sport. Of course, many members straddled both camps, and I would argue that an all-round mountaineer would have to.

Today, most Munro-baggers would fall into the Salvationist category, as did Hugh Munro, Joseph Stott, AE Robertson and many others. A common theory about Munro was that, being a Salvationist, he lacked the technical ability to climb the In Pin. This claim is shaky, as in 1906 he climbed the Pinnacle Ridge of Sgùrr nan Gillean, a route far longer and more challenging than the In Pin. The real stumbling block, with which many will relate, was the weather. In 1895, Munro had to leave Skye in abysmal conditions, and in 1897, during a yachting meet, his boat could not even anchor in Loch Scavaig due to the wild weather. Similarly, a visit with Harold Raeburn (the Ultramontane of his day) in 1905 fell through, and a further 1915 visit proved unsuccessful.

We turn now to Càrn an Fhìdhleir. Those who maintain that Munro had in fact climbed this remote summit may be surprised to learn that in January 1919, only two months before Munro's death, Ronald Burn, the second person to compleat the Munros, and on whom more detail is given in chapter 2, had visited Munro at Lindertis, where he determined that Munro had still not climbed three summits on his list.

The failure on Càrn an Fhìdhleir, as with the In Pin, certainly was not due to lack of effort. As mentioned earlier, many of Munro's ascents were made under cover of darkness due to his strict, almost fanatical recognition of the exclusive rights of landowners such that he did not like to be seen wandering on what he regarded as private land. Thus, a night-time assault on this elusive summit was attempted on 11 July 1908 by Munro and his companion William Garden. They had made a southerly approach by way of Glen Tilt and at 11.00pm and reached the remains of an old shepherd's bothy in foul weather. Here, they

> rigged up a tent with a mackintosh, under which we took our bearings by aid of compass, map and matches.[36]

By this time they were soaked and the rivers well in spate. On the ascent to An Sgarsoch, another Munro lying roughly two miles east of Càrn an Fhìdhleir, they hit thick mist and fumbled around in the rain, darkness and cloud, finally reaching the summit at just after 1.00am.

> It was now quite chilly, very dark, and, what was worse, we had been unable to keep our powder dry, and so could neither read our compass nor see our maps.[37]

As a result, the second Munro was abandoned and they struck north into the face of the wind to eventually descend to the Geldie river, now unfordable for many miles. They then headed east by way of White Bridge and Linn of Dee, the standard approach route for these two Munros today.

Finally, they trudged wearily into Braemar by 10.20am, completing a marathon night sojourn of over 13 hours. As Hamish Brown has remarked: 'They had a certain style in those days'. William Garden, on the failure of ascending Càrn an Fhìdhleir, remarked that this

> was more regretted by Munro than I, because in
> consequence it still remains one of the few three-
> thousanders undone by him.[38]

Although Munro never accomplished his dream of finishing the hills on his list, he at least had the privilege of hosting an SMC Meet at his home in Lindertis, an ambition of his for many years. Two memorable Meets were held there in 1915. This was during the First World War, and although past military age, Munro volunteered to work for the Red Cross, travelling to Malta in the winter of 1915–6 to trace the missing. He returned in June, suffering severely from malarial fever, from which he never entirely recovered. He devoted himself to the war effort by farming, raising stock and securing land for cultivation in order to boost food supply.

In 1918, after the war, he and his two daughters went to Tarascon in the south of France, where he started his own canteen for the French troops. Following a short spell back at Lindertis, he returned to Tarascon and within a month developed a chill, which progressed to pneumonia and took his life on 19 March 1919, aged just 63. A report in the local French paper read:

> This foreign gentleman, rich and elderly, who died in
> a small hotel room, had, with his sister and his two
> daughters, left Scotland, his country house and his

estates and comfortable rural life, to come to our small town and do good among us, to establish a charity and devote to it his time, nights as well as days, his wealth, his health and finally his life.[39]

Hugh Munro's knighthood was abundantly well-deserved. He died while in the service of others, a sign of his true humanity and compassion. That he spent much of his life tramping the Scottish hills in all weathers, to climb and classify summits, indicates his determination, tenacity and enthusiasm.

Before his death, he was in the process of reclassifying his list, and we will never know for sure quite what he would have altered. The Tables may have changed over the years, but the marvellous legacy of Sir Hugh Munro remains solid and permanent. In the words of the *SMC Journal* editor Joseph Stott:

It may be affirmed without fear of contradiction that so complete, exhaustive and instructive a list has never before been put together, and that it forms a contribution to Scottish orography whose value it would be difficult to exaggerate. There is little doubt that the lists will receive the study they deserve at the hands of all who are interested in the mountains of Scotland.[40]

One wonders if Joseph Stott realised how prophetic his words were and how thousands of hill enthusiasts would one day be worshipping at the altar of Sir Hugh Munro.

CHAPTER 2

Munroist Ministers

IF YOU ASKED the average Joe Public who was the first person to climb all the summits on Hugh Munro's list of 3,000-foot peaks in Scotland, other than the obvious reaction of a confused stare and a bemused look of contempt, your most likely reply would probably be Munro himself. If you asked the same question to a Munro-bagger you may well receive the same answer, or a slightly 'more knowledgeable' guess of 'Aye it was a minister... Robertson or something like that'.

The truth is that neither of these answers is correct – in fact, 'Munro' is much closer to the truth. Remember that all the summits on his list included both Munros and subsidiary Tops, and Munro climbed all of these bar three. The Rev AE Robertson climbed only the Munros, that is, 283 out of a total of 538 Munros and Tops – and while he probably bagged a good number of Tops as well, it was certainly not anywhere near Munro's tally.

The term 'Munroist' describes someone who has climbed all the Munros (not Munros *and* Tops), so yes, AE Robertson was indeed the first Munroist. A Munroist who has also climbed all the Tops is commonly said to have 'Topped up', but there appears to be no generic term to describe this exalted state. Yet another 'man of the cloth', the Reverend A Ronald G Burn, was the first to compleat both the Munros and Tops, and is therefore the correct answer to the question posed above.

For early Munroists, Topping up was viewed as almost obligatory, and indeed, seven out of the first ten Munroists did so. Nowadays, we seem more apathetically content with minimum requisites; only a scattering of modern day Munroists bother doing the Tops as well. Admittedly, many graduate to other classes of hills, such as Corbetts and Grahams, but that is another story and another chapter (see chapter 8).

Is it more than just coincidence that the first two Munroists were both clergymen? Certainly when we cast our eyes back to the 18th and 19th centuries, we find a disproportionate number of Reverends having links to hills and mountains. Names such as the Rev Hugh Fraser, the Rev Robert MacDonald, the Rev Duncan Maclean and many others all made valuable contributions to the 'Old and New Statistical Accounts' (NSA), published every half-century, giving aesthetic and topographical information on Scotland's mountains. Though none of the above actually ascended any hills, a Galloway clergyman, the Rev Thomas Grierson, was an avid recorder and climber of mountains, laying claim to at least 14 Munro ascents by the mid-19th century, rivalling John McCulloch (see chapter 1).

The high-ranking eminence and heavenly connections of Scottish clergymen, partly due to their intellectual and scholarly status, no doubt ensured that their word could not be doubted, so their contributions to periodicals such as the NSA would be highly valued. However, these qualifications do not necessarily explain the desire of some to 'get their hands dirty' and venture forth to walk the bens and glens. Perhaps the silent sanctuary of uncrowded peaks had more appeal than the sanctuary of crowded pews and brought them closer to God. As Munro guru Hamish Brown says, 'God is best found among the hills – there are few pagan shepherds'. The biblical passage imparted in Psalm 121, 'I lift up my eyes to the hills', has perhaps more literal meaning than intended. On a practical level, clergymen also tended to possess more free time than the average individual, apart from possibly teachers and other academics.

Whatever the reason, on 28 September 1901, the Rev Archibald E Robertson found his holy grail on the summit of Meall Dearg in Glencoe following a 12-year pilgrimage, and what he described as a 'desultory campaign'. Together with his wife, Kate, and friend Sandy Moncrieff, they had ascended a 'horrible loose scree gully' before a short scramble to the summit cairn. After toasting themselves with the obligatory champagne (now a rite of passage for the thousands to follow), Sandy instructed AER to kiss the cairn and then his wife! Such was the effect of the champagne that the descent was effortless:

> I never descended a scree slope with less trouble! The screes melted away under my feet.[1]

Robertson was born in Helensburgh in 1870, and his baptism to the hills occurred at the tender age of 12 when he climbed Goat Fell on Arran from his holiday home in the manse at Brodick. Not only was he alone, but he deserted the path some way up to engage in a more sporting route, scrambling over boulders and crags.

On leaving Glasgow Academy, he attended Lord Kelvin's class in Natural Philosophy (now physics) at Glasgow University, and later completed his BD course at Edinburgh University before entering the ministry of the Church of Scotland. He was assistant at two posts in and around Edinburgh before being ordained to Rannoch Parish in 1907, where he stayed until his early retirement in 1920, aged only 50. However, he continued to perform part-time chaplaincy duties until the end of the Second World War.

Robertson was twice happily married; firstly to Kate, who also shared some of his passion for the hills, until her death in the mid-1930s. His second wife, Winnifred, also enjoyed many mountain days with him, until his death in 1958 at the ripe old age of 88. Like Robertson himself, both women were of high social standing, and Winnifred was a relative of the millionaire Lord Burrell, who gifted his vast collection of expensive artefacts to Glasgow – the Burrell Collection. It is interesting that his first wife, Kate, was around 15 years his senior, and Winnifred 20 years his junior! There is no doubt that Winnifred put a new spring in his step, and a newspaper article from the late

1930s christened them as 'Mr and Mrs Mountaineer', with the young Mrs Robertson herself having bagged 210 Munros. They both claimed that 'there's nothing like climbing mountains together. It's the perfect pastime for a man and wife'. Despite her impressive tally of Munros, there is no record of Winnifred claiming compleation.

Robertson's Munro-bagging career progressed essentially in fits and starts and could be summed up as nine years of gradual summit ticking followed by a frenetic couple of years crammed into two grand walking tours in 1898 and 1899, during which he claimed nearly 150 summits. His final 20 or so Munros were spread out over the next two years. In fact, during these two years, there was a 20-month spell when he ascended only one or two Munros.

The above gives the impression that Robertson was in no great hurry to finish his 'campaign', and indeed, even at the beginning of his quest he had

> no thought of ever climbing them all, but simply from a
> desire to obtain a general knowledge of the Highland hills.[2]

It was only on his two massive three-month Highland odysseys in 1898 and 1899 that he abruptly converted from a casual plodder to devout zealot. This begs the question of the reason for this sudden change in outlook. Immediately prior to his 1898 tour, Robertson had spent several weeks on a European holiday, during which he had climbed Vesuvius. It is a common experience among Scots climbers that following trips to the 'greater ranges', such as the Alps or the Himalaya, they view the hills of home with a fresh perspective and gain a new appreciation of their beloved Scottish mountains. I have definitely felt these emotions upon return from many a trip abroad, and I see the greater accessibility and intimacy of Scottish hills as a sublime blessing. These notions are discussed further in chapter 4.

Regardless of whether these feelings were indeed shared by

Robertson, within days of his return to 'God's own country' he had boarded the train to Spean Bridge with his bicycle. That same day, he cycled to Lianachan to climb Aonach Mòr before returning to the Spean Hotel. This was the beginning of May and the start of a marathon two-and-a-half month peak-bagging extravaganza around the Western Highlands and Skye, notching up over 70 Munros.

The following day, he cycled 30 miles to the Tomdoun Inn and the next day climbed Spidean Mialach and Gleourach. He left Tomdoun on the day after, to cycle the ten miles to 'Cluny Bridge Inn' (now the Cluanie Inn) in Glen Shiel, leaving his bike at the top of the pass to ascend Creag a' Mhàim, the easternmost Munro on the long, seven-Munro South Cluanie ridge. This ten-mile cycle run is today impossible due to yet another hydro-electric mutant loch barring passage – Loch Loyne. Travelling from Tomdoun to Cluanie today, involves a 25-mile cycle or drive, or a 13-mile walk on much poorer paths. Glancing at os Landranger map 34, you will see the old right-of-way track disappear into the loch and re-emerge half a mile away, on the other side – a sad state of affairs.

There is a common impression amongst hillwalkers today, that these early Munro pioneers would have found much more difficulty travelling round the Highlands without convenient motor transport, good road and rail infrastructure, and easier access to the hills. In fact, all of these 'advantages' are essentially spurious. In Robertson's time there were more railways, quieter roads, more sea and loch access, better stalkers' paths and estate tracks, no commercial forestry blocking access and no hydro-electrification. No doubt if Robertson could see the madness that is the North Coast 500 racetrack, he would turn in his grave. I would argue that the late 1800s and early 1900s was a golden age of travel. We have lost simplicity and gained scurrility.

Robertson based himself at 'Cluny' for several days and enjoyed multiple sorties into the surrounding hills. As mentioned in chapter 1, the Cluanie Inn today is a hillwalkers' honeypot and is surrounded by more than 20 easily accessible Munros. One day, he trekked northwards through An Caorann Mor to the shapely Munro of Sgùrr nan Ceathreamhnan, 'a magnificent hill and a magnificent day'. This mountain stands above the lonely cottage of Alltbeithe, where, following his ascent, Robertson met the owner's wife, Mrs Scott, who was busy sorting and carding wool. Here, he was generously given a 'good tea' and was back at Cluanie by 8.40pm. Alltbeithe is today one of Scotland's remotest youth hostels, only open in the summer months.

There is no question that had Robertson politely requested accommodation at the Scotts' in Alltbeithe, he would surely have been accepted. Indeed, many of his overnight stays during the subsequent weeks were spent at shepherds' or keeper's cottages. Robertson, being a man of the cloth, with a distinct, paternalistic and confident air, typical of the Victorian and Edwardian higher classes, would almost expect his lower-class hosts to be accommodating.

This reflects another major difference between Robertson's Highland tour and a typical backpacking trip of today. Remote Scottish glens in his day were more populated by the likes of shepherds, keepers and crofters, living in huts or stone cottages, which today are either ruined, deserted, or in a few cases, resurrected as mountain bothies or hostels. Robertson had no need for bulky items like sleeping bag, sleeping mat, tent, stove or evening rations, which today's backpacker views as essential. His much lighter rucksack would have contained a *wettermantel* (cape), binoculars, aneroid, compass, day-food, light evening wear and baffies (slippers) – the latter for cosy evenings in his host and hostess's abode. Yet again, the 'they had it hard in those days' myth rings rather hollow.

Upon leaving his Cluanie base, Robertson stayed at a friend's farm at Balmacara (near Kyle of Lochalsh) where he boarded 'The Claymore' to Glenelg and breakfasted at Ellanreoch Farm. Sitting out torrential rain, he finally made an ascent of Beinn Sgritheall before descending to Arnisdale to be comfortably accommodated by his hosts, Mr and Mrs MacMorran, who engaged an old crofter to transport him across Loch Hourn in his boat. Robertson then climbed one of the finest, lesser-known peaks in Scotland, Ladhar Bheinn, before descending to Barrisdale for a night with the keeper, McMaster, who commented that he had some friends staying who were 'shooting rats and playing the bagpipes!'

The next day he 'walked along Loch Hourn side by a very up-and-down path' to Skiary and Kinlochhourn. Skiary was where Hugh Munro had stayed nine years before, where all they could offer him was oatmeal and foul whisky. The more discerning Robertson, however, noted that

> there was neither beer nor whisky in the place and
> the rooms were dark, damp and dirty – so I walked
> on to Kinlochhourn and arranged to stay at Captain
> Campbell's house.[3]

That afternoon, he climbed Sgùrr a' Mhaoraich and the next day crossed the South Cluanie ridge via Sgùrr na Sgìne to eventually arrive at Shiel Inn, where he proceeded to

> gobble up a cold roast of beef and a dish of potatoes,
> much to the astonishment of the girl who served me.[4]

He had not eaten meat since leaving Balmacara six days before. He was then given a lift to Totaig on Loch Duich, where he had

> some fun in hooting with an old tin horn for the ferry
> we got over to Ardelve.[5]

Ardelve Point is next to the famous Eilean Donan Castle at Dornie. This ferry is long since gone, and at that time, there was no bridge across the head of Loch Long. Later, Robertson was back at Methuen's farm in Balmacara 'enjoying all the comforts of the saltmarket at his most hospitable board'.

The enquiring reader may be wondering what Robertson had done with his bicycle for the last six days. His good friend Methuen had looked after it, and Robertson was again reacquainted with his trusty two-wheeled steed. He had a great attachment to his bike and saw the advantages of its use to gain access to the more remote hills. Although horse-powered transport was available for hire in almost every Highland glen in the 1890s, it would be prohibitively expensive and not always forthcoming when required. Robertson worried little about leaving his bike hidden in the heather as he sallied forth to climb his hills. He commented:

> Don't be afraid your bike will run away, or be stolen in your absence! Turn him loose to browse in the heather, and he will be waiting for you when you return.[6]

Robertson could be christened as the first mountain biker in Scotland, and he also enjoyed cycling as a stand-alone pastime rather than always as a means to an end. Many of today's hillwalkers – including myself – will have used a bike to access many remote Munros, and it is a sign of the times that Robertson's observations above will be eschewed by probable locking of bikes in the owner's absence.

The first three weeks of Robertson's grand 1898 tour offers a typical snapshot of the man's extended forays into the Highlands. At this stage, he was barely a quarter of the way through his intended itinerary. He was lucky and indeed privileged, as a young assistant minister, to have the advantage of long holidays for pursuing his dream of climbing all the Munros. In a sense, these extended, mainly self-propelled trips could be viewed as the embryonic seeds which would lead ultimately to Hamish Brown's continuous round of all the Munros in the mid-1970s, leading itself to yet faster and more furious efforts of fell-runners (see chapter 6). A large proportion of the outdoor fraternity look disfavourably on such feats, and even Robertson noted that

> peak-bagging and record-breaking are somewhat, I fear, looked down upon by members of the SMC.

And outside of the Club they are as a rule regarded in a same unfavourable light.[7]

Despite these observations, Robertson joined the SMC in 1893 with 45 Munros under his belt, and he enjoyed much recognition and respect from Club members. His approach to the SMC was, however, similar to his approach to tackling Munros – very much in fits and starts – and he would often go long periods with no Club activity. In spite of all this, he became slide custodian in the early 1900s and reached the dizzy heights of presidency from 1929 to 1932.

Though Robertson was 14 years younger than Hugh Munro, both were SMC members with similar interests, ambitions and identical leanings to the Tory Party. It seems odd, therefore, that they do not appear to have teamed up together, and there are no accounts of the two joining forces on the hill. Robertson did team up with many other SMC members, and part of his 'big walk' was spent on Skye, where he met up with JA Parker (the third Munroist) and Charles Inglis Clark (of CIC hut fame) to enjoy a glorious fortnight of scrambling and peak-bagging from their base at the Sligachan Hotel.

Judging by his three-page account of this trip, the first outing, the ascent of Pinnacle Ridge on Sgùrr nan Gillean, was probably Robertson's highlight of his 1898 tour and laid to rest any ideas of him not enjoying rock climbing. Despite his 'Salvationist' tendencies, he was not afraid of technical difficulty and accomplished other fine rock climbs on Ben Nevis and Buachaille Etive Mòr. Another fine day followed, when Robertson and Parker traversed the Clach Glas-Blaven ridge – probably the finest ridge traverse in Scotland other than the main Cuillin Ridge.

The next day, Skye weather resumed its normal service, and Robertson and Clark were caught out by a storm, ten feet from the top of the Bhasteir Tooth, the huge leaning pinnacle next to Am Basteir and visible from Sligachan. Wind, hail and rain forced them to retreat down a gully where a torrent of water poured over Robertson as he paid out the rope to Clark. When clear of the rocks, they ran all the way back to Sligachan, where Clark grabbed a bottle of whisky and proceeded to pour out half a tumbler of it – neat – before handing it to Robertson, who took the same. They dried themselves and slept off the effects of the alcohol, then Robertson rose an hour later to eat a dinner 'worthy of the occasion' and was 'fit as a fiddle' next day. Clark, however, was violently sick and spent the evening in bed, proving that ministers can take their drink better than other mere mortals!

Robertson's remaining time on Skye was spent climbing the other Cuillin Munros, but tellingly, he makes no mention of the Inaccessible Pinnacle. Of course, as already mentioned, the In Pin was only classed as a Top in Munro's Tables, but it is still odd, given Robertson's obvious climbing ability, that he does not appear to have attempted the In Pin until a return visit to the Cuillin in 1906.

Robertson's compleation in 1901 has been slightly tainted by a query concerning Ben Wyvis. Robin Campbell, SMC member and editor of *The Munroist's Companion*, has noted that, on consultation of Robertson's notebooks, there was a tick placed by all 283 Munros on the original list, except for Ben Wyvis. Robertson had visited this Munro on an early occasion and near the top had turned back due to heavy rain. Other unfinished peaks were also mentioned, but returned to on later dates and acknowledged in his notebooks. No such acknowledgement was ever made for Ben Wyvis; however, Robertson being a perfectionist, it is doubtful that he failed to make the ascent, and the matter is not quite in the same league as, say, Mallory and Irvine's purported Everest ascent.

On his Munro compleation in 1901, Robertson was only 31 years of age and still had many years left to walk and climb, in addition to other interests and passions. When asked what he would do now he had climbed all the Munros, his reply was to do them all again. This was more of a flippant retort rather than a reality, however, and he resorted more to rock climbing and other new-found interests. One of these was photography, which he took up seriously in 1903. Being slide custodian in the SMC, he immediately saw the need to fill a gap in the collection caused by the dearth of pictures of the north-west, and remedied this with a June tour through the northern hills, taking many excellent pictures. While I have argued previously that access, transport and 'getting around' may have been easier then, photography certainly was not. For those of us who slip an almost weightless, compact digital camera or mobile phone into a pocket, it is difficult to imagine lugging round a heavy, whole plate camera, wooden tripod legs, fragile glass plates and other paraphernalia, along with the associated complexities of setting up the equipment and taking a photograph from under a black cloth and in all weathers. Not to mention the subsequent labour-intensive hours at home spent developing and printing in a darkroom. Yes, we do have it easier today!

Another of Robertson's post-Munro passions was woodwork, which began as a necessity when working on a manse outhouse, but soon developed into an all-consuming infatuation, his diaries recording little else. Mahogany fireplaces, furniture, shelving, flooring, doors and even a coffin – nothing escaped his skilled hands. As a nod to his hillwalking days and the SMC, he constructed the table for the CIC hut on Ben Nevis, allegedly still in use today.

Throughout his long years of tramping the bens and glens, Robertson acquired an encyclopaedic knowledge of dozens of cross-country tracks and drove roads in the Highlands. Ultimately, he put this knowledge to good use and published an extensive pamphlet entitled 'Old Tracks, Cross-country routes and Coffin roads in the Northwest Highlands'. Not surprisingly, he was also closely associated with the Scottish Rights of Way Society, becoming a director in 1923, chairman in 1931 and, after reorganisation, its first president in 1946. The Society later built a bridge over the river Elchaig on the way to the Falls of Glomach as a memorial to Robertson. He was also associated with the Royal Scottish Geographical Society for many years, being elected Vice-President in 1945 and awarded an Honorary Fellowship in 1956.

In his later years, Robertson naturally assumed the role of the 'grand old man' of the SMC and was a font of wisdom to the new generation of youngsters in the Club. A most revealing and entertaining article from the diaries of a youthful J Logan Aikman (who became SMC secretary) concerns his first meeting with Robertson in the newly opened Charles Inglis Clark (CIC) hut on Ben Nevis. The following is a highly abridged summary of this meeting and I am indebted to Robin Campbell, whose book *The Munroist's Companion* contains the full account.

Aikman and his friend Tom Grieve arrive at the hut on the dreich, wet night of 22 September 1929 to find the legendary Rev AE Robertson in residence, ensconced cosily with stove and lamp lit. Immediately upon their entry, Robertson began talking cheerily with them, getting their names 'by a direct interrogation' and ordering them to 'go here' and 'do this' in a way which may have appeared objectionable but was not.

Perhaps his previous two nights alone in the hut had triggered an intense craving for company and 'craic', and he seemed to have launched into a verbose salvo of rapid-fire remarks and retorts, which were an incongruous mixture of questions, orders and random observations:

come, come, what about a meal?... soup? Excellent!... A pan, yes – Don't disturb that kettle!... Grieve, get a bigger pot out of the locker there... Add water – no, not too much!... You young fellows don't realise the easiness of climbing nowadays... we had a hard time of it... No Grieve, don't disturb that pot... I must say I am glad to see you boys – Even an old buffer like me enjoys company... Yes, I made the table and presented it... Bread? I have some loaves there... Oh! the white pudding's burst – still, it will taste as good... That soup smells good... You boys are great cooks... when did you boys start climbing? – yes, I spent ten years before

I had done all the Munros... Never could take baked
beans... I'll do the washing, you boys dry... No, no, I'll
put the coal on – Don't tickle it up that way... Now for
a smoke... It's nice to see you lads so keen – you sweep
up the floor there – Oh! this is fine...[8]

Suffice to say that 'the boys' could not get a word in edgeways,
even after the culinary commotion, when Robertson proceeded
to embark on a long-winded account of various incidents and
accidents on 'the Ben': 'You lads must learn to creep before
you can walk' was his fatherly advice. Aikman summed up the
evening:

This sort of thing went on for many hours. It was
most enjoyable, but it could probably pall before long.
However, we sat rather stunned before it all and, as the
reader can see, it was difficult to make remarks oneself,
for AER rippled on in his racy fashion.[9]

This encounter with 'old buffer' Robertson occurred almost
exactly 28 years after his Munro compleation, when he was still
only 59 – maybe an old buffer in comparison to the two young
lads, but he certainly had much mileage left in him then. In the
near third of a century that had passed, the world had changed
forever. The 'war to end all wars' had effectively repulsed much
hill activity, except perhaps for clergymen – for in 1914, another
'man of the cloth' was commencing a ten-year crusade which
would culminate in compleation of both the Munros and the
subsidiary Tops.

Other than both being clergymen and sharing a common
love of the hills, the Rev AE Robertson and the Rev ARG
Burn could not have been more different. Robertson was an
extroverted, sociable and 'clubbable' individual of high social
standing and from upper-class stock. Burn, on the other hand,
was introverted, socially hesitant and certainly not a 'man of
means'. Despite these introspective character traits, Burn did

join the Scottish Mountaineering Club, and much can be gleaned from his various *SMC Journal* ramblings; in particular, the romantic-sounding extended article 'Out of the Golden Remote Wild West' in *SMCJ* 1917.

However, it was a chance discovery by book collector GH Wright in the late 1970s, that opened the door to a much more revealing and insightful glimpse into the true persona of Burn and his beloved hills. Whilst browsing at a London bookstall, Wright picked up a bundle of ten cloth-bound notebooks and saw that they were hillwalking diaries of the Rev ARG Burn. Wright had never heard of Burn, but a glance at the diaries persuaded him that their potential historical value far exceeded their monetary worth and paid the 'trifling sum' to the vendor. Seeking someone more knowledgeable about Scottish hills, Wright approached Dr Adam Watson after seeing him in a television programme about the Cairngorms. Wright sent him the diaries in hopes that he could judge their merit and recommend a good home for them. Watson, an expert on the Cairngorms, had written the SMC guide to the range. He immediately acknowledged the value of Burn's hillwalking diaries, and they were subsequently sent to Aberdeen University, where they are held in the library's Archives Department.

Ultimately, the diaries found a commercial outlet in when Elizabeth Allan used them as a basis for her highly readable and fascinating book *Burn on the Hill*, published in 1995 by Bidean Books. The book's subtitle is 'The story of the first "compleat" Munroist'. This sentence sparks two questions: should 'first' actually be 'second'? And why the strange spelling of 'complete'? These queries are in a sense connected and have their origins in a quaint SMC tradition to describe someone as having 'compleated' the Munros, an intentional mis-spelling. One further interpretation of 'compleation' is that it applies to both Munros and Tops, which would explain the use of 'first' rather than 'second'. However, the popular interpretation of the word today refers to only Munros.

Aubrey Ronald Graham Burn was born in 1887 at Old

Deer, Aberdeenshire, the son of Rev John H Burn, and moved to Ballater in 1902. He was a small, ill-proportioned child, with a slight hunchback, making his time spent in a series of English boarding schools a thoroughly miserable experience. Excluded from sports for being too puny, he was relentlessly teased and bullied by classmates and became the butt of schoolboy humour. This teasing even followed him into adulthood, when, as an SMC member, he was forced to stand upright on the precarious summit block of the Inaccessible Pinnacle in the Skye Cuillin. Elizabeth Allan ruthlessly described him as a 'short-legged hunchback and a social misfit'.

To escape the cold reality of school life, Burn buried his head in books, escaping into a mental world of Greek mythology and romantic poetry. He excelled in Latin and Greek and gained scholarships to help him obtain a theology degree, following his father into the Anglican Church. To give an indication of the academic and abstruse intellectual heights in which Burn revelled, a paper he wrote during a period of unemployment in the early 1920s was entitled 'Conjectural emendations of Gregory of Nyssa' (No... me neither!). His interest in languages led to a profound preoccupation with Gaelic and Celtic folklore, and in his subsequent visits to the Highlands, he was unflagging in his efforts to trace the etymology and correct spelling of place names, as well as attempts to reverse the decline of the Gaelic language in the Highland glens.

On his long boarding school holidays at home in Ballater, Burn fell in love with the surrounding hills, and despite his small frame, short legs and hunch, found that he had a natural flair for hillwalking and long-distance tramping. His first major summit was probably Lochnagar, climbed with his father, but he soon built the confidence to go off alone. For such a squat individual, his speed over long distances on difficult terrain was quite unbelievable, and in adulthood he constantly amazed keepers and shepherds. He timed himself assiduously, and on occasions clocked up an incredible six miles per hour. (I struggle to cycle at that speed!)

Stamina and speed were two positive characteristics which Burn possessed in bucketfuls. However, he was completely lacking just about every other attribute or skill necessary or advantageous for hillwalking. His sense of direction was poor; his navigation skills were almost non-existent; he paid little attention to advice; he took incredible risks; his boots were in a near-permanent state of disrepair; he started out late in the day; he carried little or no food... the list could go on! His fitness and swiftness saved him on countless occasions from all these deficiencies, and his steely determination, together with a lack of fear, also helped guide him through the trickiest of situations. His head may have been in the clouds, both metaphorically and literally, but he mostly came through the other side relatively unscathed.

Despite having lived in Ballater in his younger years, most of Burn's life was spent in southern England, and the bulk of his Highland trips were made from the flat fen country of Newmarket, where he was 'the Reverend Burn' at the Anglican Church. It is quite incredible that over the course of just a few weeks per year, along with longer trips scattered over little more than ten years, he managed to scale 558 summits. Munro's Tables had been revised in 1921, and his total included all the Tops in the revised edition, plus any that had been deleted. These few golden weeks were undoubtedly the highlight of Burn's year and a store of happy memories. Allan described them as

> these were halcyon days when youth, vigour and enthusiasm were at a peak, when the hills did not seem steep, nor the way long.[10]

All ageing Munro-baggers will fully connect with these sentiments.

Although none of Burn's Highland trips were as lengthy as Robertson's three-month extravaganzas, he still relied totally on the kindness and hospitality of keepers, shepherds and estate workers who would gladly offer him food and accommodation, often free of charge. Not only did they open their homes, but also their hearts; these simple, down-to-earth, working folk became life-long friends to 'Father Burn', and in essence, became his family, for he remained single all his life. In spite of his social awkwardness, he was popular with the women in these remote cottages – keepers' wives, spinsters and daughters all took to 'dear Father Burn', perhaps like a mother to a dishevelled and unkempt child. Many of these women were desperately lonely and hung on his every word, as he relayed the latest gossip of the glen or stories from the outside world – usually whilst sitting by the fireside with dram in hand.

Unlike Robertson, who invariably observed the Sabbath by taking a day off from the hills, Burn was usually itching to be off walking, after perhaps saying the Litany in some remote cottage. The strict Presbyterian and Calvinistic proclivities of Robertson's Church of Scotland background were a strong influence, and there was only one recorded instance of him ascending a Munro on a Sunday (remote A' Mhaighdean in Wester Ross). Burn's more Anglican/Catholic leanings, however, gave him free rein to treat a Sunday as any other day, and rarely did he return in time to say the Rosary with his hosts in the evening!

Burn's diaries of recorded pilgrimages to Scotland began in 1914 and culminated in 1923 with his final summit. He also made other recorded and unrecorded trips, for which diaries have never been discovered. He also continued to visit the Highlands on post-Munro trips until 1927, by which time he was living in Glasgow and working at Glasgow University.

His maiden trip, lasting three-and-a-half weeks in the summer of 1914, was described by Burn as 'Quite the best holidays I have had', but a more nuanced view is that of a steep learning curve, verging on a baptism of fire. Right from the outset, his 'best laid schemes' were derailed (almost literally) upon discovering he had misread the train timetable and was forced to board the Edinburgh to Aberdeen train rather than the intended Glasgow to Fort William route. His original plan of a west to east multi-Munro trek was forced into the exact reverse. This produced additional difficulties, such as walking into the usual prevailing wind direction, and compounded by copious amounts of low cloud, the trek tested his route-finding skills (or lack of them) to the fullest.

Perhaps sensing these gloomy forebodings, he bought himself a Harris Tweed jacket in Aberdeen, which was not too expensive and came complete with an 'authentic peat-reek aroma'. He then boarded the train to his childhood haunt of Ballater and was soon cosy in a bed and breakfast accommodation for the princely sum of two shillings. For old time's sake, he decided to ascend the neighbouring Lochnagar on the following day, an ideal prelude to his trek. However, Burn's old Achilles Heel was quick to make an appearance, and he became hopelessly lost on ground that he should have been reasonably acquainted with, resulting in him following a path which

> degenerated into an apology for a path and ever and anon it would disappear altogether in the effort of apologising.[11]

He eventually descended to Auchallater and reached Braemar, where he gained lodgings and 'excellent brose and milk'.

The following day, Burn's resolve and determination were tested to the full. In spite of thick, low cloud draping the hills, he set off for Ben Macdui by Glen Derry, with the intention of descending south-east into Glen Luibeg and Derry Lodge. On reaching the summit successfully, he quickly became disoriented and ended up descending the Allt Clach nan Taillear, a stream which descends south-west into the Lairig Ghru. He then followed the Lairig path southwards, believing it to be the Glen Luibeg path. On the opposite side of the stream, he spotted a keeper's bothy and its resident outside cutting peat. He was assured that he was on course for Luibeg, but rather than swing east on a branching path, he continued south, eventually reaching White Bridge and the Linn of Dee. The bothy was, of course, Corrour, highly popular among and well-known to present day hillwalkers. After three attempts, Burn finally succeeded in securing accommodation at Inverey, at the late hour of 11.15pm, where Mrs Lomond gave him supper, re-lit the fire and plied him with buttermilk, before retiring at 1.00am. The house at which he stayed is now Inverey Youth Hostel.

Over the next few days, Burn's path was still plagued with low cloud and rain. He eventually ended up at Grantown after a day's trek to Spittal of Glenshee via Glen Ey and a further trek to Enochdhu, followed by 'mail motor' and train via Pitlochry. At Grantown, a Father Black secured accommodation for Burn with Mrs Romanes of 'Braemoray', a widow with two children, who Burn described as

> one of the dearest people I have ever met; a saint, if there ever was one.[12]

Such was the warmth and hospitality of his hostess that Braemoray became a 'base-camp' for his wanderings over the next few weeks, and where he would be drawn into saying mass, giving Benedictions and performing other religious rituals. One of Mrs Romanes' daughters was obviously not as taken with Father Burn as her mother; she remarked, 'He's a strange priest, such a very strange priest, mummie'.

Breaking himself free from the invisible shackles of love and loyalty to his new-found Braemoray base, Burn had a relatively carefree ascent of Braeriach and Cairn Toul in the Cairngorms before boarding a train to Dalwhinnie from Coylum Bridge. From Dalwhinnie, he tramped up by Loch Ericht to the palatial Ben Alder Lodge, receiving much care and attention from his latest lady of the moment, Lady Jardine, whose servants were sent up to Dalwhinnie specially to get him food!

Amazingly, despite wind, rain and mist, he managed an uneventful ascent of Ben Alder on the following day and enjoyed an excellent four-course dinner after a hot bath. The next day, however, saw Burn return to his customary navigational nightmarish self on the fairly innocuous Munro of Beinn a'

Chlachair. The suggested route by the keeper, Clarke, was attempted in reverse, due to Burn's inability to ford the Allt Cam, a stream which was now heavy in spate with the incessant rain. Chilled with stinging rain, he scrambled up the steep south flank of the hill, known as Garbh Bruthach (rough slope). I have seen this slope from the neighbouring Munro of Càrn Dearg, and it appears to be an almost continuous bastion of huge slabs and crags in the upper reaches; not an ascent one would even consider on a wet, stormy day.

The determined and tenacious Burn, however, proved his mettle – or foolhardiness – by climbing the slope to the flat summit plateau of the mountain. Groping around in the mist, he finally found the cairn before attempting his descent. A short while later, he believed he had discovered a second cairn, only to realise he had gone in a complete circle and was back at the summit! This should have been a warning shot to Burn, but after several other attempts to locate the correct route, he found himself on completely unknown terrain. He had descended north towards Loch Laggan and Lochan na Earba, far from his intended route. Highland hospitality again came to the rescue when, on reaching the bothy at Lubvan (now a ruin), he was given tea and a lift to Ardverikie to put him on the right road. Another nine miles of walking took him finally back to Ben Alder Lodge at 10.25pm, 'fresh as paint', with only a Munro and a sprained instep to show for his long, wet day on the hill. On the following day, Burn wisely returned to Grantown, where he stayed for four days, receiving treatment for his instep and participating in religious ceremonies, but more importantly, enjoying the home comforts of Braemoray.

The final phase of his holiday saw him board the train to Inverness and Beauly and then motor-coach to Invercannich. After walking up lovely Glen Strathfarrar and finding a bed at Braulen Lodge, he set off for Sgùrr na Lapaich, before descending south to the house at Luibnadaimh and its keeper, Finlayson. This house is now submerged under the waters of Loch Mullardoch, the massive dammed loch which replaced the original, smaller, natural lochs of Mullardoch and Lungard. Finlayson's son, Alastair, was fishing on the loch in the 1980s and caught a trout directly above the chimney pots of the submerged house where he had been born. This is what they call 'progress'.

Burn had desperately wanted to climb Mam Sodhail, the sprawling Glen Affric Munro, lying south of Luibnadaimh, gained easily from the gap between the two lochs... today, you would need a kayak to get there. Unfortunately, stalking was in progress and his plan was thwarted. Many would sympathise with his recorded reaction to this state of affairs:

> Scotland really is getting the damndest country in existence... Every h-dropping tradesman who has made his fortune, thinks he ought to have a deer forest so as to have the pleasure of shooting down defenceless creatures as if they were vermin, or worse; butchered, all of them, to make a Sassenach's holiday.[13]

The next day he reached Pait Lodge at Loch Monar, by way of Loch Mhoicean and Allt Coire nan Each, though glancing at OS Sheet 25, one wonders why he did not head directly north to include the remote Munros of An Socach and An Riabhachan, or indeed, why he had not included them with Sgùrr na Lapaich the previous day. They all lie on one continuous ridge; the 'easy' option of traversing this ridge today involves taking a motorboat from Mullardoch Dam to the western end of the loch and traversing the ridge from west to east. The following day, Burn headed west, finally reaching Strathcarron Station, where he boarded a train to return him to Grantown and the 'leisurely genteel atmosphere' of Braemoray, where he spent the last few days of his holiday.

Casting a cold, critical, objective eye over Burn's inaugural Highland odyssey, there hangs a nagging doubt that circumstances are not auguring well for his quest. His serious navigational difficulties on three hills, his instep injury, the dreadful weather, his limited Munro tally and the whole journey undertaken in the opposite direction to that intended... even wearing the finest, retrospective, rose-tinted glasses, these gloomy indicators fail to give the slightest hint that he would one day fulfil his dream. Of course, the weather, and his injury to some degree, were factors outside his control that contributed to his low Munro count. However, this debrief must also take into account Burn's specific positive character traits. His resolve and tenacity, in addition to his gritty optimism and 'glass half full' outlook, were all-pervasive and ultimately the seed to his success.

Burn's surviving diaries and *SMC Journal* accounts can only give a snapshot of his many mountain wanderings; a detailed chronology, if even desirable, is completely impossible. Therefore, a concentration on specific aspects of his trips, such as memorable incidents, memorable people and SMC dealings, is more appropriate. In mountaineering, the term 'memorable incidents' usually conjures up the more negative aspects, such as accidents, near-accidents or unintentional consequences of various actions. We have already seen the unintended consequences of Burn's poor route-finding skills on three occasions, but there are several other recorded incidents where Burn got into serious difficulty and had some narrow escapes.

By far, the most noteworthy of these occurred during the 1917 SMC Easter Meet at Lochawe, when Burn had been an SMC member for just one year. Following two unsuccessful attempts on Ben Cruachan, Burn decided on 11 April to tackle the two easier Munros of Beinn Eunaich and Beinn a' Chochuill, separated from the Cruachan massif by a high bealach, the Lairig Noe. Burn approached the two hills by the big southern corrie and followed the stream up to the bealach on the ridge between the Munros. Conditions were fairly typical for a spring day in the Scottish mountains; a generous covering of fresh snow along with treacherous ice-covered rocks to add spice to the ascent. From the bealach it is about a 900-foot climb to the summit of Beinn Eunaich along an obvious ridge; it has the odd steep section but nothing taxing.

Yet Burn seemed to make a meal of the ascent, losing the sling of his ice-axe and tottering gingerly between icy slabs and snow. Crampons had yet to be invented, and he relied completely on his axe and hobnail boots. On eventually reaching the summit cairn, he checked the aneroid height before beginning his descent. Part way down the ridge, he again wanted to check the height with his aneroid, but he could not find it. Knowing that he had used it on the summit, he toiled back up to look for it, only to discover it in his 'jacket pooch' all along. Uttering a few obscenities, he again embarked on his descent. Somewhere down the exposed ridge, he made an odd decision. In his words: 'I thought I'd try a glissade'.

The term 'glissade' describes a fast method of descending a snow slope by either standing or sitting and simply sliding down the hill in a controlled fashion. The key phrase here is 'in a controlled fashion'. Burn had only recently been introduced to winter climbing, courtesy of the SMC, and had gained some positive and enjoyable experiences of glissading.

A fundamental point concerning this apparently reckless means of descent is that it should only be attempted on a long, concave slope, with few or no protruding rocks and a visible run-out at the end. A wide, bowl-shaped corrie with a flat bottom is usually ideal... an exposed, rock-indented ridge, with steep drops on either side, is nothing short of suicidal. Yet Burn was actively contemplating this potentially fatal tactic.

His own considered analysis of the situation is telling in itself:

> Now the slope extends over 200 feet down to a
> bank topped with boulders. But the lie of this slope
> is outwards to the northwest bottom of the hill. The
> slope over the ridge is very steep, and this glissadable
> slope is tilted to the northwest bottom of the hill.[14]

These thoughts would deter most mountaineers from even thinking of a glissade, but Burn was not most mountaineers.

He began his sitting glissade, soon gaining speed on the

frozen, icy snow. Attempts to brake, using his ice-axe, proved fruitless, despite desperate jabbing with the axe into iron-hard ice. Then, without warning, he took a right turn over to the precipice on the right flank of the ridge. He had now lost any semblance of control and tumbled helplessly over the edge, careering over rocks and boulders without feeling them. Then he lost his axe.

Now I felt I was done for, and would probably be killed. Fervently I breathed out, 'Oh God help me' in the midst of my mad career.[15]

Perhaps his 'direct line' to the 'big man in the sky' helped, as literally a second later, Burn came to an abrupt halt. There was no obstruction, or lessening of steepness to cause it, 'just a miracle', he surmised. Burn had not a bone broken, and he was not even in shock. On standing up, he began to laugh. Apart from a few small cuts and bruises on his face, along with a bruised ego, he seemed absolutely fine. The first thing he did was to pick up his missing bawbees (Scottish sweets), which had tumbled out of his pockets! Burn then examined the place where he had stopped and quickly came to the realisation that if he had continued his plunge, 'neither archangel nor luck could steer me through scatheless'. Looking back at the slope he had just tumbled down, it was not just its steepness which was significant, but the fact that he had fallen clean through a foot-wide gap between two partly buried boulders – another miracle.

He then made the long climb back up to the ridge, retrieving his ice-axe in the process and wondering how he was still alive. At 4.30pm, he reached the bealach and wisely decided to give the second Munro a miss. Despite his desperate fall from grace, he still had the heart for an aesthetic appreciation of the corries, ridges and peaks of Ben Cruachan, opposite the glen, which he finally ascended on New Year's Day, 1920.

Exactly a year before Burn's great glissading gaffe, his ambition to become a member of the smc was realised at the

1916 Easter Meet at Fort William. In a sense, he was being vetted for membership, but oddly, his hill activities whilst there were accomplished alone, based on advice and 'orders' left by Maylard and Green, two prominent SMC members. Burn took their neglect and offhand attitude as a sign of their confidence in his judgement. Whether that was true or just wishful thinking, Burn's SMC membership was in no doubt. Although his association with other SMC members was fairly superficial, he obviously had a positive impression of them and remarked:

> They are all so companionable and nice. They have no Gaelic, being Glesca, but keen on the hills.[16]

However, as mentioned earlier, Burn took a good deal of gentle ribbing and teasing from some of them, no doubt due to his unorthodox style, social awkwardness and general eccentricity.

Over the New Year holiday of 1917–8, Burn managed to arrange a snow and ice climbing trip with renowned SMC member Harold Raeburn. It is not certain whether this was influenced by his substandard snow and ice climbing skills and subsequent glissading disaster from eight months before, but Burn's elation at meeting and being tutored by such a climbing legend as Raeburn was profound. Harold Raeburn was the 'Ultramontane' of his day and an expert on snow and ice, as well as a brilliant rock climber, with numerous routes bearing his name.

The meeting was based in Perthshire. Over the course of several days, the pair completed some excellent climbs on the Munros of Ben Vorlich, Ben More and Stob Binnein. Raeburn proved a thorough and patient tutor and was impressed with Burn, as was Burn with the great man's tolerance and superior skills. Burn declared those few days as 'the happiest New Year I've ever spent in my life'. On one of Raeburn's rest days, Burn boarded the train to Luib in Glen Dochart and ascended Sgiath Chùil and its two associated Tops. On his return, he made his acquaintance with various keepers and shepherds who were friendly with some of Burn's 'extended clan', from whom he received the customary Highland welcome and a 'slap-up tea'.

These keepers, shepherds and estate workers were, in essence, the glue that held together Burn's many trips. Without them, he would not only be lacking in food and accommodation, but in true Highland hospitality, conviviality, warmth and heart that was desperately appreciated after a long day in the hills. The network of working people throughout the Highland glens were Burn's extended family, and he would have sat at the fireside of dozens of remote cottages, content in the knowledge that he was welcome in the bosom of honest, warm-hearted folk. There were the Campbells at Pait Lodge (Loch Monar), the Stoddarts at Cluanie Lodge, the Scotts at Alltbeithe in Glen Affric, the Finlaysons at Loch Mullardoch, the Macdonalds at Glen Strathfarrar... the list goes on.

If there was one family in particular who made a lasting impression on Burn, it would probably be the Scotts of Alltbeithe, with whom Robertson had stayed here in the summer of 1898. The building, now a youth hostel, has since been extended and stands at the head of Glen Affric, arguably the most scenic glen in Scotland. In Burn's day, the keeper, Angus Scott, had moved north from the Borders following a previous marriage and had married Christina, an island lass. Between them, they had a large brood of seven children; it is perhaps easy to see why Burn would have so many cherished memories of this large, happy, Highland family.

One of the Scott children, Katie, was in her late teens when Burn first visited Alltbeithe. She made a lasting impression on him. Her high cheekbones and finely sculpted features contrasted with her shy and diffident nature aroused feelings in Burn which would never leave him. Even in his 70s, many years in the future, he would talk wistfully of Katie, like some lost dream-child he knew was unattainable.

There was a standing joke in the Scott household about Katie sewing a button on Father Burn's jacket, only for it to detach itself a day later, but her sewing skills must have improved, as on a later occasion Burn remarked,

> I spent the time in getting dear Katie to mend my knickers, which she did very well. After sad goodbyes I left at 12.10. I gave £1 to Mrs Scott and 10 shillings douceur for Katie, who was surprised and pleased to get it.[17]

Now you may be wondering why an innocent teenage lass would be tending to the stitching requirements of an elder priest's delicate undergarments. However, I suspect (and hope) that by 'knickers' he was referring to 'knickerbockers', commonly also known as 'plus-fours' or 'breeches'. These itchy, tweed leg coverings are still the standard uniform of keepers and members of the hunting-shooting-fishing fraternity, and up until the early 1990s, were still 'standard issue' for many hillwalkers, including myself, although by then they tended to be constructed from less irritating fabric.

Such was Burn's deep attachment to the Scott family, and Katie in particular, that he returned to Alltbeithe even when he had completed all the Munros and Tops in the area. Following a successful New Year SMC Meet in 1919–20, however, he was to suffer a shattering disappointment. Early 1920 had gone well, with Burn's successful ascent of Ben Cruachan, but events went downhill from there. On conclusion of the SMC Meet on 5 January 1920, Burn boarded the train to Glen Finnan, a glorious day when the Scottish peaks were mantled with snow and adopted an Alpine appearance. He then trudged nine miles over the high pass between Streap and Sgùrr Thuilm to arrive at the Stewarts of Strathan at the entrance to Glen Dessarry, an old haunt with which he was familiar. That evening was a fairly typical one for Burn and his hosts; they enjoyed ceilidhs, stories and songs round the fireside amongst dear friends. However, there one song in particular touched Burn deeply. Its mournful air and sad lyrics were a lament for the old deer-stalking way of life, particularly, for a stalking friend who had perished in the Great War.

This seemed to set the scene for the next few days. The following morning, Burn said his farewells to the Stewarts before heading over the bealach to Glen Kingie and the shepherd's house at Kinbreack, now a bothy. Still early in the day, Burn decided to plough on, but had difficulty in his attempt to cross the frozen river Kingie and was soon up to his waist in ice-cold water. A painful cramp forced him back to Kinbreack, where a teacher girl and a daughter of the householder tended to his needs. Later in the day, Mrs Maclean, the householder, appeared, having just waded the river at the steppingstones! Faced with a house, now full of wet garments, a meagre food supply and an uninvited guest, Mrs Maclean could hardly be filled with joy, but in Burn's words she was 'just her usual kind self... full of apologies and fresh peats'.

The next day, in torrential rain and after a two-mile detour to cross the Kingie, Burn squelched his way eastwards through Glen Kingie and on to Glen Garry. His ambitious plan to reach Cluanie Inn was shelved due to flooding, and he opted for a night at the old haunt of the Tomdoun Hotel. To add to his woes, he had a cold coming on and felt rheumatic pains across his shoulders. Even a hot bath was not forthcoming. It was almost noon on the following day before his clothes were dry enough to wear and he set off for Cluanie by the old road, passing the west end of Loch Loyne. Sustained by a mug of cocoa at Cluanie Inn, he continued northwards through the long pass of An Caorann Mor, the 'magnet' of Alltbeithe at its end drawing him onwards. However, a strong headwind, deep snow and encroaching darkness all conspired to slow his torturous progress, and it was after 7.00pm before he arrived at Alltbeithe. Then the bombshell dropped. The Scott family had departed in November, leaving Alltbeithe occupied by another keeper, Paterson.

On that dark, stormy, January evening, it must have felt that Burn's world had come to an end. The promise of the usual warm Scott welcome and his reacquaintance with his 'dear Katie' had evaporated to nothing. Burn remarked:

Paterson is here permanently, and Camban shut. The glen is not the same to me now. And other keepers are leaving other glens.[18]

This was the beginning of the mass post-war exodus of countless keepers and their families from the remote glens, who had been finding it harder and harder to make a living. Nothing about the Highlands would ever be the same again.

Despite this enormous disappointment, Burn stayed at Alltbeithe for a full week, pottering about on the hills, before leaving and eventually tracking down the Scotts, who had moved to Fasnakyle at the entrance to Glen Affric. He, of course, received a grand welcome from Mrs Scott, and even secured Katie's services of mending some holes in his clothes!

There would be a long spell of seven years before Burn visited the Scotts again, only to discover Angus Scott now almost totally housebound with rheumatoid arthritis. Christina and Burn laughed, joked and reminisced about old times in Alltbeithe, and Burn was especially pleased to see that his enthusiasm for Gaelic had been passed on to Katie, who was trying to get a place of her own in the Highlands. Katie was now a confident young lady who would eventually go on to work in the North British Hotel in Edinburgh before 'coming home' to Strathglass, where she would marry a local man. A letter of thanks, which she had written to Burn for the gift of some books, was folded neatly inside his diary and treasured for 45 years. This 1927 visit would be the last time he saw the Scotts.

Following the SMC Skye Meet in May 1923, when Burn was given moral support on his final Cuillin Munros and Tops, he finally 'compleated' his life's ambition on Beinn a' Chròin, near Crianlarich, alone and with no fanfare. He wrote:

On 20th July with the two tops of Beinn a' Chròin
I completed all the hills over 3,000 feet, ie, all the
mountains and tops contained in both editions of
Munro's Tables, 558 in all (including, therefore, those
omitted from revised tables). I believe I am the first and
only one to have done everything.[19]

In Burn's humble and unassuming way, this said it all. He had fulfilled his lifetime's dream at the age of only 36. Although he made several visits to the Highlands after this time, the 'head of steam' which had motivated him up until then had dispersed, and his life beyond 'compleation' was not entirely happy or fulfilling.

His lectureship at Glasgow University ended rather unceremoniously in 1929 and he returned to his father's rectory in England, where he lived in relative poverty. On his father's death in 1937, he returned to Scotland, where he spent several wretched months in an Edinburgh hostel. His luck turned, however, when he secured the job of Reader of Greek and Latin proofs for Oxford University Press, a post which he relished and in which he remained until 1967, when he was almost 80. He died in 1972, leaving £50 in his will for Katie Scott, though now, being married, she was no longer a Scott. Katie died in 1981.

It is fitting to end this chapter with the words of both Robertson and Burn, the first two Munroists.

In conclusion, let me say that I look back upon the days I have spent in pursuing this quest as among the best-spent days of my life. Amid the strange beauty and wild grandeur of rock face and snow slope, scaling Tops where literally almost foot hath never aforetime trod, I have indeed come face to face with the sacred sanctities of Nature, and he would be indeed dull of heart who could see her beauties thus unfolded, feel her hand on his brow, her breath on his cheek, who could see and feel that unmoved. – Reverend AE Robertson[20]

The recollection of the everlasting hills abides to cheer the spirit in its long months of exile. – Reverend ARG Burn[21]

CHAPTER 3

Fire and Freedom

THIS CHAPTER COVERS the period from the Rev Burn's 'compleation' in 1923 to the outbreak of the Second World War in 1939. The first half of the 20th century was of course dominated by two world wars and severe economic depression in the late '20s and throughout the '30s. It is not surprising, therefore, that only another six people compleated the Munros up to the outbreak of World War Two in 1939.

The third Munroist, James Parker, an engineer and an active SMC member, was President in 1925–6. His first Munro, in common with a host of others, was Ben Lomond in 1883, and he compleated with Ben Hope 44 years later in 1927. His first and last Munros are the most southerly and most northerly, and apart from the rather lengthy time in between, his round is typical of many of today's Munroists. Ben Hope has probably seen more champagne corks popping than any other Munro.

When discussing his next objective after his compleation, Parker dismissed the idea of doing a repeat round in favour of the 'Twenty Fives', referring to Scottish summits of 2,500 feet and over. He commented: 'Fortunately they have not yet been listed, and probably never will'. Little did he realise what a contra-prophetic statement that was. The next Munroist, Rooke Corbett, went on to compile a list of these very heights, not surprisingly christened 'the Corbetts'. The listing of hills according to height has had a long and intricate history that is discussed fully in chapter 8.

Parker's interest in the Corbetts appears to have waned,

however, and there is no official record of him ever climbing them. Instead, he completed all of the 3,000-foot peaks in England, Wales and Ireland, an addition which is now called the 'Furth of Scotland'. These summits are sometimes erroneously referred to as the 'English Munros' or 'Welsh Munros', possibly more as a convenience rather than a deliberate error. The term 'Munro' for a 3,000-foot summit can logically only be applied in Scotland, as Hugh Munro did not classify the 'Furth of Scotland'. Not surprisingly, however, the purists' demands have resulted in a classification of these hills into 'Mountains' and 'Tops'. By general consensus, England has four mountains, Wales eight and Ireland seven. Including subsidiary Tops, the corresponding totals are England, six; Wales, 15; Ireland, 13. Surprisingly, the 'Grand Slam' of Munros, Tops and the Furth (including Tops) did not come until 1949, by the 13th Munroist, William Docharty (see chapter 8).

Munro-bagging and SMC membership were intimately tied together in these early days, and it is telling that only one of the first eight Munroists (J Robertson in 1938) was not a member of the 'Club'. The SMC of this time was a male-dominated brotherhood, with a classist and sexist tradition seemingly welded into its very foundations, and it was not until 1947 that the first woman, Mrs P Hirst, fought her way into this male monopoly and became the tenth Munroist. Her husband, J Hirst, also compleated; in doing so, they became the first married couple to finish the Munros. Despite the formation of the Ladies' Scottish Climbing Club in 1908, it would take many years before women were accepted as equals, especially single women or women whose husbands did not indulge in mountaineering. Mountaineering history was still very much 'his-story', and 'her-story' would sadly have to wait a while. The modern term 'white, privileged male' perfectly describes a typical participant in the mountaineering scene in the mid-1920s.

However, another neglected stratum of humanity was poised to shake the foundations of the walking and climbing fraternity and would reverberate deeply and persuasively down the years. By the dawning of the depressed '30s, as the dole queues lengthened and the jobless total topped three million, thousands of working-class folk escaped the soul-destroying vacuum of unemployment and looked to the hills for fresh inspiration and challenge in their bleak lives. Their down-to-earth and refreshingly couthy contribution to the outdoor scene was a timely reminder that the 'great outdoors' was not a playground for only the privileged upper classes, but for everyone.

The spearhead of this proletariat outdoor movement was the city of Glasgow, which enjoyed the advantages of being on the doorstep of magnificent wild country, such as the Campsies, Trossachs and 'Arrochar Alps'. The desire to escape the shackles and grimy tenements of industrial Glasgow amid the despairing darkness of economic depression was like a fire in the hearts of countless working folk, and the freedom of the open road and distant hills acted like a magnet. Many a wistful eye would gaze through a tenement window and across the deserted Clyde shipyards to the distant, blue hills of the Campsie Fells hanging on the horizon above the smog of the city. Yet these 'distant' hills were only ten miles from the centre of Glasgow, easily attainable in a long day's walk. On a clear day, the often snow-capped summit of Ben Lomond, the most southerly Munro, could be picked out another ten miles beyond.

One particular young, working-class climber was so captivated by Ben Lomond that he would ascend it regularly, week after week. In April 1940, he broadcasted a talk on the Home Service of the BBC entitled 'A hundred times up Ben Lomond'. To the listeners, embroiled in the depressing days of war and Nazi oppression, Ben Lomond and its symbolic representation of natural landscape must have seemed a breath of fresh air and freedom, not only from city squalor but from the anguished angst of war. The individual in question was the legendary Jock Nimlin, a life-long socialist, pioneering climber and a true luminary amongst the lower-class outdoor fraternity of the time.

In reply to those who would remark that even Ben Lomond must grow dull with repetition, Nimlin responded:

When I reached the summit for the hundredth time,
I felt the same thrill as when I reached it for the first
time, fourteen years ago. All the mountains of the
Highlands seemed to rise up in welcome. On that first
climb they were strangers to me; but now they are old
friends. I've climbed on so many of them since then:
Ben More, Ben Vorlich, Ben Cruachan and a host of
others. They form a skyline which has become nearly
as familiar to me as the skyline of Glasgow – but much
more pleasant to look at.[1]

His intimate attachment to his home city of Glasgow is
abundantly apparent when his eyes turn from this mountain
skyline south to the city, where

distance lends enchantment to the view; and if you
should ever see Glasgow from that distance when its
haze of smoke turns purple in the setting sun, you'll see
an enchanted city.[2]

One final comment he makes, perhaps sums up his and a host
of others' reason for climbing:

I forgot fears, worries and depression in the clean
mountain air. A feeling like that is all the reward you
want for the labour of climbing 3,000 feet.[3]

In common with Jock Nimlin, hordes of other disillusioned,
unemployed youngsters escaped from the city to forge the open-
air movement prevalent at the time. A few of these pioneering
individuals would also go on to make their mark in the world,
including the likes of Tom Weir, Alastair Borthwick and Ben
Humble. Tom Weir in particular became a household name,
and his classic television series *Weir's Way* eventually rose to
the giddy heights of cult status, latterly watched by thousands
on late night TV. Born in Springburn, one of the most elevated

parts of Glasgow, Weir vividly remembered his first childhood view of sparkling white peaks, beckoning tantalisingly on the northern horizon, lighting a fire within him which would last a lifetime and eventually earn him a living.

The Outdoor revolution, though primarily fired by economic circumstances, was also nurtured by a wealth of literary offerings in the way of books and newspaper articles. Books such as *Rambles around Glasgow* and *The Highlands with Rope and Rucksack* helped to inspire a new generation of walkers and climbers. Several series of newspaper columns, such as 'Tramp Royal' in *The Evening Times*, 'Hobnailer' in the *Daily Record* and 'Citizen Ramble' in the *Evening Citizen*, reached a wide and receptive audience.

On the subject of newspapers, the seemingly unassuming publications were put to a multitude of uses beyond mere reading in the 'thrifty '30s', especially by the outdoor devotee of limited means. Walter Elliot, of the newly formed Lomond Climbing Club, a keen smoker, would roll his cigarettes in strips of paper torn from a copy of the *Scottish Daily Express*, arguing that this paper produced a finer smoke than any other. Others of a more prosaic and practical mind immediately saw the advantages of newspaper for warmth and insulation, and in Alastair Borthwick's classic book *Always a Little Further* he recounts the tale of Choochter, Ginger and Wee Jock finding an unoccupied tent, which they immediately claimed. The following morning, Choochter narrates:

> We woke early... six o'clock. We'd nae blankets, and I was sleepin' in a *Glasgow Herald* and a sheet o' broon paper. Ginger woke first: He was in an *Express*, but the pages is far ower wee. Wee Jock, meanwhile, having a kilt as well as a *Glasgow Herald* was still fast asleep.[4]

The previous evening, pangs of hunger were eradicated by 'getting tore intae a poke o'chips', a finger-licking Glasgow delicacy no doubt double-wrapped in pages of *The Evening*

Times. The book's subtitle promises 'a classic tale of camping, hiking and climbing in Scotland in the '30s', and is rightfully regarded as a minor masterpiece, beautifully capturing the spirit and humour of this unique period.

The earthy humour of these cash-strapped, colourful characters was not only a result of their Glasgow upbringing, but a survival mechanism, which went far in helping to cope with their meagre circumstances. Humour was the glue that sealed relationships and the vital spark that ignited life-long friendships. The severely limited means of these folk took improvisation to new levels. Accommodation in hotels and guesthouses was out of the question, and even tents were unaffordable to many. Barns, ruined cottages, caves and that most ubiquitous of habitats, the 'howff', were all used in equal measure. A howff was a natural rock shelter, or possibly a cave, which was subjected to much human alteration and improvement, often using nothing more than a flattened baked bean can or ice-axe for the construction. The Shelter Stone howff at Loch Avon in the Cairngorms is perhaps the five-star example of luxury howffing accommodation and is well-used by today's climbers. Closer to the Clyde basin, the lower, bouldery slopes of the Cobbler, a prime climbing venue of the '30s, provided a host of ideal howffs.

Jock Nimlin and his climbing companion, Ben Humble, both exalted in the spartan charms of howffing. Humble extolled the creative opportunities offered by these natural shelters:

> Mountain camping is all very well, but the inside of
> a tent is always the same and once in there is nothing
> to do. Each howff is different, each has its building
> problems, each its own charm, each its own memories.
> And there is always so much to do, for howffing
> refinements are endless.[5]

Nimlin himself talked of his experiences at the Shelter Stone in the New Year of 1936, with four companions in sub-zero temperatures:

With two men on either side encased in eiderdown
bags, I slept in coat and sweaters, with feet stuffed into
a rucksack. True, my teeth were chattering when
I wakened, but I had enjoyed eight hours sleep, and
four other sets of teeth were chattering in unison.[6]

Eiderdown sleeping bags – indeed, any kind of sleeping
bag – were a precious luxury which only the few could afford
or acquire by illicit means. Two blankets sewn together was
about the best 'sleeping bag' available, and failing that, the
above-mentioned newspapers gave a modicum of protection
from the cold.

The creation of the Scottish Youth Hostels Association in
1931 added further momentum to the great Outdoor revolution.
Aimed primarily at young people, the association endeavoured
to promote the health, recreation and education of all through
relatively cheap lodgings in remote surroundings. Hostels
such as Alltbeithe in Glen Affric, Loch Ossian and Glen Doll,
are all surrounded by wild country and numerous Munros.
Some die-hard outdoor individuals, including Jock Nimlin,
however, shunned the militaristic, institutionalised nature of
hostels, preferring the freedom and independence of barns and
howffs... and besides, they cost a shilling per night! Lights out
at 11.00pm was certainly not suitable for those who revelled
in the atmosphere of a candlelit howff, enjoying the 'craic' and
camaraderie of like-minded souls. Howffs also had the distinct
advantage of being on the hill and only a stone's throw away
from the best rock climbs.

Rock climbing was the real passion of many 'howffers', and
not surprisingly, much of their attention was focused on the
Arrochar hills and in particular the triple-peaked rock bastion of
the Cobbler. This grand wee hill was not a Munro, but possessed
endless possibilities for new climbs and was within striking
distance from the industrial heartland of Glasgow.

For the lucky souls who were engaged in employment, the
great escape to the countryside would begin on a Friday evening,

or possibly not until Saturday. A large proportion, however, blighted by the Depression, were unemployed, and some of these would spend almost the whole week living wild, returning to Glasgow only to collect their meagre dole hand-out. In the present day of relative privilege and luxury, it is difficult to imagine the sheer tenacity and grit these hardy and pioneering souls must have possessed.

Jock Nimlin was not slow to realise that most of his contemporaries on the hill would benefit greatly from being members of a mountaineering club, not only to give them guidance and education on best practice, but also as a shared collective to channel the drive and passion of its members. Nimlin's socialist ideals also extended to his leisure pursuits. The middle-class and privileged credentials of the SMC were not an option, so in 1929, Nimlin formed the Ptarmigan Club, the first working-class mountaineering club in Scotland. Other rival clubs began to spring up in the wake of the Ptarmigans, including the cult Creagh Dhu Club in 1930 and the Lomond Club in 1932. The Creagh Dhu Club was more selective in its membership, and new members were accepted only with the agreement of the entire membership. It has been said that it was easier to be a member of the House of Lords than the Creagh Dhu.

The origins of all these clubs could be traced to one unassuming spot on the western side of Craigallion Loch, about three miles north of Milngavie and on the route of the current West Highland Way. In a wooded hollow, about halfway up the loch and backed by the imposing cone of Dumgoyne, burned the legendary Craigallion Fire – a fire that allegedly remained lit throughout the 1920s and 1930s, until the outbreak of the Second World War. The fire was described by Tom Weir as 'a kind of university of knowledge on the great outdoors' and indeed became a focal point and a beacon of faith for the thousands of embittered and disillusioned city refugees who would find hope, humour and humanity in the warm glow of kindred spirits and of the fire itself.

The Craigallion Fire's situation on a popular walkers' and climbers' trade route to the Campsies and beyond ensured that it had a constant stream of visitors on many a Friday, Saturday or Sunday night, and the tang of woodsmoke and sound of laughter when approaching the fire on a dark night must have lifted the spirits of many a gangrel. Newcomers to the ring of faces were always welcomed with open arms and offered a mug of tea from the half-gallon pot, bubbling away merrily on the fire. As the evening wore on, the firelit faces became names... usually nicknames, but never surnames. Names like Bones, Sparrow, Peaheid and Scrubbernut, all beloved characters and all connected by bonds of friendship and a passion for the outdoors. Jokes, stories, experiences and political ponderings would all be forthcoming and merge seamlessly into songs and 'fire-chants', such as one based on the old hymn, 'Rock of Ages' :

> Long May old Craigallion Woods
> Send forth abundance of their goods
> May the fire be always lit
> So that we may come and sit.[7]

The ring of 'fire-sitters' was on one level, a ring forged by the communal love of the outdoors, but on a deeper level it was forged from freedom; freedom from fascism, freedom from the divisions of social class, freedom to roam and above all, freedom to enjoy the outdoors, unfettered by the bonds of irresponsible land ownership and petty bureaucracy. The Craigallion Fire was the symbolic equivalent of the Kinder mass trespass in the Peak District in 1932, when walkers were denied access to areas of open country, and realistically and metaphorically, it marked the opening of the Great Outdoors for everyone. At the outbreak of the Second World War, the fire was finally extinguished due to blackout regulations. Like a Phoenix rising from the ashes, however, a new, metaphorical fire would soon burn brightly in the form of post-war euphoria and optimism.

At the site of the old fire, a long overdue memorial was

finally erected by two descendants of the original fire-sitters in 2012 and is passed each year by thousands on their pilgrimage from Glasgow to Fort William on the West Highland Way. An inscription round the base of the central plinth reads:

> Here burned the Craigallion Fire. During the Depression of the 1930s, it was a beacon of companionship and hope for young unemployed people who came from Glasgow and Clydebank seeking adventure in Scotland's wild places. Their pioneering spirit helped to make the Scottish countryside free for all to roam.[8]

Finally, it would seem appropriate to end this chapter with the wise words of WB Yeats:

'Education is not the filling of a pail, but the lighting of a fire'.

CHAPTER 4

Topography and Topology

THIS CHAPTER DEPARTS from the preceding historical and people-related aspects of the Munro phenomenon to concentrate on the prehistorical and topographical aspects. The aim is to be comprehensible rather than comprehensive and to throw light on such questions as: How were the Scottish mountains formed? Why are they so unique? Why are Munros over 3,000 feet? How are Munros and Tops distinguished?

If you have little interest in the physical and topographical side of Munros and mountains in general, then this chapter could be skipped without loss of continuity and perhaps returned to later. However, you probably would not have picked this book up if you did not have some interest in these matters, some of which are, in fact, fundamental to an understanding and appreciation of Scotland's unique and incredibly varied landscape.

Some philistines have dared to remark that Scotland and the UK do not have any real mountains, just hills. Leaving aside the thorny question of the distinction between a mountain and a hill, this viewpoint is, in a certain sense, justified. Certainly by global standards, Scottish mountains (or hills!) are not high. Compared to the Himalaya, the Andes, the Alps or even the Pyrenees, the Scottish mountains are only foothills. Yet the Scottish Highlands have been elevated in another sense to a world-renowned tourist destination, a Mecca for the almost unique British pursuit of hillwalking. One of the aims of this chapter is to explain why this has happened.

In a nutshell, the Scottish mountains are the worn-down remnants of a massive mountain chain that existed many millions of years ago. This dauntingly brief synopsis suggests that these mountains are currently in a state of gradual erosion or destruction, as opposed to a state of construction. For example, the vast mountain range of the Himalaya is currently in the process of construction; Mount Everest is growing in height by several millimetres per year. The cause of this growth is the collision and subsequent pressure of two opposing plates underneath the earth's surface which, like carpets pushed together from opposite directions, are buckling up in the middle.

The great mountain chain from which the Scottish mountains were eventually derived was formed in exactly this manner: the Caledonian Mountain range was formed over 400 million years ago and became established over 130 million years. These timescales are mind-boggling enough, never mind that Scotland's first rocks (Lewissian Gneiss) were formed 2,600 million years ago – more than half the age of the earth. The Caledonian range was of Himalayan scale, both in height and extent, and its remnants range through modern Scandinavia, Greenland, Eastern Canada and the Appalachian Mountains in the Eastern USA – at the time, these areas were part of one huge land mass.

This mountain genesis, or orogeny, was also the genesis of a horizontal pressure, resulting in the obvious south-west to north-east grain of the Scottish Highlands and Southern Uplands. This grain is most apparent today in the Highland and Southern Upland Boundary Fault lines, together with the Great Glen Fault. Not only is this alignment also evident in Scandinavia and North America, but these other mountain ranges have distinct similarities to Scottish mountains. The Gross Morne National Park in Newfoundland, for example, has an uncanny affinity with the Cairngorms, and many mountain areas of Norway could be mistaken for parts of the Highlands.

Since the beginning of the Caledonian Mountains, four other major, distinct, physical events occurred, each contributing to the Scotland we see today. The first was the gradual separation of Eurasia from North America caused by the drift of tectonic plates between 200 million and 65 million years ago. The gap that formed between these masses is the Atlantic Ocean, still widening today at a rate of about a centimetre per year. At the end of this period, Scotland was still attached to Greenland and Scandinavia. However, as the Caledonian range continued to tear apart, Greenland too became severed, leaving a line of prolonged volcanic eruptions between Ireland and Greenland and through to Iceland. These massive volcanoes continued to erupt intermittently for 10 million years, producing today's remnants of igneous rock on Arran, Mull, Ardnamurchan, Rum, Skye and St Kilda. The lava produced, poured out in successive flows over millions of years, spread far and piled high as a tableland with a west-to-east tilt.

The second major event occurred around 30 million years ago and consisted of a gradual uplifting of the tableland to form a much higher undulating plateau that stretched far beyond St Kilda to the Continental Shelf. This plateau had a general slope to the south-east, with a watershed much closer to the western boundary. The ultimate consequence of this would be the extraordinarily indented west coast, with its numerous sea lochs and fiord-like scenery. The rivers flowing to the east and south-east gradually carved out glens, now valleys such as the Lairig Ghru, Glen Nevis and Glen Coe. Subsequently, many of these eastward-flowing rivers were captured and redirected by older rivers. For instance, Glen Coe once channelled a river originating in Ardnamurchan and flowing east across Rannoch Moor to the North Sea. It was then intercepted by a south-west flowing river along the fault line now containing Loch Linnhe and Loch Leven. The head of Glen Coe became a watershed, turning all drainage back to the west, as is the case today.

The next event would give Scotland an appearance that we might recognise today, when the land link to Scandinavia was submerged and the Minch was created by the flooding of seawater between Scotland's western seaboard and the Hebrides. This happened between 10 and 15 million years ago and created the western sea lochs.

But by far, the most important contributor to the present Highland landscape was the covering of the land by glaciers and ice sheets, constituting the fourth and final event that began 600,000 years ago. The advance of polar ice came in four phases, the last one beginning 27,000 years ago and ending 10,000 years ago, popularly known as 'The Ice Age'. At maximum glaciation, a massive ice-cap, 1,500 metres thick, stretched from the northern tip of Norway to the south of Ireland, and its western extremity was only a few miles short of St Kilda. At this time, Scotland, Ireland and Europe were still connected by land bridges, and the Scandinavian land bridge would fluctuate over thousands of years.

Most knowledge of Scotland's glaciation is based on the evidence from the last phase, as each phase tends to wipe out evidence from the one prior. All ice ages have two significant consequences: rises in land and sea levels. Once the enormous weight of ice is removed, the land begins to lift up, and raised beaches appear around the coast. However, the melting ice became water and so raised the sea level also, flooding the land bridge between Scotland and Ireland, between Britain and Europe, and filling the glens between Mull and Morven, Skye and Glenelg, Arran and Kintyre, and also separating the Outer Hebrides into the component islands we see today. Valley glaciers were the last to retreat, gradually withdrawing to the upper glens, then to the high corries, where they slowly melted away to just a few vestiges of snow and ice, clinging on in the shadowy recesses of the remotest north-facing corries.

Over the course of thousands of years of retreating and advancing ice, the upland plateau, already dissected by numerous faults and water courses, was further eroded by ice action, producing corries, cliffs, hanging valleys, narrow rocky arêtes, buttresses, ice-scoured boiler plate slabs and U-shaped valleys... in short, the landscape we see today. From a human perspective, mountains appear changeless and timeless, but even now, post-glacial erosion, wind, water and ice action continue to have an influence on the slow but sure alteration of the landscape. We are just observers for a brief moment in a vast timescale of continuous renewal and destruction.

The preceding few paragraphs are no more than a sweeping generalisation of the creation of Scotland's mountains, and scant mention has been made of the underlying geology. The geological jigsaw representing Scotland is so convoluted that there are still many pieces missing. The great fault lines separate an amazing assortment of rock types, from Dalriadian Schists to Moinian Schists, from granite and gabbro to Lewisian Gneiss and Old Red Sandstone. This incredible diversity of rock, squeezed into such a small area as Scotland, has resulted in a host of distinctive and localised landforms. From the rolling grassy ridges of Perthshire to the lonely sandstone sentinels Of Coigach; from the vast, rounded, granite domes of the Cairngorms to the serrated, gabbro ridges of the Skye Cuillin, Scotland has more landscape variety packed into its small area than any other country of comparable size in the world. Two other contributary factors to the uniqueness and beauty of the Highland landscape are water and climate. On the deeply indented western seaboard, the numerous sea lochs complement the mountainous terrain vividly and dramatically, and inland glen lochs do the same. The notoriously changeable Scottish climate, dominated by Atlantic air streams, is ironically a boon and a blessing. The often swift change from curtains of mist and driving rain showers to brilliant sun, blue sky and sparkling air delivers the immeasurable bounty of a richness and refined subtlety of landscape colour that is totally absent in drier climates.

In all this uniqueness and variety, the single unifying theme linking Highland landforms is their ultimate creation from a highly dissected tableland. The Scottish mountains have formed through the negative actions of sculpting by ice, water and wind out of a pre-existing upland plateau, rather than a positive action of construction, such as the uplifting caused by the collision of tectonic plates. This chiselling and carving process over thousands of years has produced mountains of a more rounded and gentler appearance than other mountain ranges, and their lower altitude has accorded them an intimacy and accessibility that is almost unique in the world.

Walkers and climbers can connect and relate to the landscape in a way that is less demanding and taxing than can be found in, say, the European Alps. Given reasonable levels of fitness, most people can climb to the top of even the highest Scottish mountain without carrying a cumbersome array of technical equipment, and the ascent can be completed in a few hours. The majority of people can know and experience this landscape through the simple act of putting one foot in front of the other. To gain this same level of intimacy with the Alps would require many decades and a thorough acquaintance with technical mountaineering skills and techniques.

It is largely only in Britain, and in particular, Scotland, that the term 'hillwalking' is used. In England there is fellwalking, in the USA there is hiking, in the Himalaya and other high ranges there is trekking, in New Zealand there is tramping. But the difference is more than in name only. These overseas walkers are rarely trying to summit particular peaks; rather, they are generally walking 'through' mountainous terrain, to reach say, Everest Base Camp, or hiking part of the Appalachian Trail. There is a culture of hillwalking in the UK, and especially Scotland, that exists in no other country.

The view from the summit of a typical Munro often gives the impression of wave after wave of ridges and peaks on a frozen sea. Moreover, there is a distinct uniformity of summit altitudes extending out to the far horizon. This fact should not be completely surprising, given that the mountains embody the erosional remnants of formerly extensive upland surfaces. So in a meaningful sense, the heights of these mountains are strongly correlated with the height of this pre-existing elevated surface. This association gives the first clue as to why Munros have a minimum height of 3,000 feet. The Munros range in height from 3,000 feet to just over 4,400 feet. A reasonable question to ask is: 'Are Munro heights scattered randomly within this height range?' The answer is a definite no – the greater the height, the fewer Munros there are. Talking numbers, only a quarter of all Munros are over 3,500 feet, and only nine are above 4,000 feet. If Munro heights were randomly scattered throughout this range, then we would expect the median height to be around 3,700 feet (halfway between the two extremes). In reality, the median height is about 3,270 feet. If the heights of all 282 Munros are arranged in order, the middle two Munros (Ben More Assynt and Broad Cairn) each have a height of 3,274 feet, which in metric, is surprisingly close to an even 1,000 metres (998 metres). In other words, Munro heights seem to be clustering or bunching around the thousand-metre mark.

Being mindful of the aphorism, 'lies, damned lies and statistics', a cynic would argue that the concentration of Munros is bound to fall off with increasing height, as there are obviously no hills above the maximum height. What the statistics suggest to geologists, however, is that the average height of the prehistorical, upland plateau, in areas dominated by Munros, was probably around one thousand metres. Notice the proviso, 'in areas dominated by Munros'. A comprehensive analysis would include hills under 3,000 feet, which is beyond the scope of this brief investigation.

The question as to why Hugh Munro and the SMC decided on a minimum height of 3,000 feet is an interesting one, and it has never been fully addressed. As we saw in chapter 1, the notion of this favoured height had been bandied about before Hugh Munro produced his list, and he and the SMC adopted it as a height threshold to separate lesser peaks from principal peaks. Though this height seems linked to the height of the original tableland, it is doubtful whether this connection ever entered the mind of Hugh Munro or the SMC. The majority of 'principal peaks' in the Highlands are above 3,000 feet, so this minimum seems entirely reasonable. However, it will not have passed most people that '3,000' is a 'nice round number', and it is uncannily fortuitous that the imperial system of length unwittingly resulted in this almost perfect minimum datum line. The unit of length known as the 'foot' was originated by the ancient Greeks and Romans as simply the length of a typical adult male foot. So, in a sense, ancient Romans are indirectly responsible for the Munro list we see today!

If the metric system had been in predominant use in the late 19th century, then Munros would almost certainly have been defined as mountains over 1,000 metres in height, and we would have a more manageable 137 Munros rather than the current 282 – almost half the actual number. There are those who argue that Munro heights should be 'metricised' and redefined as mountains over 900 metres in height – the closest metric 'round number' height to the actual minimum height of 914.4 metres (3,000 feet). However, the resulting list of around 305 mountains cannot, in all honesty, be termed Munros, and the name 'Metros' is often given to this list.

The idea of naming a list of hills according to their height originated in Scotland with the advent of Munros, and since then, a host of other named lists have appeared, such as Corbetts and Grahams. These lists are discussed in chapter 8.

We now turn our attention to Hugh Munro's list and try to gain some insight into how he may have distinguished between Munros and subsidiary 'Tops'. The question is not clear-cut, and even Hugh Munro himself conceded:

> The decision as to what may be counted as Tops, although arrived at after careful consideration, cannot be finally insisted on.[1]

The aim here is to throw some light on various attempts to quantify and rationalise Munro's thinking without getting bogged down in a morass of technicalities. For a more detailed analysis, the interested reader is referred to the SMC publication *The Munroist's Companion*, edited by Robin N Campbell.

Since the original publication of Munro's Tables in 1891, there have been another four distinct versions (1921, 1974, 1981, 1997), each with different numbers of Munros and Tops.

This obviously begs the question: Why are these totals such a 'moveable feast'? The reasons are threefold. First are changes arising from simple mistakes and anomalies. Second are changes resulting from a fresh perspective on the Tables, in light of, say, better quality maps or a broader and more progressive interpretation of Munro's methodology. Third are changes arising from new height measurements which may indicate that a certain elevation is above or below 3,000 feet.

A good example of the first type of change relates to the Skye Cuillin, where the 1891 Tables listed Sgùrr Dearg as a Munro and its partner, the Inaccessible Pinnacle, as only a Top, when the Inaccessible Pinnacle is the higher of the two. Strangely, the 1891 Tables contain another seven such 'binary pair' anomalies, where the lower summit of two twin peaks is accorded Munro status. A clue as to the existence of these anomalies can be found by glancing at an old OS map of the Cuillin (OS Landranger 32). These older maps name Sgùrr Dearg, but omit the Inaccessible Pinnacle, and the presence of a name seemed to be an important consideration for Hugh Munro in deciding Munro or Top status. This business of names has more important and contentious consequences, as we shall see later.

The second type of change has probably resulted in more bickering and heated exchanges than any argument about Brexit or Scottish Independence. As Hamish Brown puts it, we take our sport seriously, but treat politics as a joke. He was probably referring to football, but for many, Munro matters are more serious than life or death! The 1981 revision of the Tables threw a particularly cantankerous cat amongst the pigeons and sparked an ongoing bone of contention, which still retains meat even today – more on that later. A personal story is relevant here.

In the summer of 1981, I was engaged in an extended Munro-bagging trip in the Northwest Highlands, hoping to reach the giddy heights of a hundred Munros. Six days into the venture saw me sitting at the cairn of Spidean a' Choire Lèith on the superb Liathach ridge in Torridon under cloudless, blue skies. My limited knowledge at this point, gleaned from the 1974 edition of the Tables, told me that I was sitting atop the only Munro on Liathach – which I believed until two young lads appeared at the cairn. We naturally exchanged pleasantries before discussing the more serious matter of Munros... then the bombshell was dropped. 'Liathach now has two Munros', they both proclaimed in unison. Believing I was the butt of a practical joke, I laughed until I noticed they were deadly serious. When they additionally pronounced that a new edition of Munro's Tables had been published and another three Tops had also been promoted to Munros, including Sgùrr Fiona on An Teallach, a mountain I had yet to climb, my amused expression turned to one of gob-smacked astonishment.

After arranging to meet them on Beinn Alligin the following day, I completed a magnificent traverse of the Fasarinen Pinnacles, to arrive eventually on the 'new Munro' of Mullach an Rathain, flushed with the heady excitement of a wonderfully exposed ridge scramble and of course the knowledge that I had two more Munros under my belt. Full acceptance of this fact was finally established when I descended and made a beeline for the Torridon village shop, an unlikely venue from which I secured a copy of the 'new Tables' and verified the changes in black and white.

As a postscript to this tale, I decided to splash out a hefty £22 for dinner, bed and breakfast at the Torridon Hotel, partly to celebrate Liathach's new Munro and partly to escape the jaws of the rampant midges, which had devoured me on the previous night's camping. A few pints were sunk with 'the bearers of good news' in the Ben Damh bar that evening, and the following day we completed our arranged traverse of Beinn Alligin. Little did we know, however, that its then-single Munro, Sgùrr Mhòr, would also become two in 16 years with the 1997 revisions.

One reaction to this tale is the legitimate question as to how Munro's Tables can be tampered with by changing prior Tops to Munros. Surely, the Tables are a historical document and should remain sacrosanct? Interfering and altering the 'holy writ' of Munro is viewed as blasphemous and beyond the pale by many purists. However, the opposing view states that because Hugh Munro left no explicit criterion for distinguishing between Munros and Tops, the field was open to make changes, albeit with prolonged and careful consideration.

It is to this prolonged and careful consideration that we now turn, but firstly, an attempt to gain some insight into Munro's thinking on these issues. Undoubtedly, he placed a high emphasis on the amount of 'separation' between two summits in order to decide if one or both of them deserved full Munro status. The separation depends on such factors as distance and drop between the two summits, which will later be discussed in full. Other factors influencing his thinking were the presence of a name on the map (as mentioned previously) and even if a particular summit had a cairn! Munro did ponder long and hard on these issues; he once visited his hill mentor, Sir Colin Phillip, on Arran, where 'hills and tops were discussed for three days and three nights with but little intermission'. Unfortunately, none of these discussions was ever recorded, and interpretations of Munro's methodology remain little more than informed guesswork.

Returning to names, one aspect of this influence survived the 1921 revisions, indicating that Munro was in favour of its retention. The aspect concerns mountain groups with singular range names, such as Liathach, Beinn Alligin, Beinn Eighe, An Teallach and Ben Wyvis, to name a few. Each of these ranges contains several summits, none of which have the same name as the range. For example, Liathach is comprised of two main summits, neither of which is called Liathach (as the earlier tale shows). More to the point, in all these cases, Hugh Munro assigned only one Munro. On the other hand, mountain ranges with collective names, such as the Mamores, the Grey Corries and the Fannichs all contain numerous Munros, despite the fact that the separation, in drop and distance, between some Munros in these groups is less than that of some summits in the previous groups. So perhaps if Liathach had instead been named 'The Torridons', he would have assigned it two Munros!

The preceding discussion has obvious relevance to the 1981

and 1997 revisions of the Tables, both of which have initiated much argument and controversy. Before reaching any hasty conclusions, however, we need to examine some serious attempts to quantify, rationalise and justify adherence, and indeed non-adherence, to Munro's guidelines, scanty though they are.

Throughout the years, various SMC members have made attempts to establish criteria for distinguishing Munros from other Munros, Munros from Tops, Tops from other Tops and even Tops from minor tops. We shall focus almost exclusively on the first two in the following discussion. The three individuals who have probably made the most valuable, useful and usable contributions are John Dow (the fifth Munroist), Frank Bonsall and David Purchase, the latter producing the most comprehensive, detailed and user-friendly analysis.

As a sufficient separation between summits is generally deemed to be the most significant factor in distinguishing Munros, we will examine this notion in some detail. As already mentioned, distance and drop both contribute to separation. The 'drop' for a particular summit is simply the minimum height we would need to descend to reach an adjacent higher summit, and the distance is the minimum distance we would need to walk to reach the same summit. However, a third factor also requires consideration: terrain. The more awkward the intervening terrain, the longer it will take to walk or scramble between the two summits. Think of 'walking' between say, Sgùrr Alasdair and Sgùrr Mhic Coinnich in the Skye Cuillin, and walking between Creag a' Mhàim and Druim Shionnach on the South Cluanie ridge. The first involves tricky scrambling, down climbing and even possible abseiling; the second is a mere stroll. John Dow summed up these three factors as distance, dip and difficulty, which appeals greatly to my fondness for alliterations. Dow commented that a formula (or, in more modern parlance, algorithm) could be found to determine distance and dip, but the 'difficulty' aspect of the terrain is more subjective to each hillwalker, which seems entirely reasonable. Obviously, the time taken to walk from one summit to another depends on these three factors, and Frank Bonsall subsequently derived a formula for this time based on distance and dip, or drop, using Naismith's Rule.

W Naismith was the founder of the SMC, and his name will always be linked with his famous hillwalking rule: an hour for every three miles, plus half an hour for every thousand feet of ascent. In actuality, Bonsall's time separation equation was determined from the lower of two summits to the nearest higher ground, not necessarily to the nearest higher summit. This was to avoid certain anomalies that are beyond the scope of this discussion. Bonsall concluded that if the time separation was 30 minutes or more, then the lower summit was deemed to be a Munro. If the time separation was less than 30 minutes, then the lower summit was a Top. Omitting the Cuillin from Bonsall's analysis, which wisely he did, there is remarkable agreement between his theory and Munro's reckoning. Bonsall found that only 12 Tops in Hugh Munro's list had a separation of more than 30 minutes. Currently, this total stands at only seven, courtesy of the 1981 and 1997 revisions. David Purchase has since created a slightly more sophisticated analysis that produced a more definitive list, given later. For the record, Mullach an Rathain on Liathach, the newly christened Munro that I bagged unexpectedly in 1981, has a separation of 38 minutes.

So according to Bonsall, seven Tops should be Munros. But what about Munros that should be Tops? He was more coy in this respect and asserted that the majority of Munros have separations of 26 minutes or more, but that seven Munros have separations less than 23 minutes. These seven have now shrunk to just one: Càrn Ghluasaid (more on that later). It could be concluded that Bonsall's analysis rates pretty highly in comparison with Hugh Munro's reckoning, but David Purchase's scrutiny, though partly based on Bonsall's study, made significant improvements. In a strong sense, Purchase's novel approach was to allow the existing Munro list to dictate the criteria for their inclusion, rather than the other way round. He did this by first plotting the Munros and Tops on a distance-drop graph and then drawing a straight line between the two axes, separating Munros and Tops in such a way as to match the current Tables as closely as possible. The line was drawn between the two points: 'zero distance, 150-metre drop' and 'four-kilometre distance, zero drop', meaning that any hill having a drop of 150 metres or more, or at a distance of four kilometres or more, *must* qualify as a Munro. A second line was also drawn from the 30-metre point to the four-kilometre point to separate Tops from minor tops.

Essentially, any 'point' lying above the line signified a Munro, and its distance above that line signified its associated merit for being a Munro. In other words, summits well above the line are more deserving of Munro status. Hills close to the line are deemed to be within a 'zone of fuzziness', and their status should rightly remain unchanged. Whereas Bonsall ranked Munro merit on the basis of time separation, Purchase ranked them on this vertical distance above the line, which he calls the 'excess'. Bonsall's approach tended to emphasise distance over drop, but Purchase's analysis gave drop rightful priority over distance, in agreement with Dow. As for 'difficulty', a factor which really only applies to the Skye Munros, Purchase again wisely omitted the Cuillin from his analysis, indicating that these summits are in a class of their own.

The great beauty and benefit of David Purchase's approach is its combined simplicity and sophistication together with its grounding in Hugh Munro's own ideology. As a mathematician to trade, I applaud his efforts wholeheartedly and view his undoubtedly time-consuming endeavours as the seminal statement on this subject. He also extended his analysis to Percy Donald's list of 2,000-foot hills in the Southern Uplands and English, Welsh and Irish Hills, where he used 100 metres as a minimum drop for 'mountain status'. It is interesting that he uses metric units for both drop and distance, despite the Munros themselves having a minimum height in imperial units. Indeed, he is the main proponent of the controversial suggestion that Munros should be redefined as mountains over 900 metres. This is one crucial aspect on which I disagree, and maintain that if we alter the absolute height threshold, we are not just moving the goalposts, but changing the game.

It is a curiosity that we live in a country where we have allegedly adopted the metric system, yet still universally have road signs marked in miles and where many people still think in feet, inches, stones and pounds. This strange halfway house has also crept into hill measurements and in particular the odd practice of expressing absolute heights in imperial and relative heights in metric. The most obvious example of this is in the definition of a Graham. A Graham is defined as a Scottish hill under 2,500 feet, having a minimum absolute height of 2,000 feet and a relative height, or drop, of at least 150 metres. This definition is a rough metric equivalent of the Corbett criterion, relating to Scottish hills under 3,000 feet with a minimum height of 2,500 feet and a drop of at least 500 feet. Since 500 feet is equal to 152.4 metres, it was deemed suitable to use the round figure of 150 metres.

It is not coincidental that this 150-metre reascent threshold was used by David Purchase, and it has now become the standard minimum drop required for a summit to assume 'mountain status'. Both Corbetts and Grahams use only an objective drop criterion to determine inclusion, which implies that they are well-defined summits with totally justified criterion for existence, unlike the subjective nature of Munros. It is interesting that if the 150-metre drop criterion was the only criterion used to define Munros, then the 14 Munros east of Glen Shee would drop drastically to only three (Lochnagar, Glas Maol and Mount Keen), indicating the 'rolling plateau' and 'smaller drops' nature of the terrain.

David Purchase's analysis was undertaken after the contentious 1981 Tables revision and no doubt was greatly initiated by the furore following it. So what caused this outcry? Other than the 'tampering' aspect already mentioned, contrarily, there was a feeling amongst some that the revisions had not gone far enough. In adopting the 150-metre drop criterion of promoting any Top to Munro which satisfied the minimum drop, only two out of five such Tops were upgraded to Munros in the 1981 changes: Mullach an Rathain on Liathach and Garbh Chioch Mhòr in Glen Dessarry. To add insult to injury, a further two Tops with a drop of less than 150 metres were promoted. One was deserving of its promotion (Sgùrr Fiona, on An Teallach, with a drop of 145 metres), but the other, Sgòr an Iubhair in the Mamores, with a drop of only 77 metres, was a resurrection from a previous deletion (and promptly deleted again in the 1997 revisions!). But the biggest bombshell of 1981 concerned Liathach's mighty neighbour, Beinn Eighe, with its magnificent cluster of six distinct 3,000-foot summits. Its only Munro was Ruadh Stac Mòr, certainly the highest summit, but rather a whaleback outlier, lying off the main ridge. Spidean Coire nan Clach, a peak at the centre of the range, with a whopping drop of 168 metres, could easily lay claim as being the true representative of Beinn Eighe itself, yet it was left as a Top. Also, in Glencoe, the summit of Stob Coire Raineach on the Buachaille Etive Beag ridge laid claim to being the Top with the biggest drop, at 177 metres, and it too languished in its lower status. The last '150-metre drop' summit to remain unpromoted was Tom na Gruagaich on Beinn Alligin, the third of the Torridon trio, including Liathach and Beinn Eighe.

The 1981 revisions will forever be unfairly associated with Hamish Brown and JC Donaldson, who were asked by the SMC to recommend changes in the wake of map metrication and the OS resurvey. These proposals were subsequently discussed with the SMC at a meeting, then put to a vote. The result in, Hamish Brown's own words, was 'a botched-up compromise', with which he was clearly unhappy. On discussing the issue with Brown, he had no hesitation claiming that the SMC lost a unique chance to do the job properly.

Perhaps partly in reaction to the inevitable flap and fluster following the 1981 changes, Alan Dawson, creator of the 'Marilyn' hill list (see chapter 8), decided to compile his own list of 3,000-foot Scottish hills and called them the 'Murdos'. In keeping with the mixed metric/imperial fashion, he defined a Murdo as a Scottish mountain of 3,000 feet and above, with a minimum drop of 30 metres. The 444 Murdos obviously had a massive overlap with the (then) 517 Munros and Tops. Alan Dawson's disdain for the SMC is apparent in his remarks that

> their intermittent tinkering has resulted in a list of
> Munros that is neither Sir Hugh Munro's original list nor
> a systematic revision. It is not based on any particular
> criteria, so it has become just a list of mountains
> published by the Scottish Mountaineering Club, loosely
> based on an original idea by Sir Hugh Munro.[2]

Despite the 'botched-up compromise' of the 1981 revisions and certainly in the wake of the 1997 revisions (of which a discussion will follow), I find these comments a trifle harsh. Hugh Munro's original list was never intended to be 'set in stone', as Munro remarked himself. Whether hills are switched from Top to Munro, or vice versa, does not remove them from the list, and very few original Tops have been removed completely. The list of Munros and Tops is still essentially Munro's own list, not 'loosely based' on it. I am sure that if Munro were alive today, he would have approved of any changes, but would no doubt be chuckling to himself in amazement as to how serious the problems of his innocent list have become in some people's minds.

According to the late Irvine Butterfield, Munroist number 105, and acknowledged authority on Munro-related matters, the 1921 revision of the Tables suggested that a 250-foot drop criterion was beginning to emerge from the analysis as a suitable criterion for mountain status. Irvine subsequently produced a list of the 304 mountains satisfying this condition along with another 133 Tops satisfying a hundred-foot drop criterion, giving a total of 437 summits of 3,000 feet – or 440, allowing for three 'doubtful' Tops. As 100 feet is approximately 30 metres, this final total is close to Dawson's Murdo count of 444.

In 1997, it was Derek Bearhop's turn to run the gauntlet and take any flak for revisions to the Tables. If the 1981 revisions were a 'halfway house', then surely the 1997 revisions would see the job done properly? Yes and no. The good news was that the remaining three '150-metre drop' summits were promoted to Munros, which was an essential move in order for the SMC to retain any credibility. In addition, another five Tops, which appeared on David Purchase's list of 17 Tops in descending order of priority for promotion, were also upgraded. However, the five chosen appear to be an almost random selection from his list, with two of them (An Stùc of Ben Lawers and Sgòr an Lochain of Cairn Toul) sitting second and third from the bottom! The inclusion of an extra Munro on Buachaille Etive Mòr, Bidean nam Bian and the Five Sisters ridge, however, was a bold and (almost) correct decision; when all factors are taken into account, the SMC seemed to have redeemed a modicum of dignity.

David Purchase's original list of 17 Tops most deserving of promotion has now been reduced to nine, five of which have an 'excess' (height above his critical line) between 45 metres and 131 metres. The other four have an excess below 16 metres. The first five, in order of merit, are Glas Leathad Beag (Ben Wyvis), Sgùrr na Lapaich (Mam Sodhail), Sail Mhòr (Beinn Eighe), Stob na Doire (Buachaille Etive Mòr) and Cairn Lochan (Cairn Gorm). It is a moot point if any of these are likely to be promoted in the near future – if at all. My own preferences include Stob na Doire, with a drop of 145 metres, and in my view (and David Purchase's) more deserving than Stob na Bròige, which has both less height and less relative height, though its position at the termination of the Buachaille Etive Mòr ridge has no doubt influenced the decision. Another thoroughly deserving candidate, and my second contender, is Sgùrr na Lapaich in Glen Affric. This too stands proudly at the end of a ridge, over two miles from its parent summit of Mam Sodhail and totally dominating Glen Affric. This summit has always sat uncomfortably with the SMC as ripe for promotion, and maybe one day it will gain its true glory. Finally, only one out of 13 possible Munros was recommended for demotion to Top in the 1997 revision, Càrn Ghluasaid of Cluanie, with a shortfall of just 52 metres (distance below the critical line) and a drop of only 60 metres.

By this point, many readers will be thinking that the whole issue regarding the status of Munros and Tops is being taken far too seriously and that the proponents of these opposing viewpoints need to 'get out more'. This is a fair criticism, but there will always be a see-sawing between the traditionalists and modernists, with a good dose of unflexing rigidity on both sides. Part of the title of this chapter is the word 'topology'. Mathematically, this is the study of spatial relationships, which are unaffected by continuous changes of shape. Although I intended to hijack this meaning and replace it with something like 'the study of Tops', the true meaning possesses a message, crucial to the point I wish to make. What is unaffected by the continual change of the status of Munros and Tops? It is essentially the spirit of Sir Hugh Munro. Regardless of the additions and deletions to the Tables, his legacy remains secure, and his memory will forever be enshrined in the name given to Scotland's 3,000-foot mountains.

We now turn to the third and least contentious factor governing the ongoing changes to the Tables – the checking of mountain heights. As already seen in chapters 1 and 2, many of the early pioneers, such as Heddle, Munro, Robertson and Burn, all used pocket aneroids to gauge the heights of Munros, and prior to that, map-makers such as William Roy used simpler barometric methods in conjunction with geodetic surveys. Munro gleaned most of his height information from the government OS maps of the time, which consisted of both one-inch and six-inch scales. The one-inch maps had contours, but only at 250-foot intervals and included few spot heights, whereas the six-inch maps had no contours, but numerous names and spot heights. It is almost certain that Munro would have owned most or all of these maps, and considering their obvious deficiencies, it is remarkable that his Tables contained so few height anomalies.

The real catalyst which prompted a fresh scrutiny of mountain heights was the Ordnance Survey's shift to metric from imperial in 1974. That the OS had 'progressed' from giving heights in feet, to one decimal place, to heights in metres, to the nearest metre, with the corresponding massive increase in possible error, was a nightmare for those wishing to determine true heights and illustrated the Survey's more lax principles. As 3,000 feet is 914.4 metres, it followed that any mountain shown as 914 metres or 915 metres could be under or over 3,000 feet and would require checking. There were five such hills, two marked as 914 metres and classed as Corbetts (Beinn Dearg in Torridon and Ganu Mor of Foinaven) and three marked as 915 metres and classed as Munros (Sgùrr nan Ceannaichean, near Moruisg, Ben Vane and Beinn Teallach). Even before metrication, conjecture had ebbed and flowed over the status of Foinaven; the prospect of a 'new Munro' could propel the popular press into frenzied speculation – such was the popularity of Munros. It was only a matter of time until the issue would be settled once and for all, but who would carry out the measurements, and how would this be done? The OS appeared to be the obvious answer, but remeasuring mountain heights was not number one on their priority list, as it was only of real concern to a specific breed of hillwalkers.

The Munro Society (TMS; see chapter 8), formed in 2002, represented that 'specific breed'. In 2006, they took on this weighty – or should it be 'heighty' – challenge. Perhaps 'weighty' is an understatement, because any new height measurement would have to be accepted by the SMC, the custodian of Munro's Tables, which would not accept any changes unless verified by the OS; however, the OS was not involved with The Munro Society – a classic Catch-22. In addition, the sheer cost in money, time and labour was a monumental consideration that would require serious thought. Personal GPS devices did not possess the required accuracy, especially for height, and the machines that were up to the task had a huge price tag and could only be operated by experts in the field. After much to-ing and fro-ing, a surveying firm was found that was prepared to carry out the task for free – in view of the likely publicity generated if a new Munro was discovered. The firm's only stipulation was that the operators and equipment be safely escorted to the summit by TMS members who would help with load carrying.

Few will realise the parley and palaver involved in making a height measurement. Leaving aside the act of transporting equipment and manpower to the summit, there then follows several hours of work before the next stage of the process. Obviously, the equipment must be erected on the highest point of the mountain, but often the high point is far from clear, and it is not necessarily at the cairn or trig point. Cairns may have to be partially dismantled in order to find solid rock or earth underneath, then reassembled on completion. Even when all the necessary measurements have been made, a checking and ratification process involving the OS and the SMC must take place after the descent from the mountain.

One uncontrollable factor is the weather, and although both 914-metre summits were successfully remeasured in 2007, poor conditions plagued both 'heightings'. By far, the greatest media interest was in Foinaven, which was strongly tipped to be a new Munro. So much so that on the morning of the press conference to announce the result, a *Daily Mail* reporter climbed Foinaven in order to claim the first ascent of a new Munro. His glory was short-lived, however, when the height was announced as only 911 metres (2,989 feet), nearly 11 feet lower than the existing map height. Beinn Dearg also remained a Corbett at 913.6 metres, and media interest naturally waned somewhat. The 11-foot discrepancy on Foinaven suggested that other Munros and Corbetts bunching around the 3,000-foot mark would benefit from further measurement, and a sizeable list of 21 possible candidates was drawn up, ranging in height from 909 metres to 918 metres and arranged in order of priority. However, the hired surveying firm, perhaps miffed by the negative results on Foinaven and Beinn Dearg, was no longer willing to provide its services for free, but offered 'reduced rate' prices instead. These still proved too expensive for TMS, and by 2008 there appeared to be another impasse.

The hand of fate took an emphatic positive swing when press coverage revealed that three 'hobbyist' surveyors had validated a Welsh mountain as being over 2,000 feet, decreeing it 'Welsh Mountain' status. Not only had the measurements been accepted by the OS, but the main surveyors, John Barnard and Graham Jackson, were both Munroists, who were promptly invited to join TMS and who agreed to undertake 'Heightings' for under £600 per mountain, a sum acceptable to TMS. Things were once again looking up... pardon the pun.

Of the five 'priority hills', the remaining three were checked in 2009, but produced only one negative change. Sgùrr nan Ceannaichean was found to be 913.5 metres and so reverted to its previous Corbett status, as it had been before the 1981 changes. By this time, the media were beginning to lose interest, and the press conference elicited fewer reporters. However, the reclassification of Sgùrr nan Ceannaichean persuaded TMS to continue with its agenda for the larger cluster group of 21 hills. Hoping for a Munro promotion, they concentrated largely on some higher Corbetts around Drumochter and Gaick Pass in 2010, but all remained in the shorter category with no significant height changes.

The general lull in proceedings was revitalised when an offer was given to finance the heighting of three hills in the remote Fisherfield Forest by Alan Haworth, a Labour Peer and Lord Haworth of Fisherfield. Haworth was a TMS member, and his generous offer could not be refused. In July 2011, an army of TMS members and the usual technical crew took on the task. Logistically, the challenges of such a remote area were considerable, but crucially, the weather was unusually kind, and the heightings were carried out with few problems – even the midges kept a low profile. The three hills were all on the list of possible contenders and included the magnificent Corbett of Beinn Dearg Mor, and the two Munros of Ruadh Stac Mòr and Beinn a' Chlaidheimh. The hoped-for Munro promotion of Beinn Dearg Mor was thoroughly demolished when its height was reduced by four metres to 906.4 metres. There was no significant change to Ruadh Stac Mòr, but Beinn a' Chlaidheimh flipped back to its pre-1974 state, as a Corbett, when it was found to be 914.0 metres – now the highest Corbett. This brought the number of Munros to their current number of 282. Whether Lord Haworth's financial involvement in this latest venture raised the profile of the event, or for other reasons, media interest was high; the Press Association Report on the TMS findings appeared in over 40 newspapers, including a handful of foreign publications.

The ensuing years have seen no further major changes, but a trip to Skye in the summer of 2013 saw the demotion of Knight's Peak on Sgùrr nan Gillean from a Top. Certain press outlets, unaware of the Top distinction, wrongly reported that a Munro had been demoted. One final quirky development occurred in July 2015 when a German TV production company arrived in Scotland to make a documentary on some more idiosyncratic and out of the ordinary facets of Scottish culture. A significantly large group of people who climbed mountains because they were above a specific height, and spent considerable time and effort checking these heights, was viewed as prime quality material for their programme. So, on the lower slopes of Ben Lawers, TMS and the usual gang staged a simulated heighting, with all the usual surveyors, poles and equipment, complete with customary rain, mist and midges.

The Munro Society is to be congratulated for its determined efforts over the course of several years to successfully undertake this series of heightings; in particular, its coordinator, Iain Robertson, deserves attention. Robertson is one of the oldest surviving Munroists; he became the 55th in 1963, even predating 'old man of the hills', Hamish Brown, who was the 62nd Munroist in 1965. Robertson was also one of the founding members of TMS. More detailed information on the heightings outlined in this chapter can be found in the book *Scaling the Heights*, published by TMS in 2018.

This chapter ends on a rather sad note... well, only sad if you are a nerdy mathematician like myself. Prior to the two most recent demotions of Munros to Corbetts, the total number of

Munros was 284 and the number of Corbetts was 220. These two numbers are astoundingly special from a mathematical viewpoint. They are known as 'amicable numbers', meaning that the sum of the proper divisors of each is equal to the other. Not only that, but they are the only pair of amicable numbers under a thousand. I will not endeavour to demonstrate this, but in the spirit of maths textbooks of old, I will leave it as an exercise for the reader. The recent changes by The Munro Society have destroyed the elegant, profound amicability of Munros and Corbetts; in order to restore this delicate, mathematical harmony, two Corbetts will require eligibility for Munro promotion... so keep measuring!

CHAPTER 5

Boomers and Baggers

AN ANGUISHED YELP followed by a string of gross expletives drifted up from the swirling mist below. Then, as if to disguise the colourful language, a disembodied voice shouted up – 'Watch yersels, the rocks are gey slippy!'

'It sounds like it's no oorselves we need to watch, Jack', shouted back Martin, who was holding up the rear. This remark induced a ripple of laughter from the group, lightening the edgy atmosphere surrounding our precarious descent.

'Stob Bàn' translates as 'white peak', a name owing to the smooth, white quartzite rock, of which it and the Grey Corries is composed. When wet, or damp, it is potentially lethal for walking or climbing on, as Jack, one of our instructors, had painfully discovered. Only ten minutes earlier, we had ascended the same route with no problems, but descending awkward and slippery terrain always requires more care. Minutes later, with thankfully no more profanities, we reached the neat pile of colourful rucksacks which we had left on the bealach below the next summit of Stob Choire Claurigh.

That morning, we had vacated the dubious, spartan delights of Lairig Leacach Bothy, over a thousand feet below, and plodded up the wide, grassy corrie to the bealach, from which the almost incident-free ascent of Stob Bàn was made, free of our heavy backpacks. The ensuing 1,200-foot climb up Stob Choire Claurigh, with full packs, seemed endless, and the ever-present low clouds ensured no scenic reward for our efforts.

'OK... ten-minute stop here... get some grub inside you,'

shouted Jack as we flopped down at the summit cairn, hearts thumping. Chomping away at my Mars bar, I began chatting to Stephen Brown, a broad Lancastrian with an even broader, almost permanent grin.

'Well, that's 80 Munros up,' he nonchalantly remarked. I stared at him blankly, my puzzled expression obvious.

'What's a Munro?', I asked curiously. Stephen launched into a rambling discourse on Hugh Munro, Tables and related matters. Unable to absorb the fact that he had notched up an amazing 80 of the 3,000-foot Scottish mountains, I began to view him as some kind of superman, but all the time I was thinking: if he could do it, so could I.

Four days before, a minibus had brought our group of two instructors and eight clients from Glenmore Lodge to Ben Alder Lodge, from which we embarked on our backpacking trip that would ultimately end at Ben Nevis and Fort William. The aim had been to traverse as many mountains en route as possible, and despite the abysmal low cloud, we had kept to the itinerary. A quick calculation, with Stephen's help, showed that this was our fifth Munro of the trip (Ben Alder, Stob Coire Easain, Stob a' Choire Mheadhoin, Stob Bàn and Stob Choire Claurigh). As I had already climbed Ben Lomond previously that year (my first Munro), that made my tally to date a giddy six Munros.

That innocent conversation with Stephen in August 1978 was my baptism, my rite of passage into a long, illustrious and chequered Munro-bagging odyssey, from which there was no return and no cure. Thereafter, as we stumbled along in the mist. Every summit traversed was accompanied by my urgent questions regarding its Munro status… I was stricken with acute Munroitis. The remaining two full days of the course saw my tally double to 12 Munros, with the highlight being the narrow, curving, rocky spine of the Càrn Mòr Dearg arête leading to the summit of Ben Nevis. Other than tantalising glimpses of a few wild corries and ridges, through parting mist, the low cloud remained permanently clamped to the mountain tops, and it was not until the morning of our last half day, whilst camped at

Lochan Meall an t-Suidhe, that the sun decided to pay us a visit. The glorious colour and splendour of the Western Highlands finally revealed itself, and I was hooked for life.

A fortnight later, I had moved from the Central Belt up to the village of Fort Augustus to begin a seven-year spell of teaching at the Abbey School. This physical relocation was also a mental relocation, and in a deep sense, it was my coming of age. Fort Augustus is often described as the geographical centre of the Highlands, a focal point from which the diverse range of mountainous country can be accessed with relative ease. For me, it also became a mental and spiritual hub, about which the rest of my life has revolved.

Not surprisingly, my Munro count entered overdrive during the Fort Augustus years, and almost exactly ten years after the Grey Corries baptism in 1978, myself and several friends were glugging champagne on the summit of Ben More on Mull, celebrating the culmination of a decade's quest and the end of an era. In doing so, I had entered the hallowed ranks of that elite band of brothers and sisters, known as Munroists, at number 594. Less than 200 souls had accomplished this quest when I had sat on the summit of Stob Choire Claurigh all those years before. In the intervening decade, over 400 more names had been added to the list. In other words, more than twice the number of people had climbed all the Munros in the space of ten years than had done so in the nearly 80 years since the first 'compleation' in 1901. Today, the annual increase in Munroists is around 200. The pre-war trickle had grown to torrential proportions by the 1980s, and has continued growing ever more rapidly in the passing years. So what caused this veritable flood?

In the years following World War Two, a renewed sense of freedom and optimism fostered the belief that anything was possible. Increased leisure time, the meteoric rise in car ownership and a healthier economy inspired many to seek the open countryside for fresh air and fresh challenges. This newfound affinity with the Great Outdoors gave rise to an increased awareness of training and safety, and in 1948, the

Scottish Centre of Outdoor Training was formed at Glenmore Lodge, which would facilitate trips such as the one described at the start of this chapter. In particular, courses for young people were initiated in which all facets of outdoor education were introduced, from sailing to abseiling, rock climbing to rescue techniques, summer hillwalking to winter ice-climbing, canoeing to cross-country skiing; the list goes on.

In the 1950s, the first ascent of Everest and the dawn of manned space exploration captured the public's imagination and symbolised man's struggle against the odds and the elements. For the average person, Everest was an impossible dream; meanwhile, the Munros provided a challenge that was not insurmountable – the Munros could be one's own personal Everest. In fact, that decade produced 20 Munroists, adding to the 15 prior to the end of the 1940s.

The post-war baby boom was in full swing, encapsulating anyone born between 1946 and 1964 under the term 'baby boomer', or just 'boomer'. The baby boomer generation has been blamed – fairly or unfairly – for many of today's ills, but no one has yet blamed them for the Munro-bagging boom... until now. Being born in 1954, I am well and truly a central member of this hippy-happy clan of 'world movers and world forsakers'. The exponential rise in Munro-bagging came to a head in the '70s and '80s, just as the boomers were hitting their 20s and 30s, the prime time for walking and climbing and establishing a toe hold on the first rung of the Munro ladder. The late 1960s mantra of 'Turn on, tune in and drop out' was slowly but surely being replaced with the Munro equivalent: 'Tune in, get out and climb up'. Long hair, beads and beards became, in the Highlands, grey hair – and even no hair – boots and beards. The possession of a beard is almost obligatory for a male Munro climber, but more on this later. The drug- and LSD-induced euphoria of the Woodstock era was giving in to a new and healthier hill-induced euphoria, where addiction was to reach new heights, in a metaphorical and literal sense. Sex, drugs and rock and roll were being sacrificed on the altar of

Hugh Munro, where the only 'rock and roll' was the rock you were sitting on and the cheese roll you were eating. The School of Hard Rock had closed for the summer... and what a summer it would be! The psychedelic, hallucinogenic summer of love gave way to the transformation of hippies into hillwalkers and a whole new mind-expanding scene.

This mind-expanding scene of Munros and Munro-bagging were, however, still well below the media radar in the '60s and even '70s; the Munro floodgates would not fully open until as late as 1985, when the first Munro guidebook appeared on the shelves. Rewind 20 years to 1965 when a book was published, described by *Climber and Rambler* magazine as 'nothing less than a monumental work': *The Scottish Peaks* by WA Poucher. The book could easily lay claim to be the forerunner to the avalanche of hillwalking books that would hit the market in the following decades. Poucher's book became a bestseller, and it is a testimony to its huge popularity that the book held its own despite the inevitable competition of scores of glossy, coloured rivals appearing 15 years later. The photographs were all black and white, but Poucher's reputation as a world-renowned landscape photographer and his fellowship with the Royal Photographic Society ensured that his book's photographic quality was second to none. In addition, his membership of the Climbers' Club and the Fell and Rock Climbing Club, together with his considerable 'hands-on' experience of hillwalking and climbing, gave *The Scottish Peaks* a masterly and professional air that far exceeded its rivals, if indeed it had any rivals.

The Scottish Peaks was way ahead of its time, not just for its photographic quality, but for the inclusion of one-inch-to-the-mile Ordnance Survey map reproductions with specific mountain routes indicated by dotted lines. In addition, many of the photographs had superimposed route lines and names marked on them. These two visionary concepts would not become the norm for another half-century and are now evident in post-millennium publications such as Ralph Storer's *The Ultimate Guide to the Munros* (Luath Press, 2008) and Tom Prentice's

The Cuillin and other Skye Mountains (Mica Publishing, 2019).

Poucher's writing style is somewhat dated, so on reading snippets from the book, there is a feeling that a knowledgeable, elderly uncle, complete with pipe, is talking to you in front of the roaring log fire of some Victorian hotel. He eulogises over 'mountains in snowy raiment' and weighs the advantages of nailed and Tricouni boots over new-fangled Vibram soles. Some of his observations and advice verge into the terrain of the 'mildly eccentric', such as his strong recommendation to wear red stockings as an aid to location, should you find yourself in need of assistance and subsequent rescue. And yes, he is referring to stockings rather than socks, as later advice encourages that each be worn together, for increased comfort and warmth, and reduced friction. The question as to how these stockings are prevented from sliding down the leg is not addressed, and the use of suspenders and corset is perhaps moving into a new avenue of exploration beyond the scope of the book... and this one!

An odd, but probably unconnected parallel with the above concerns Poucher's day job as an employee for Yardley's perfume company. Rumours of green eye-shadow, often worn by Poucher, were dismissed by myself as nonsense, until my outlook changed on one eventful day in 1982. I had just completed my only continuous traverse of the Cuillin ridge on Skye and was enjoying a slap-up meal in the Sligachan Hotel when I noticed an elderly gentleman ensconced in the corner, green eye-shadow darkening below his brows. Whether it was the eye decoration or true facial recognition, or a bit of both, I am unsure, but I had no hesitation in duly approaching him to corroborate my intuitions. I was of course correct in my perception and am now the proud owner of a signed copy of *The Magic of Skye*, another of Poucher's classic works, complete with sublime, monochromatic images of the 'Coolin' (his spelling). So if you should come across a lone gentleman in red stockings and green eye-shadow, it is not a temporal vision, but the ghost of the late Mr WA Poucher, a colourful character in more ways than one.

When *The Scottish Peaks* hit bookshelves in 1965, it would have bypassed the baby boomer generation, whose literary leanings then would hardly have progressed beyond *The Beano* and *New Musical Express*, with perhaps a selective, expletive-ridden interest in *Lady Chatterley's Lover*. I first discovered the book in a Fort William book shop in 1978 and purchased it for the princely sum of £3.50. I can honestly admit that the book was an immense source of inspiration and awakening to my newer, simpler, more profound delight in hills and mountains.

As if 1978 was not enough of a formative year for me, another book appeared that year which arguably did more to kickstart the Munro phenomenon than any other publication. The title *Hamish's Mountain Walk* may not exactly entice the average bookstore browser, but the subtitle, 'The first non-stop climb of all the 3,000-foot Scottish Munro peaks', whilst not exactly snappy, said all that needed to be said. This book by Hamish Brown has probably been read and re-read by most Munroists more than any other, and even today it continues to inspire countless future Munroists. It has survived several reprints and new editions and has deservedly become a classic of mountaineering literature. *Hamish's Mountain Walk* is currently available in paperback and published by Sandstone Press. The book is discussed in more detail in the following chapter, which deals almost entirely with non-stop Munro rounds and records.

As Hamish Brown is such an instrumental and central character in Munro-bagging culture, it is fitting at this point to examine his persona in more detail. When I first met Brown in his house, overlooking the Firth of Forth, in early 1994, I was endeavouring to get to know and understand the man and his many facets – it is a general misnomer that Munros are his only interest in life. Morocco, tall ships, canoeing, travel, birds, flowers, music, history, Scottish culture, post offices, cemeteries... he has passions along with Munros. When I met him back in 1994, Hamish was 60 years of age, but over 20 years later, he was still writing books and as full of wonder for the natural world as he ever was. His two recent books, *Walking the Song* and *Chasing the Dreams* (Sandstone), possess the same immediacy and sparkle as his 1978 epic work and will continue to inspire future generations of walkers and climbers.

During our chat in 1994, Brown produced a hefty volume outlining his experiences on the Scottish hills over his lifetime. This was just a summary of his stravaigings, however, and his 'office' housed a further 36 bound volumes in diary form. In the Foreword to *Walking the Song*, he divulges that he is now on Volume 73, just 23 years later! It is obvious that he has kept more detailed diaries in his later years, probably due to failing memory. As he put it:

> Memory is a strange thing, certainly for me, with a
> greater facility for forgetting rather than remembering.[1]

Join the club!

Brown's biggest interest and investment beyond Scotland is likely Morocco. For several decades, Brown has made regular three-month annual excursions to the Atlas Mountains, where he stays with a local family and guides private groups into the mountains. His increased dissatisfaction with the complexities and bureaucracy of modern living in the UK have been replaced with quiet contemplation in a relatively unfrequented haven of peace and solitude. His thirst for a 'back to basics' way of life is quenched in Morocco, and he often finds himself depressed on return to the petty sham of so-called civilised Britain. In *Walking the Song* he comments:

> On the first morning of every visit to Marrakesh I still
> climb to the rooftops at dawn and look south to the
> mountains of my life.[2]

On hearing this, it would almost appear that the Atlas mountains have replaced his beloved Munros as the mountains of his heart, and in a strong sense, this is true. In fact, in the mid-1990s, Brown 'put feet to the dream' and accomplished a three-month, 900-mile traverse of the Atlas range, a first, and the Moroccan counterpart to his continuous Munro traverse. Both trips were the natural consequence of his love affair with Munros and Morocco; his book *The Mountains Look on Marrakesh*, an account of the traverse, is the Moroccan equivalent of *Hamish's Mountain Walk*.

It would be fair to say that Brown has crammed more into his life than most people, and there is no doubt that his diaries and journals still contain enough quality material for dozens more books. As travel writer Kev Reynolds remarks on Brown's *Chasing the Dreams*:

> Perhaps the title of this book should be 'Living the Dream', for Hamish's dream is one that thousands aspire to but rarely capture.[3]

Hamish's Mountain Walk and Poucher's *The Scottish Peaks* were just two of around a half-dozen publications which could be regarded as the most influential and inspirational in the exponential growth of Munro-bagging in the 1970s and 1980s. The next trailblazing book came in 1980, with the launch of *The Big Walks*, compiled by Ken Wilson and Richard Gilbert. The walks were big and so was the book – a large, glossy coffee-table tome, which would set the scene for a host of future publications. Richard Gilbert became Munroist number 101 in 1971 and wrote most of the contributions, while Ken Wilson's publishing prowess, eye for detail and propensity for cutting no financial corners ensured that the final result, though expensive for the time (£16.95), would have the impact intended and achieve 'classic' status. The book had followed in the wake of *Hard Rock* and *Classic Rock*, two similar sized publications devoted to rock climbing routes. Before the end of the 1980s, another four productions basked in the glow of success generated by the previous three: *Classic Walks* and *Wild Walks*, which continued to positively encourage the hillwalking passion, as well as *Extreme Rock* and *Cold Climbs*.

The chief selling point of all these books is the collection of absolutely stunning photographs by a variety of photographers.

A single, high-quality, colour image of the Highland landscape can inspire and excite more than a thousand words of florid prose and has the immediacy and impact to encourage the average bookshop browser to part with serious money – I know I did. By today's standards, the photographic quality in *The Big Walks* is not exceptional; the difference between it and *Wild Walks* in 1988 is obvious. Nevertheless, what red-blooded hillwalker could fail to be moved by the double-spread image on pages 72–3 of two walkers about to embark on the grand, snowbound crest of the Càrn Mòr Dearg arête, leading to the summit of Britain's highest mountain? This is the view I should have had back in 1978 – minus the snow, of course.

Despite these books covering the rest of the UK (including Ireland) and Scotland, their only failing was their lack of comprehensiveness. The articles were essentially a hand-picked selection of the best mountain walks, cherrypicked to suit the overriding theme of each book (big, classic and wild). But the books had no pretensions of being comprehensive; their mission was to motivate, inspire and kindle the fire of enthusiasm in the hearts of potential hill-goers, and this they did, with unbridled success.

Two books were to hit the shelves within months of each other in 1985–6 which comprehensively covered the mountains over 3,000 feet, and both were destined to become bestsellers and 'bibles' among Munro-baggers. In today's climate of Munro popularity, it is hard to believe that before 1985, there were no Munro guidebooks and only a list of Munros published in Munro's Tables by the SMC. So the SMC publication *The Munros*, edited by the highly respected Donald Bennet, was ordained to occupy the bookshelf and rucksack of every self-respecting Munro climber and quickly disappeared from bookstores, like 'snow off a dyke'.

The Munros was the first of the SMC's new 'dust-coverless' hardback guidebooks, designed to survive the scrapes and knocks of outdoor use. Yet it was no pocket guide, and its relative weight and bulk placed it more in the bookshelf category rather than in the pocket of a rucksack. Its user-friendly and simple layout, with a Munro or a Munro group occupying a single or double page, with good quality colour photographs and easy-to-follow maps, all ensured its accolade as the bestselling Munro guidebook, despite the competition of later years. Quite simply, it was the original and best. The accompanying route descriptions, free of aesthetic embellishment, are straightforward and generally describe the most popular or direct routes by existing paths, appealing greatly to novice hillwalkers. The contributions by such SMC 'notables' as Donald Bennet, Peter Hodgkiss and Hamish Brown give the text a professional stamp and authority. The division of the Highlands into 17 sections, with an overview map showing all the Munros in that section, is an innovative idea and vitally useful for planning the ascent of groups of Munros; it also offers the best approach routes for cars. The SMC Munros guidebook has seen several revisions and re-editions, and it is deservedly destined for many more years of shelf life.

Literally months after the publication of *The Munros*, in the Spring of 1986, another book appeared that would be a serious contender in the hillwalking publication market. *The High Mountains (of Britain and Ireland)* by Irvine Butterfield (Diadem) was also aimed at Munro-baggers, but extended its repertoire to include the 3,000-foot peaks of England, Wales and Ireland, commonly known as 'the Furth'. The author, a Yorkshire man, became the 105th Munroist in 1971. His track record is impressive: he was an early member of the Mountain Bothies Association, a founding member of the John Muir Trust, the Scottish Wild Land Group and the Mountaineering Council of Scotland, and the first president of The Munro Society.

The book demands obvious comparisons with *The Munros* and is similar in many respects, notably in the mapping style and the division of the Highlands and the Furth into manageable regions. In style, presentation and number and quality of photographs, however, it is superior and its only real drawback is its fairly hefty size, placing it more in the category of coffee table books. Irvine was a traditionalist and did not agree with many of the recent changes in Munro's Tables. Although he describes the ascent routes to the 'new Munros', he does not include them in his initial overview at the beginning of each chapter. Subsequent editions of the book were titled *The High Mountains – Volume 1*, and it was Irvine's intention to produce a second book about Corbetts and other smaller hills. Due to financial problems, time and other factors, this book failed to materialise. *The High Mountains* has been out of print for many years.

The High Mountains could be considered Irvine Butterfield's seminal work, but on the cusp of the millennium, in 1999, he produced, with the help of many others, what could be regarded as the ultimate Munro-bagger's coffee table book. *The Magic of the Munros* was a breathtaking photographic tribute to Scotland's 3,000-foot mountains and Irvine's lasting 'swansong'. The book, published by David and Charles, is in large, panoramic format, ideally suited to its plethora of outstanding photos interspersed with Irvine's informative text. Each of six specific Highland regions opens with a painting by mountain artist Paul Craven and an overview by Irvine. The photos are taken by a selection of mainly Munroists, including Iain Robertson, Richard Wood, Tom Rix, Jim Teesdale and many others, including Irvine himself. By the time the book was launched, the Munro bandwagon was unstoppable, with Munroists now having broken the 2,000 mark. It could be argued that the book was 'preaching to the converted', but there is no doubt that it contributed to inspiring a whole generation of young Gen Xers and Millennials to take to the hills. I can imagine flicking through this hefty tome, years from now, when old age and arthritis have taken their toll, and basking in the warm glow of past forays in the hills. *The Magic of the Munros* has an assured place on the coffee tables of hillwalkers for many years to come.

One influential book in this market has the unique advantage of photographic content produced by a professional photographer. The author of *The Scottish Peaks* was also an accomplished mountain walker, which is perhaps fortuitous and unique. In the early 1990s, a young photographer by the name of Colin Prior was set to take the world of landscape photography by storm. Although his photography was not specifically aimed at the Munro and mountaineering market, the sheer quality of his images engendered an inspirational response, bordering on the sublime. The world 'ultimate' is often bandied about freely and carelessly, but many believe that Colin Prior's best images are the ultimate in landscape photography.

Honorary Scot Magnus Magnusson remarked on opening the pages of Prior's first book, *Highland Wilderness*, that it was

> like the feeling he had as a boy when he first saw
> CinemaScope in all its eye-stretching splendour.[4]

Prior's work is landscape photography at its limits, both technical and in terms of extreme lighting conditions and the backbreaking measures required to be in the right place at the right time. For the vast majority of mountain walkers, being in the right place at the right time is down to pure luck. If the light is right and the view is fine, then we snap away and move on. For Colin Prior, every photograph is the result of a long, hard series of events and observations, including patient checking of light and weather conditions, failed attempts and summit bivvies.

It is said that genius is one per cent inspiration and 99 per cent perspiration. I would add another two qualities and declare that Prior's photographs are the result of devotion, dedication, inspiration and perspiration in equal doses. To produce images like Prior's, a love of landscape is essential, as well as an eye for composition, the finest equipment, and knowledge of the best time and season to take the photograph. All good photographers are aware of the 'golden hour', when a low sun accentuates the finer details in a landscape and shades of red and gold give an ethereal quality to the surroundings. To see this first-hand is one thing, but to capture it perfectly in a single image is the result of a long, exhausting apprenticeship with no shortcuts. Colin Prior has served his apprenticeship to the full and has spent countless hours on the Scottish mountains in all weathers to achieve his goal of capturing these elusive images. For mere hillwalking Munro-baggers, the goal is to reach the summit, our photos just a record of our accomplishment. While Prior's goals differ, our intrinsic love of the wild landscape unites us. Of course, Prior is no stranger to mountaineering. In winter, crampons, ice axe and head torch are as essential to him as his wide format camera and tripod. In any season, the combined attributes of commitment, patience and tenacity are equally important; so much has to come together for each image to materialise.

Prior's two main books, *Highland Wilderness* and *Scotland: The Wild Places* (Constable), have undoubtedly inspired and encouraged potential Munro climbers. A recent box set of his best work is now on sale for a cool £100! Prior's profile has grown to the extent that his name is now almost synonymous with Scottish landscape photography, and his panoramic calendars are often sold out within weeks. Not surprisingly, Prior has several imitators, the best probably being Alan Gordon, whose 2007 photographic book, *The Scottish Mountains*, with accompanying text by Hamish Brown, is definitely worth a perusal.

Other than image quality, the key difference between Colin Prior's photographs and those from other books already mentioned, is their lack of people. Prior's photos are stripped back to the bare essentials of form, texture, light and wildness. Walkers would only detract from these fundamental elements. Having no foreground interest of the human variety allows the viewer to become totally immersed in the scene and, indeed, become part of the scene. Looking at a Colin Prior image is as close as one might get to actually being on a Munro without actually making the trek. Lying on my deathbed many years from now (hopefully!), I can imagine myself looking at the double page 'cloud inversion' image on page 56–7 from *Highland Wilderness* and thinking that if there is no heaven beyond, then it is at least there in front of me now, to be carried to the grave.

In the roughly 30 years of literary and photographic Munro influences, from Poucher to Prior, the Munroist tally had snowballed from trickle to torrent to tsunami. Another media aspect found living room audiences in the Spring of 1991. *The Munro Show* was a prime-time television programme presented by the already popular Muriel Gray; it first aired exactly 100 years after the launch of Sir Hugh Munro's Tables. The programme followed in the wake of Gray's book, *The First Fifty – Munro bagging without a beard*, a title indicating more than a suggestion of humour. The connection of Munros and beards goes back to an article in the *SMC Journal* by Munroist number 5, J Dow, who jokingly remarked that he was the first person to climb all the Munros without the assistance of a beard. He went further, however, in maintaining the scurrilous proposition that bearded men 'cannot, in a civilised society, be reckoned' and therefore that the 'glory and honour' of the first Munroist should go to him.

I doubt that these ramblings by a crusty old SMC stalwart had any bearing on the title of Muriel's book. What she was really saying was that women could climb Munros as well as any man, bearded or otherwise. The fact that

> a self-confessed eight stone peroxide-blonde girl with spindly shanks and a nose that turns blue if not kept at constant room temperature[5]

could have notched up 50 Munros was indeed a crucial spur to all potential female Munro-baggers. Such female frivolity as that found in her book could not be passed unchecked, however, and the male reply came in 1994 in the form of Hamish Brown's *The Last Hundred – Munros, Beards and a Dog* (Mainstream). He makes the point that

> I'm no Oor Wullie look-alike in puking colours and the Gray and the Brown would probably agree to differ on a whole range of topics.[6]

Despite their playful and colourful differences, both are united by the Munros, which are 'a great shared blessing'.

The Munro Show, now available on DVD, had a huge impact on the numbers taking up Munro-bagging. The Irish comedian Ed Byrne was an 18-year-old Glasgow student when he first watched the programme, which was the spur for his current 'bagging' interest – he has well over a hundred Munros under his belt. Ed confessed that 'hillwalking will never be hip', yet here was this woman who had interviewed people like Morrissey and Paul Weller. What was she doing stoating about on a drizzly mountain? What indeed.

Of course, TV programmes about Scotland's wild country were not new; prior shows included the likes of *Weir's Way*, *MacGregor's Scotland*, *Wainwright in Scotland* and the esoteric *Where Eagles Fly* series by the late Hamish MacInnes. The main programmes since *The Munro Show*, have been Cameron McNeish's festive seasonal offerings which concentrate on long walks through the Highlands, as well as Paul Murton's *Grand Tours of Scotland* travelogues.

The Munro Show, was quirky, fun and self-effacing, and it avoided the stereotypical 'random' encounters with locals evident in other outdoor programmes. The format involved two distinct walks over one or more Munros, separated by a short, flashy feature on a hill-related issue. The opening scene of a group of diverse, colourfully booted dancers against a background of a subliminal montage of mountain images, complete with a 'get up and go' rap soundtrack, broke all the rules of outdoor programming. Near the end of the programme, the contrasting image of famous Gaelic poet, Sorley MacLean, seated in a traditional Scottish schoolroom and instructing, with scholarly precision, on the semantic subtleties of the mountain's name, chalked on the blackboard, was a stroke of genius.

The prime ingredient of the show, however, was Muriel Gray herself. Her flamboyant enthusiasm, impish humour and irreverent banter were crucial in creating a marvellously refreshing and highly watchable series. She resembled a female version of 'Oor Wullie' with her blonde, spiky hair and lithe frame, darting up mountains dressed in colourful fleece jackets, all the while spouting forth her canny, funny observations, such as her description of Scotland's narrowest and scariest mainland ridge, the Aonach Eagach, as a 'brown underpants job'. A feminist, Gray would no doubt have had a field day with the stark Victorian image of Walter Poucher, though with his red stockings and green eye-shadow, they would strike a colourful scene on the hill together.

The show brought the sport of Munro climbing to the most chronic couch potatoes, and more essentially, it transformed Munro-bagging from a macho, male-dominated pastime discussed in the pub to the common domestic level of the living room. Women were climbing Munros too, and many without the moral support of a bearded, male companion. Yet only around a fifth of Munroists are female, so there is room yet to expand the hobby's scope.

While on the subject of humour (and beards), a bi-monthly 'hillzine', *The Angry Corrie*, was launched in 1991, edited by Dave Hewitt and co-compiler Alan Dawson, who also produced the series of booklets containing relatively obscure lists of hills, of which more in chapter 8. The series of booklets contained relatively obscure lists of hills, of which more in chapter 8. *The Angry Corrie* was essentially a *Private Eye* for hillwalkers and contained a raucous collection of offbeat articles, cartoons, letters and satirical observations about anything remotely connected to Scottish hills, and Munros in particular. A few serious articles helped to complement the magazine's humorous bent. The magazine's focal character was 'Murdo Munro' – 'he's a bugger of a bagger' - a stereotyped impression of the lone, male Munro-bagger, complete with beard, glasses, woolly hat and cagoule. The 'fanzine' was entirely self-funded, featuring no advertising and reliant on contributions from various sources. It subsequently developed a cult following, despite its reduced availability in selected outdoor shops and pubs, such as the Clachaig Inn. It has been out of circulation for several years – whether resting or deceased remains to be seen. Hewitt's blog,

'Hill Informed', is also worth a look.

This chapter would not be complete without a brief discussion on Munro guides and outdoor magazines. As already mentioned, prior to 1985, there were no guidebooks to the Munros... today there are at least half a dozen to choose from. Apart from possibly Cameron McNeish's large format book, *The Munros*, complete with excellent photography and beautiful relief mapping (1996, Lomond Books), most of the other offerings had no major influence on Munro-bagging popularity.

However, one series of books, entitled *The Ultimate Guide to the Munros* by Ralph Storer (Luath Press), published in 2008, broke the mould of the guidebook genre in one specific area – humour. As stated previously, the series took inspiration from Poucher's *The Scottish Peaks* by including OS maps and photographs with superimposed routes. The 'Ultimate' tag related to the inclusion of all practicable ascent routes described for every Munro. Thus, the 'one Munro–one route' scheme of other guidebooks was completely demolished; its back cover blurb of 'the only guide to the Munros you'll ever need' is pretty close to the truth. However, it is Storer's creative use of corny characters, such as F-Stop, Chilly Willy, Terminator and Baffies, each representing a specific aspect or trait of Munro-baggers – camera buff, winter expert, etc – and his overall light-hearted and irreverent approach to route descriptions that sets this series of books apart from its competitors. The one drawback is its six-volume coverage of all the Munros, resulting in a hefty price tag of nearly £100 for the set.

Some have argued that the days of guidebooks are numbered due to the advent of online hillwalking sites and mobile apps. Such is the current popularity of these technical innovations and their immense influence in the Munro-bagging sphere that their origins, use and importance will be discussed further.

By far the largest and most influential website in the Scottish walking world is Walkhighlands, set up in 2006 by Paul and Helen Webster. The idea for the site originated during their continuous 4,000 mile walk across Europe in 2003–4. The mission of Walkhighlands was and is to encourage the enjoyment of walking, and it is the best online information source and social network for Scottish walkers.

With the site's ample success, in 2011, Walkhighlands teamed up with ViewRanger, an online app that introduced many features, including allowing users to download routes directly to their smartphone. The merger also meant that phones could now be used as a walking guide, complete with GPS (Global Positioning System) functionality, interactive maps, navigational aids and location sharing. There is even a system for automatically labelling the names of surrounding peaks on a summit panorama photograph.

There is no doubt that these websites and applications have inspired a new generation of hill-goers, and interest in Munros has itself inspired some of their functionality. Walkhighlands is not only a site for Munro-baggers, but features over 2,000 routes, many of which are low-level walks and rambles. Yet the Munro influence is strong: the site lists the Munros alphabetically, by height, by popularity, by region and by rating, as well as providing a Munro map which allows users to track their progress through the list. The site also features podcasts with place names, correct pronunciation of Gaelic names, 3D visuals and GPS downloads – the resources seem endless. What would Sir Hugh make of all this?

A significant facet of Walkhighlands is the social aspect, which allows users to share their experiences through stories, photos and videos of their walks. Over half a million subscribers check in with the site every month, an indicator of its phenomenal success! I often feel I am in the minority now with my 'old-fashioned' map and compass while I observe younger walkers peering at their phones in order to ascertain the correct route or identify a distant peak. However, from a safety point of view, carrying a paper map and compass, and having the necessary skills for their use, is an absolute must. Many incidents and accidents today are the outcome of a total reliance on electronic gadgets and the subsequent failure of walkers to navigate without them.

Turning briefly to outdoor magazines, in 1961, the first monthly periodical devoted entirely to mountaineering hit newsagents. *Climber and Rambler* was the only serious contender in the market for many years, and it rebranded to *Climber and Hillwalker* in the 1990s before dropping its hillwalking articles and settling as simply *Climber*. In the intervening years, a host of other competitors have jostled for shelf space, such as *Footloose*, *High*, *The Great Outdoors* and *Trail*, the latter two dominating today's hillwalking market. The outdoor magazine trade is notoriously fickle, and to have any hope of staying afloat, the quality of articles, photography and production must be cutting-edge. Comparing a 30-year-old outdoor magazine with one today is like chalk and cheese. Moving with the times is sometimes not even enough – being ahead of the zeitgeist is almost essential for survival in an intensely competitive market. In general, outdoor magazines appeal more to a younger audience, so they have an assured place in motivating the next generation to great heights.

The baby boomer generation produced the exponential rise in Munro-bagging in the later decades of the 20th century. The general trend seemed to indicate a tenfold increase in Munroists roughly every 20 years; ten Munroists by the late 1940s, 100 by 1970 and 1,000 by the early 1990s. Of course, this exponential rise could not last, and the tally of around 4,500, by 2010 was less than half of the exponential forecast of 10,000. Today's leisurely, linear increase of roughly 2,000 per decade – or 200 a year – is still a substantial rate of increase, and the total of 7,000, would no doubt move Sir Hugh to an astonished look and a wry, disbelieving shake of the head.

CHAPTER 6

Rounds and Records

ON 13 AUGUST 1967, a Sunday, two brothers, Brian and Alan Ripley, together with a friend, David Summerfield, stood on the lonely summit of Ben Hope, the most northerly Munro, and gazed southward. The tangled knot of hills and glittering lochans led their eyes to a vast horizon of distant ridges and hazy mountains that would form their future for the next three to four months. For these three visionaries, this moment was the dawn of a dream, a dream soon to become the rhythmic reality of placing one foot in front of the other. They were on the cusp of putting feet to the dream of climbing all the Munros in one continuous push, a feat never before accomplished. Ben Hope means 'peak of the bay', derived from the Norse 'Hop' (bay), but these three young men's anticipation and belief was reflected in the 'hope' of their inaugural mountain.

In spite of enormous 60-pound packs and daily distances of 17 miles, the ebullient enthusiasm of youth took them over Ben Klibreck, Ben More Assynt and Conival, the other scattered and isolated Munros of Scotland's far north, in three days. Apart from minor but expected annoyances, such as aching shoulders, sore feet and midges, their baptism was complete; they struck on southwards to the greater ranges with fire, hope and optimism in their hearts.

The equivalent youth of today would no doubt be posting blogs of their adventures so that interested parties in the outside world could follow along. For Summerfield and the Ripley brothers, of course, this was not an option; any news of their progress was mainly discovered by Mountain Bothies

Association (MBA) bothy visitors who might happen upon notes left by the three in these unlocked shelters. The MBA had only been in existence for two years, but already had secured many semi-ruined cottages in remote corners of the Highlands, which were subsequently renovated for use by walkers and backpackers. In the past, these stone dwellings would have been home to shepherds and keepers who were often delighted to accommodate passing travellers, such as the early Munro-bagging pioneers, outlined in previous chapters. This pioneering spirit was still truly alive in the '60s and '70s and was totally embodied in Summerfield and the Ripleys' bold dream.

In any Munro round, continuous or otherwise, the Cuillin ridge on Skye is often viewed as a major obstacle to compleation, not least because of the infamous Inaccessible Pinnacle. When news came of Summerfield and the Ripleys' success on 'the ridge', there was a general feeling that the key to the whole venture was turning in the lock. However, the Cuillin had thrown up a demanding gauntlet, with a wet, misty traverse in deteriorating conditions and enveloping darkness, on the final peak of Sgùrr nan Gillean. The final descent into the wrong corrie added an extra three miles to an already backbreaking day. This bitter-sweet moment in the expedition was perhaps its turning point, but not in a positive sense. Not long after the Cuillin traverse, David Summerfield had to give up due to financial problems, altering the group dynamic and casting a long shadow over the remainder of the trip. Nevertheless, the two brothers ploughed on alone, traversing the Cairngorms to eventually reach the most easterly Munro of Mount Keen on 12 October, two months after they summitted Ben Hope. Their planned time of 105 days, finishing on 25 November, still seemed reasonable, and on their return westwards they were buoyed by fine weather on the remote Tarf and Tilt hills, where they enjoyed a memorable night in the MBA Tarf bothy, known affectionately as the Tarf Hotel.

However, the notorious unpredictability of late October weather in the Highlands dealt them a poor hand; cold, blustery conditions, with huge snowdrifts and icy rivers, accompanied them all the way to Dalwhinnie. Fortune appeared to favour them again, however, as Irvine Butterfield recalled reading in an entry in the Culra bothy logbook that the pair had traversed all six Munros of the Ben Alder group in just over six hours, an incredible feat. Things were again looking up, and their continued westward push across the Grey Corries to Ben Nevis was followed by a magnificent traverse of the – then – 11-Munro Mamores ridge.

The brothers' initial purist ideals of using no motorised transport other than island ferries slowly faded as the combination of heavy packs, blisters, supply restocking, deteriorating weather, shorter daylight hours, stalking problems and financial worries began to take their toll. To reach Ben More on the island of Mull, they reluctantly accepted a lift, and buses were sometimes used on long road stretches. Once their resolve was first broken, affairs continued to go downhill. In Glen Etive, Alan started suffering from swollen ankles, and the weather took a massive turn for the worst, with positively arctic conditions making any hill ascent attempt suicidal. On Ben Dorain on 10 November, the wind was so strong that they were reduced to crawling on hands and knees, forced to retreat just 500 feet from the summit. The two still continued bravely on to Bridge of Balgie in Glen Lyon, but with 230 Munros under their belts, the Ripley brothers were finally forced to pack it in. Alan's ankles were still considerably swollen, and upon return they were both diagnosed with acute iron deficiencies. The brothers had come within a whisker of realising their dream, and it is natural and instructive to scrutinise their situation in order to ascertain what went wrong. Hamish Brown noted that Brian's diary entries read like a graph with ups and downs, but each down falling a bit lower than the previous as the burden grew heavier.

The brothers were both members of the Karabiner Club based in Manchester, and had they succeeded in their venture, they would have joined an illustrious club of other Manchester-born Munroist notables, such as John Rooke Corbett, the fourth

Munroist and first Englishman to compleat, and Paddy Hirst, the first woman compleater. From Manchester, the Ripleys had limited experience of the Scottish Highlands; combined with their relative youth, this unfamiliarity strongly contributed to their failure. However, one vital aspect, probably not missed by the reader, was the August start. The date had been dictated by other commitments, such as Brian's Himalayan trip the following year, during which he was tragically killed by falling stones on a 25,000-foot peak. Their late start had obvious repercussions relating to stalking, weather and daylight. Pack weight was another factor that limited the brothers' progress, and the iron deficiency diagnoses indicated dietary problems associated with food quality. Considering all these factors, it is astonishing that the Ripleys achieved as much as they did, a reflection of their true fortitude and determination. Far from returning to Manchester with their 'tail between their legs', they were upbeat and had 'no regrets'.

All the above considerations would have weighed heavily on the mind of Hamish Brown five years later as he prepared for his own continuous assault on the Munros, planned for 1974. Hamish's initial inspiration is the classic tale of escaping from the cold, soulless clutches of dead-hand officialdom and bureaucracy, to the fun, freedom and fresh air of a challenge that would ultimately change the course of his life. Brown was in charge of Outdoor Activities at Braehead School in Fife until its closure, when he became County Adviser on Mountain Activities, a desk-bound role, where his 'every fibre rebelled at the incarceration'. One hot, stuffy day in the office, bored by the grinding monotony of paperwork, he spread out a map of Scotland on the floor and the seed of a continuous Munro round became sown in his mind. No more desk work was done on that pivotal, hot afternoon.

Unlike the Ripley brothers, Brown benefited from a wealth of experience tramping 'round the Scottish hills; he had already compleated three rounds of the Munros. Philip Tranter, one of Brown's mentors, was the first to compleat a second round in

1964, but Brown's unique three had already placed him in the record books. His knowledge of the ground was unsurpassed, and his careful analysis of the Ripleys' account armed him with the necessary wisdom and benefit of hindsight to better prepare for success. Two crucial factors in the planning were where and when to start. Essentially, Brown turned the Ripleys' itinerary upside down, favouring a southerly start earlier in the year. Realising that the Ripleys' August launch was a prime reason for their subsequent failure, Brown chose an April start for the best chance of success. His intended compleation time of three to four months ensured that he would not interfere with stalking interests, but perhaps more importantly, he would not encroach upon the fickle weather conditions of a Scottish autumn. As to where he would begin, Brown wisely selected Ben More on the island of Mull, which would cut out one long, unnecessary arm mid-journey. In subsequent continuous Munro rounds by other individuals, Ben More has become the standard starting point, as it halves the necessary sea crossing – important if shunning ferries and resorting to kayaking or swimming. Brown used ferries, but self-propulsion on the ground was one of his strict conditions, so he planned to bring a folding bike for long road sections.

He was well aware of the Ripley brothers' dietary problems and recognised the crucial importance of nutritious food and high calorie intake, along with their associated morale boost. Although today's dehydrated food has improved greatly compared to the 1970s, in Brown's era it was generally unpalatable muck. He gave it a wide berth, other than a few exceptions, such as dried apple flakes. Fresh food and tinned produce would form the bulk of his intake, and a backup team was essential for supplying much of his diet. In addition, 42 parcels, each containing non-perishable food, candles, matches, toilet paper, film and books, were deposited at strategic points throughout the Highlands, many requiring a major expedition just to deliver.

No amount of preparation, however, can prepare for all eventualities of a large-scale expedition. 'Expect the unexpected' is a maxim central to all major ventures, and it is the unexpected which turns a venture into an adventure. Prolonged poor weather, for instance, can induce low morale, and in the final analysis, it is often this low morale rather than the poor weather itself which kills off the expedition. The spirit has to move the body... with no will, there is no way.

All expeditions experience low points when morale is at rock bottom, and Brown's was no exception. His lowest point came just over two months into his trek, on 10 June 1974, when he had only 100 Munros left to climb. He had left Oban bothy at the east end of Loch Morar, heading for the wilds of Knoydart. As bad weather closed in, he began to get wetter and colder, realising that hypothermia was not far away. A brief clearance revealed his intended hills plastered with snow, well below the 2,000-foot level... was this really June? Erecting his tent there and then was the only sensible option, but upon eventually locating a less wet spot, Brown made the grim discovery that the tent pegs were back at the bothy. The only solution was to grovel about in the icy wetness, collecting rocks to secure the tent. At the back of noon, he stripped off everything and crawled into his sleeping bag. He remarked: 'It took half an hour and a couple of brews before I stopped shivering'. His main concern was that the bad weather would continue and prevent him from scaling the Knoydart Munros, thus upsetting his schedule. Worry tends to breed more worry, and this anxiety became the lowest point of Brown's whole trip. However, the high points of *Hamish's Mountain Walk* predominated by far, and the expedition was ultimately a positive and uplifting experience.

It is not the purpose here to describe Brown's trip in even slight detail, as his subsequent book, *Hamish's Mountain Walk*, gives a blow-by-blow account in his own fresh and chatty style. Brown's descriptive writing has a sharpness and immediacy that breathes the sparkle and beauty of the mountain scene onto the page, but he also imparts countless recollections, reminiscences, historical snippets, opinions and humorous anecdotes, enriching and enlivening the general flow. The book has undergone many reprints and editions, from its genesis in 1978 as a Gollancz hardback, through to its current Sandstone Press paperback reincarnation, and will always have a deserving and assured place in the pantheon of classic mountaineering literature.

The inside cover and facing page of the original hardback show Brown's route from Ben More, on 4 April, to his finish at Ben Hope, on 24 July, a 112-day odyssey; a 'grand tour of the Scottish Highlands'. The snaking, contorted, dotted route line weaves, loops and curls its way eastward to Mount Keen, before returning west, eventually out to Skye and the Cuillin. Finally, it staggers northwards, in further twists and convolutions, to its termination at Ben Hope. It is reminiscent of a snail's random perambulations, leaving a tenuous, silvery track. Yet these musings are justified, in a sense, as Brown himself remarked: 'It had been a disciplined, slow progression'. Slow like a snail, but disciplined rather than random. Part of enjoying a long period in the wilderness is the discipline of slowing down, both physically and mentally, and learning to see, feel and appreciate simplicity. As Brown wrote: 'There was a marvellous rhythm in this simple life'.

Brown's 'dancing days of Spring' ended on that final summit of Ben Hope, where the Ripley brothers had stood, seven years before, contemplating their impending saga. Hamish now looked back with fondness, regretful that his journey was done yet fortified with an even stronger love for his native land. In his words:

More than ever I love my own land – its sweeping and often bewildering changes and challenges, its joys and delights, its incomparable peace and beauty.[1]

The ending of Brown's historic, ground-breaking walk was low-key, with no fanfare. One wonders what kind of ballyhoo would have been generated if Brown had competed the adventure today, looking through the prism of our intense media attraction to Munro-related preoccupations, even as muted as the measuring of a mountain's height! It would be another four years, on release of *Hamish's Mountain Walk*, before the general public became even vaguely aware of Munros and Brown's monumental feat. Its publication was the first book that had ever been written concerning purely the Munros, other than the SMC's dry and dusty Munro's Tables.

It was perhaps apt and timely that four years after the book's publication, the 'continuous round' baton was passed to a woman. Kathy Murgatroyd, in parallel with and inspired by Brown, packed in her job as an Outdoor Education teacher with the Grampian Regional Council in December 1981 to spend a season ski instructing in the Alps. This gave her the necessary finance and fitness to embark on her marathon Munro quest beginning on 1 May 1982. Like Brown, she started on Ben More, Mull, but finished with Sgùrr Mhic Chòinnich in the Skye Cuillin, thus beginning and ending on islands. Again, like Brown, Murgatroyd used a bicycle for the road sections, but adopted a more modular approach, using fixed bases, to climb groups of Munros with a lighter pack. Her later finish, on 11 September, resulted from alterations to her planned route due to stalking problems. On the whole, Murgatroyd had great luck with the weather, remarking that she had completed half the Munros before she even got her feet wet. In fact, a June heatwave and nutritional deficits were to prove her biggest hurdles – indeed, it was unusual to blame good weather for difficulties in a Scottish summer! Murgatroyd received regular weekend support from her boyfriend, Ivan Young, and like Brown, she used preplaced food parcels to maintain sustenance.

Murgatroyd's relatively slow round of 134 days ensured ample time for quiet reflection. She remarked that her hearing became so acute that she could hear a butterfly landing and taking off from an adjacent rock. When I met Murgatroyd in the early 1990s, she reckoned it was 'disgraceful' that no other woman had yet compleated a continuous Munro round; that disgrace would finally be remedied in 2005 by Lorraine McCall. Her finish on Skye placed her as Munroist 292, and although she first experienced unbridled elation, it was soon followed by tears and several months of adjusting into a 'normal existence' once again. Though my own longest walks have only lasted four weeks, I can understand these sentiments. The peace, beauty and solace of a long-distance walk is a precious, personal possession that is not easily surrendered.

Early on in Murgatroyd's walk, she was sitting at a table in the Crianlarich youth hostel, when in walked a man with a familiar face: Hamish Brown. It was the first time the two had met. Brown remembers seeing an attractive, sun-tanned female face in the corner (the tan more a result of her season of Alpine skiing than of the Scottish summer) and making a beeline for her table. Both Brown and Murgatroyd were reticent to divulge their Munro round intentions when on their respective missions, and Murgatroyd displayed this reticence by not letting the cat out of the bag and disclosing her objective, tempting as it was. A second curious quirk of fate occurred almost at the end of her walk, on Skye, with only the Cuillin left to finish her round. Yet again, by chance, she met Brown in Glenbrittle; unsurprisingly, pride got the better of her and she 'spilled the beans'. One can only imagine the stories, laughs and experiences they must have shared together.

These chance meetings were the genesis of a recurring theme that would crystallise fully in the following years: 'continuous compleaters' meeting by chance, or otherwise, and sharing tales, offering advice and generally confiding in one another. During Murgatroyd's walk, she met a man named David Herdman halfway up a Munro; he was also attempting a continuous round, no doubt inspired by Brown's book. They parted ways after swapping stories. Sadly, the old chestnut of nutritional deficiencies defeated Herdman, and he bowed out of his quest with only 12 Munros to go. He mounted another continuous attempt in 1982, but that too was unsuccessful. I would hazard a guess that there are likely more unsuccessful attempts than successful ones.

In 1984, George Keeping, from Preston, compleated the third continuous round in 136 days. His round was noteworthy for two reasons. Firstly, he did not use a bicycle, and secondly, he extended his walk for an extra 29 days to include the English and Welsh 3,000-foot summits. His choice of Ben Klibreck as his first Munro was odd, as it entailed an extra northwards loop to include Ben Hope, the most northerly Munro. However, his finishing Munro of Ben Chonzie, in Perthshire, gave him a clear run southward for his extension into England and Wales. The Munro leg of his jaunt ran from 14 April to 27 August, and the unusually dry spring and summer of that year was a significant factor in his overall success. He made use of the usual food parcel strategy, and incredibly, he only took two complete rest days in the course of the entire walk.

It is interesting that no one to date had attempted to break Hamish Brown's 112-day 'record', though it should be noted that Brown never intended for his walk to be any kind of record-setting project. Inevitably, however, the record-breaking mentality reared its head, and the 112-day time was taken on by another 1984 pioneer, Rick Ansell. Ansell, from Hertfordshire, made a clean sweep of all the mainland Munros in exactly one hundred days, from 3 May to 10 August. In his own words, 'the mainland Munros in one bash, using no support, no bicycles, canoes or food parcels'. His reason for omitting the island Munros on Mull and Skye was that the ferries would have spoilt the purity of the walk... or was he possibly not feeling competent enough to traverse the Cuillin ridge?! Nevertheless, in terms of ethics and fitness, this was a fine performance, no doubt helped by the brilliant weather – Ansell reckoned it only rained four times during the entire walk. Whether extensions to include Mull and Skye would have resulted in a time less than 112 days is purely speculative, but later that same year, an expedition commenced that would not only smash Brown's record, but constitute a monumentally greater challenge.

A young 29-year-old accountant, Martin Moran, decided his destiny in life was not to continue sitting behind a desk in a stuffy office. Four years earlier, in 1980, he had handed in his notice with the intention of attempting a solo round of the Munros in the winter of 1980–1. His plans were cruelly thwarted, however, when he damaged a knee while training, just six weeks before the intended departure date. With bridges burned and 'spirit crushed', Moran's anguish was absolute. Yet in retrospect, his knee injury was perhaps a cloud with a silver lining; in the intervening years, Moran and his wife, Joy, made a pact to tackle the winter Munro challenge together, a wise decision, that would play a crucial part in any ultimate success. In the wisdom of hindsight, Moran realised that his original plan for a lone, solo attempt was 'ill-considered' and in all likelihood destined for failure.

The true enormity of a winter Munro round cannot be underestimated. The days are shorter, the weather considerably more unfavourable and unpredictable, the objective dangers more acute, extremes become the norm and the potential for morale to plummet is massively inflated. Moran noted that winter wind alone can be a killer on Scottish mountains. A compass and good clothing may see you through mist and cold,

> but against the wind there is no answer. It slows the pace, saps the strength and sucks away the body heat – a triple threat in a single foe.[2]

I would add a fourth threat and say that it also strips spirit and morale, the real driving force that can ensure the continuity of any expedition. But blessed with the moral, emotional and practical support of his wife, Joy, Moran's chances of success were greatly enhanced.

Luckily, Moran was re-engaged at his accountancy office following his knee injury, and he spent the following four years in a blend of recovering, working, dreaming, scheming, scribbling and planning. Moran's plans ultimately concluded in the sale of their terraced house in Sheffield and the hiring of a Ford Transit motor home. His transformation from a hollow, faceless pawn in the accounting world to the recognised and respected icon of the climbing world, had begun in earnest. One of Moran's main reasons for embarking on a winter Munro challenge was to raise his profile and gain a professional reputation, which hopefully would lead to the creation of his own mountain guiding business in Scotland. Moran already had much experience guiding in the Alps, but his dream was to be self-sufficient and to put his own individual stamp on things – in short, he was getting a life.

As with his predecessors, one crucial aspect of Moran's planning was the timing of his quest. In the Alps, a climber can only claim a winter ascent between 21 December and 20 March (winter solstice to spring equinox), and this tight, 90-day winter window was the period Moran decided on. This schedule implied a daunting average of more than three Munros per day, not including rest days and the inevitable storm-bound days in the middle of winter. Was it possible? But Moran had a new advantage: the use of a motor home, though detracting from the purity and ethical honesty of a purely self-propelled journey, would provide comfort, flexibility and morale, essential at the end of a long, cold, exhausting day on the hills.

With the unpredictable and often localised nature of winter weather, a motor home gave the Morans flexibility to choose Munros according to the prevailing conditions, but this certainly did not imply a haphazard drive round the Highlands, picking off hills here and there. The general plan was to begin in the Southern Highlands, where the bulk of the Munros are easily accessible, coinciding with the shortest winter days. The Central Highlands would follow, including the more remote regions of Ben Alder and Lochaber, before the Cairngorms and rounded eastern hills, planned to coincide with heavier snowfall and consequent reasonable Nordic ski compatibility. Finally, the great ridges and remote peaks of the Northwest Highlands were the 'icing on the cake', with the Cuillin ridge on Skye providing the greatest winter challenge of all. The slightly longer daylight of later February and March gave the best chance of success for these difficult peaks, the most demanding part of the trip. A typical day would see both Martin and Joy leaving the comfort of their motor home to ascend a couple of Munros together before Joy returned to their mobile base camp. Moran would continue on, perhaps over another one or two Munros, then descend to a new location where Joy would be waiting with tea, supper and a large dose of warmth and affection! Joy, incidentally, managed a highly respectable 120 Munros during the trip.

In contrast with other continuous Munro marathons, up to this point, distinct media interest followed the Morans' extended winter adventure, and this was not accidental. Moran intended for the venture to be partially an exercise in self-promotion, so he drummed up a reasonable level of media participation – a presence which engendered a more pressing need to succeed. The trip was not sponsored, but Berghaus provided clothing and equipment for the Morans, and they raised £20,000 for the charity Intermediate Technology. Moran's ultimate success in the venture could be put down to his fast, lightweight movement; efficient, morale-boosting backup and his fortune in having chosen one of the most settled winters for a decade, with the incidence of gales and snowfall little over half their averages. The trip began on Ben Lomond on 21 December and finished on Sgùrr Èilde Mòr, in the Mamores, on 13 March, a record-shattering total of 83 days. On ten of these days, no Munros were climbed at all, while on three days Moran mounted nine Munros. None of these bald statistics can convey the joy, despair and full sweep of emotions and experiences felt by the Morans, but their adventure is fully documented in the marvellously readable *The Munros in Winter*, published in 1986 by David and Charles and now available in paperback by Sandstone Press.

About halfway through the trip, the pair had a planned rendezvous with some famous names in mountaineering and adventuring at the Clachaig Inn, Glencoe; namely, Chris Bonnington, Hamish Brown, Alan Hinkes and the Crane brothers. Alan Hinkes became the first and only British mountaineer to ascend all 14 of the Himalaya 8,000-metre peaks, and Richard Crane had run across the Himalayas. Perhaps it was Hinkes who once joked that the Himalaya was good training for a Scottish winter. Bonnington, meanwhile, successfully ascended Everest only two months after the Glencoe meeting.

The following day's planned traverse of the Creag Meagaidh range descended into a 'circus' when Bonnington's skis were stolen from his car roof rack and Brown's dog, Storm, abruptly disappeared in thick snow. The final insult: Martin reached the road at 6.30pm and waited at the lay-by whilst Joy waited at an identical lay-by, two miles up the road.

A few days before the Clachaig meeting, an incident occurred, which can only be described as tragically prophetic. The Morans were using their Nordic skis in a white-out on the final, broad snow ridge, leading to the summit of Ben Wyvis. A dull crack and shudder were their only warning as they both fell through the cornice on the ridge crest and began to ride an enormous slab avalanche down into Coire na Feola. It was every winter climber's worst nightmare and lasted only ten seconds, but Martin felt a lifetime of emotions passed him by. Both were shocked, but incredibly, unharmed. However, 34 years later, on 26 May 2019, Martin, six clients and an Indian liaison officer were all swept to their death by an avalanche on Nanda Devi in the Himalaya. In those intervening years, the Morans had created and developed a highly successful mountain guiding business in Lochcarron, living their dream.

Less than a month before Moran's triumphant finish, a young man named Craig Caldwell had just been dropped off from his father's car at the Megget Stone near the Talla Reservoir in the Scottish Borders. There, he began the short climb up Broad Law, one of seven Corbetts in the Southern Uplands. This was no mediocre, ordinary day's hillwalking, however it was the subdued start to a continuous year of climbing all the 498 Munros and Corbetts in a single, self-propelled journey. Caldwell's ambitious trip would surpass any previous marathon Scottish walk, both in terms of its scale and duration, and would set a new benchmark for future expeditions. The previous autumn, Caldwell had given up his small business selling sports equipment and began planning and packing for what he would describe as the happiest year of his life.

The Corbetts are far more widespread throughout Scotland,

taking in the Southern Uplands, six separate islands and areas such as Morvern, Ardgour and Moidart. Planning the ideal route, therefore, was crucial to success. In a nutshell, Caldwell's route began with a massive clockwise sweep from south to north, starting with the easier Border and Argyll hills, before island hopping, via Arran and Jura, to the Outer Hebrides to claim its lone Corbett of Clisham. Following the Stornoway to Ullapool ferry crossing, he then tackled the hills of the far north before working his way south, through Torridon, Applecross and the big glens, eventually to Skye and Rum, coinciding with late spring and early summer. The hills of the south-west Highlands then followed, before autumn and winter saw him cover the Cairngorms and eastern hills. He concluded with the easier hills of Perthshire and the Southern Highlands, compleating on Ben Lomond and in sight of his home city of Glasgow.

The above itinerary, as if not demanding enough, was completed during the wettest summer since 1897. Out of Caldwell's 300 active days on the hill, only 55 were totally clear. Enduring endless weeks of rain, wind, mist, midges and gut problems can only be the product of a passionate love and obsession with Scotland's wild country, and Caldwell possessed it in spadefuls. An excellent support team, including his parents and friends, ensured relatively trouble-free logistics. Apart from island ferries, Caldwell's trip was entirely self-propelled; he used a bike for road sections and some tracks. Like Martin Moran, Caldwell used his efforts to benefit a charity; he raised an astounding £18,000 for the Erskine Hospital for ex-servicemen.

Caldwell's marathon venture lasted from 16 February 1985 to 27 February 1986, and his mammoth book of the trip, aptly called *Climb Every Mountain* (Macdonald), appeared four years later in 1990. Interestingly, four years was the timescale between Hamish Brown's conclusion of his Munro round and his book, and the parallels invite obvious comparisons. Though perhaps not as poetically deft as Brown, Caldwell's book is stamped with a freshness and individuality, and his obvious love of Scottish history is a recurring theme. Despite the atrocious weather,

Caldwell's sense of humour enlivens the daily narration of events. Like *Hamish's Mountain Walk*, Caldwell's book would be an ideal fireside companion – along with a malt – in old age, when advancing years have put paid to youthful wanderings but the spark of springtime joys remains.

Considering the monumental scope, duration and challenge of Caldwell's trip, I feel he did not perhaps receive – or want – the respect and recognition that he undoubtedly deserved. Caldwell was not only the first person to complete a continuous round of the Corbetts, but he included the Munros as well, and overall, his expedition was by far the longest continuous self-propelled Scottish journey ever undertaken – and in mainly miserable weather. It is a general truism that most mountain marathoners are modest people who shun media attention and whose ultimate satisfaction is derived from the peace, escape and solitude, offered by wild places.

During the late 1980s and 1990s, there was a marked proliferation, not only in the number of continuous rounds, but also in the nature of the undertaking. Mountain marathon journeys began to fall into one of three categories. First were the walking (and often, part cycling) trips, which included the Munros, but increasingly included 'add-ons', such as the English and Welsh 3,000ers or the Corbetts. Second were purely winter endeavours, such as Moran's trip, and third were record-breaking running marathons, which concentrated almost entirely on the Munros. Of the five 'compleat' continuous rounds discussed so far, four fall into the first category (Brown, Murgatroyd, Keeping, Caldwell) and the remaining one in the second category (Moran). The third category did not make its entrance until 1988, and it has since progressed in leaps and bounds. The running phenomenon will form most of the second part of this chapter, but first we shall examine further developments in the first category, concentrating almost exclusively on 'Munros plus add-on' trips. Other 'Munros only' rounds are mentioned in the table at the end of the chapter.

On 'compleation' of the Munros, many a bagger will seek

a fresh challenge, such as the Furth of Scotland, Corbetts or Munro Tops. It is natural, therefore, that the mountain marathoner would also include these in their increasingly challenging repertoire. Craig Caldwell had already accomplished the Corbett add-on, but at that point, the Furth and Tops were still 'up for grabs'.

George Keeping had included the English and Welsh 3,000ers in 1984, but it was not until 1986 that the Irish 3,000ers were also included. Ashley Cooper, from Clitheroe in Lancashire, was a 24-year-old unemployed graduate when he visited friends in Malawi, who introduced him to some of the staff of LEPRA (The British Leprosy Relief Association). Armed with the knowledge that £10 can, in most cases, cure one of the world's 15 million leprosy victims, Cooper decided on the spot to put his idleness to some use, and the seeds of a Munros and the Furth trip were planted. Unfortunately, the summer of 1986 was little better than that of 1985, and out of the 107 days Cooper spent covering the Munros section of the trip, only 14 were free of rain or snow. At the time, his venture drew relatively little publicity, but his 313-peak, 1,420-mile, self-supporting marathon raised over £6,000 for LEPRA; Cooper strode right into the record books.

In my book *The Munro Phenomenon*, I commented:

It is interesting and almost strange that no one has yet attempted all the Munros and Tops in a single expedition.[3]

I hardly expected that one individual, upon reading this, would be inspired and rise to the challenge just a year after the book's publication. That individual was Chris Townsend. It would not be an exaggeration to say that Townsend is to wilderness walking as Chris Bonnington is to mountaineering. Townsend is quite simply one of the world's most experienced long-distance wilderness walkers, and he is well-respected in the outdoor world. He has successfully completed dozens of marathon backpacking trips, including Land's End to John o'

Groats, the Pacific Crest Trail from Mexico to Canada, the whole length of the Canadian Rockies, a north to south Scandinavian trek, the 3,000-mile Continental Divide Trail and many others. Given Townsend's phenomenal track record, his success on the Munros and Tops challenge was pretty much assured and well within his capabilities. Townsend had compleated the Munros in 1981 and had accomplished two 500-mile walks over 147 Munros and seven coast-to-coast crossings of Scotland. In 2015, he completed a 700-mile walk along the watershed of Scotland, one of only three known people to have accomplished this.

Chris's overall plan was similar to Hamish Brown's and many others, starting on Mull's island Munro of Ben More, followed by a huge loop east to Mount Keen and back, before the final trek north to Ben Hope by way of Skye and the north-west Highlands. His total time for the walk was 118 days, quite remarkable, considering that he included all the Tops and did not use a bicycle. His walk was only six days longer than Hamish Brown's, who climbed Munros only. The weather was generally cool, damp, cloudy and windy, with rain on roughly half the days, but Townsend did enjoy some sunshine – a typical Scottish summer. His wife, Denise, provided excellent backup, and he survived mainly on dehydrated food – unlike Hamish Brown. The following year, his fascinating account of the trip was published by Mainstream under the title *The Munros and Tops: A record-setting walk in the Scottish Highlands*, another addition to the growing list of marathon mountain rounds.

The Munro Phenomenon seemed to have caused a few ripples in the outdoor world, and early in 1997, I received a letter from a certain Peter Lincoln, from Mold in Flintshire, who was planning a 'mammoth expedition through the Scottish Highlands', partly blaming his decision on my 'inspirational writing' – praise indeed. In short, Lincoln was hoping to climb all 722 Munros, Corbetts and Grahams in one continuous journey. It had taken just over a year for Craig Caldwell to do Munros and Corbetts, and Lincoln reckoned, in his letter to me, that 16 months would be the likely timescale for his extensive trip. Lincoln was a teacher who used the long summer breaks to indulge in a stunning variety of overseas long-distance walks, such as three Pyrenean traverses, a 500-mile backpack along the Canadian Rockies, a traverse of New Zealand's southern Alps and a couple of lengthy sections of the Pacific Crest Trail, to name a few. His shorter winter and Easter breaks were spent mainly in Scotland, and he had completed all the mainland Munros and about half the Corbetts.

So, in July 1997, Lincoln packed in his teaching job and packed up his rucksack to embark on the most ambitious walk ever undertaken in the Scottish Highlands. His journey was entirely self-propelled and amazingly completed in only 359 days, on the Corbett of Morrone, on 2 July 1998. Considering that a large proportion of his trip included the winter months, this time is quite incredible; Lincoln's resolve and fitness, together with largely favourable weather, would have helped a great deal.

Lincoln's original letter to me included this query: 'I would like to clarify with you that such an expedition is without precedent'. At the time, as far as I was aware, there were no other individuals engaged in such a monumental undertaking, and so I hopefully put his mind at rest by acknowledging his contention. Little did anyone know, however, that in 1995, a modest young man from High Wycombe named Andrew Allum had commenced a gargantuan walk that would last over two years. Allum's extraordinary aim was to climb the English and Welsh 2,000-foot peaks, the Donalds (2,000-foot hills in the Southern Uplands), the Grahams, the Corbetts, the Munros and the Munro Tops! To refer to this aim as ambitious is a vast understatement, as the above itinerary probably constitutes the 'ultimate' mountain marathon adventure in Britain.

Allum essentially worked his way from south to north, completing the Donalds in early 1996, and reaching his final summit of Scaraben, a Graham, in the far north-east of Scotland in July 1997, just around the time when Peter Lincoln was embarking on his own trip 'without precedent'. Allum's mega-walk was only broken by four rest periods totalling six weeks.

Despite the enormity of the undertaking and the illustrious star quality of the challenge, little is known about Allum; the dearth of publicity was evident. There is no doubt that Allum embodied the true spirit of an unassuming pioneer who did not undertake his venture for public fame or acknowledgement, but rather for the enjoyment and lifelong satisfaction that can only be experienced through prolonged exposure to the natural world.

We now turn to the second type of mountain marathon journeying, that of purely winter outings. However, a short preamble is appropriate here. A Land's End to John o' Groats (LEJOG) walk, though a major trek for most mortals, has fast become a bog-standard route for the long-distance walker. In 2003, Steve Perry, from Todmorden, Yorkshire, completed the route in 223 days, rather longer than the average three to four months. But this was no average walk and no average individual, because Perry's walk included all 303 peaks over 3,000 feet in Wales, England and Scotland. Although George Keeping had traversed the British 3,000ers in a continuous walk in 1984, Perry was the first person to combine the feat with a LEJOG walk.

On arrival at John o' Groats on his own at the end of September, Perry's elation with finishing was tempered by the flat emptiness that invariably accompanies the end of a long communion with the outdoors. This was partly mitigated by his phoning of friends and family, informing them of his success. One of these friends had met up with Perry only a fortnight earlier, and told him that he had been to John o' Groats after their meeting to leave a surprise hidden among some bushes. Sure enough, Perry found a plastic bag with a note inside:

> Congratulations Steve – if you're reading this note it means you must have finished! If you go to the John o' Groats Hotel I've booked you a room and there's a free bar for you all night.[4]

Naturally, Perry was overjoyed, but his joy soon turned to disappointment when he discovered the hotel now closed for winter. A rather peeved call to his 'friend' revealed that it was an outlandish joke. Who needs enemies when you have friends like those?! However, Perry shrugged off the disappointment and booked himself into another hotel for a well-deserved night of luxury. Two days later, a reception crowd of a hundred well-wishers and a brass band were waiting for him at Todmorden railway station, all organised by Perry's fiancée, Sarah Peach.

Long suffering Peach became used to Perry's wanderings and realised that he was not one to let the grass grow beneath his feet. She knew that once he had an idea in his head, he would not let go, and that his next idea would be more challenging than his 2003 trip. These exact thoughts had already entered the mind of a man named Mike Cawthorne, who 'on a whim' in 1986 had compleated all the Munros in a single sweep with no support or planning. His follow-up expedition had to be a winter challenge, but he quickly dismissed the Munros, saying:

284 winter mountains on foot and with no backup
seemed a madman's charter, only a fool would attempt it.[5]

Instead, he settled on the 137 thousand-metre peaks and thrashed out his vision during the winter of 1997–8. The resulting book of the venture, called *Hell of a Journey* (Mercat Press), was shortlisted for the Boardman Tasker prize for Mountain Literature 2000 and is up there with *Hamish's Mountain Walk* as one of the true classics of the genre. It was this book and Martin Moran's *The Munros in Winter* that inspired Steve Perry to contemplate the 'madman's charter' of an unsupported winter Munro round.

Perry soon realised that the 'official' 90-day winter window between 21 December and 20 March would constitute an unrealistic challenge and opted for a more manageable 121-day alternative, from 1 December until 31 March. It was actually Martin Moran who suggested this longer period, and he commented that 'doing the hills without the flexibility offered by a vehicle would have been unappealing'. Even with the longer timescale, the enormity of Perry's proposed undertaking could not be underestimated. Like Mike Cawthorne, he would be burying numerous food caches in advance and tackling the challenge largely alone. Martin Moran's observation of the wind slowing the pace, sapping the strength and sucking away body heat was thrown into stark relief as Perry battled his way up Ben More on Mull in wind-driven hail on 1 December 2005, the first Munro of his extreme winter challenge. Luckily, his baptism by fire mellowed into some fine, settled December weather, during which he enjoyed 29 consecutive days on the hill. A slight blip at the end of December forced a rest day, but a traverse of the celebrated Aonach Eagach ridge on New Year's Day heralded more superb conditions, and Perry completed a grand circuit of all ten Munros in the Mamores in an incredible 15-hour romp.

His luck inevitably took a downward turn, however, whilst based in the remote Culra bothy in the Ben Alder area. A slip on ice and subsequent fall onto a sharp rock resulted in a painful chest injury which he feared might end the trip. Despite exhaustion from a long traverse of the four Munros west of Ben Alder, Perry hardly slept from the pain. The next morning brought a massive thaw and incessant rain, but he still managed to haul his aching body round the South Laggan Munros – the worst day of his trip. Matters only worsened when he reached the Allt Cam, a stream, which in the morning had been a relatively easy crossing, but by late day had burst its banks and was a raging torrent of dark, peaty water, easily waist- or chest-deep. This was the same stream that the Reverend Burn had been unable to cross back in 1914. With determination, grit and sheer bloody-mindedness, Perry crossed the swirling mass with a final lunge for the far bank after swimming with the current. He was soaked to the skin, and the final two-mile walk to the bothy was accompanied by a bone-chilling headwind that froze him to the marrow. As he remarked, 'I don't know how I would have coped that evening without the bothy fire'.

A nurse at Dalwhinnie confirmed one broken and one cracked rib and advised a week's rest, which translated to one day only, when he rested because of gales. More rain, sleet and blizzards followed, until a ridge of high pressure coincided with the eastern hills and Cairngorms, creating 'the best winter weather I've ever experienced in Scotland'. The mixed weather eventually took Perry to Skye, where six long days and the services of Lorraine McCall and Neil McAdie were needed for him to complete its 12 Munros. (Lorraine McCall became the third woman to complete a continuous round of the Munros in 2005; Kate Weyman was the second in 1990.) Perry's lowest point occurred during his six days between Camban bothy, near Alltbeithe, and Achnashellach, when abysmal conditions of driving snow and wet sleet made every step a huge effort, and he would often still be trudging through deep snow in total darkness at 11.00pm.

Incredibly, Perry reached his final Munro, Ben Hope, on March 31, exactly as planned. The weather was a repeat of his inaugural Ben More ascent, the last thousand feet shrouded in a blizzard. Friends had accompanied him to the peak, but a Grampian Television crew was forced back due to the appalling conditions.

Less than 13 years later, on 5 February 2019, in almost the same spot, Steve Perry and pioneering, legendary Scottish climber Andrew Nisbet had just completed a winter climb on the north-western cliffs of Ben Hope, when they found themselves in serious difficulties. Perry managed to send a distress call, but their bodies were not found until ten hours later. Martin Moran and Steve Perry, then the only two individuals to have accomplished continuous winter Munro rounds, both died in separate climbing accidents within three months of each other. This tragic coincidence cast a long shadow over the Scottish mountaineering fraternity and was a seemingly ominous omen for whomever might next attempt to fill the vacuum left by the winter Munros challenge.

Yet the very next winter, 2019–20, a freelance filmmaker from Glasgow, Kevin Woods, became the third person to compleat the challenge. Woods took 97 days and used a van to travel between different ranges. He was already an experienced mountain guide and had compleated a third Munro round only a month before he embarked on his winter epic. Woods started his trip on Ben More on Mull and used his van, bothies, friend's houses and his tent to sleep, and he completed the first half of the challenge in 'quick time', giving him 'time in hand to finish the Munros ahead of the virus'. Of the COVID-19 pandemic, he commented,

> There's not much difference between being in the hills
> and being at home – both are physically isolated.[6]

Woods finished his round on Ben Lomond and plans to write a book and make a film of his trip.

Of course, the picky purists will complain that he used motorised transport to travel between mountain groups and strayed beyond the official 90-day winter window. Martin Moran's original winter round in 1984–5 used similar tactics, but in the quicker time of 83 days. So the plum prize of a purely self-propelled winter round, within the tight 90-day window, is still an outstanding challenge, which no doubt will be overcome in the future – given an inordinate amount of fortitude, sheer grit and luck.

Martin Moran's 'record' of 83 days to compleat the Munros remained so until the late 1980s, when fell runners began to turn their attention to this enticing challenge. Up to this point, mountain runners had concentrated their efforts mainly on 24-hour challenges, such as Ramsay's Round, Bob Graham's Round and Paddy Buckley's Round, in Scotland, England and Wales. These 24-hour challenges were one thing, but the time and organisation required for a sustained multi-week marathon run offered a whole new level of difficulty. Although many of the needs of walkers and runners overlap, runners require more specialist backup in the form of pacers and injury support groups. Notable fell runner Mark Elsegood took up the challenge in 1988, but used a car to drive between Munro groups; he compleated the round in 66 days.

As a quirky aside: the following year, a unique first was accomplished by a young lad from Wigan called Paul Tattersall.

Tattersall became the first person to traverse the Munros with a mountain bike – 'with' being the operative word, as in many instances, the bike had to be carried rather than ridden. For example, on the Cuillin ridge, Tattersall dismantled his 35-pound bike and carried it on his back, which provoked even the free-thinking Hamish Brown to quip: 'Anyone who takes a bike up the Cuillin needs a psychiatrist'. I wonder what Brown makes of present-day Danny MacAskill, who has taken Cuillin ridge cycling to a whole new level. Tattersall himself admitted that the bike was as much a nuisance as it was an advantage, and it is probably fair to say that his 81-day trip will stand as a monument to, if not eccentricity, then downright unconventionality. Tattersall has since moved to Gairloch, where he practises his first love of rock climbing and works as a qualified mountain guide.

Returning now to running, two bold, record-breaking journeys were undertaken in the early 1990s which set the gold standard for many years to come and were a prelude to the truly astonishing record rounds of the 2000s. Hugh Symonds, a maths teacher from Sedbergh, Cumbria, supported by his wife and three children in a motor home, achieved a continuous, purely self-propelled round of the Munros in 67 days, beginning on Ben Hope and finishing on Ben Lomond. He then ran south to England, traversing the four 3,000-footers of the Lake District, before continuing to Wales to complete its 15 3,000ers there, ending on Snowdon, 83 days after his Ben Hope start. This was the same time that Martin Moran had taken for his winter Munros round. As an afterthought, Symonds then crossed over to Ireland, running its seven 3,000-footers, an incredible mission which culminated on the romantic Brandon Mountain, the most westerly 3,000-foot mountain in the British Isles (and on my bucket list). His total time for the impressive 303-hill round was 97 days.

Symond's resulting book of the venture, entitled *Running High*, is subtitled 'The first continuous traverse of the 303 mountains of Britain and Ireland'. This is not strictly true, as Ashley Cooper had accomplished a walking round of the Munros and the Furth in 1986, which included ten more summits and a much longer time schedule. However, Symond's ethics were purer, sailing a yacht to Mull and rowing to Skye, using a ferry only for the Ireland crossing. The ultimate accolade came from legendary fell runner Joss Naylor, who described the run as 'perhaps the greatest athletic achievement ever'. Further testimony to the enormity of the feat was given in a subsequent television programme aired about the run.

Incredibly, Symond's gained half a stone in weight during his run; due appreciation must go to his wife, Pauline, who was responsible for supplying him with over 5,000 calories per day – more than double of that recommended for an adult male! As far as I am aware, no other runner has attempted the Munros and the Furth in a single push, and Symond's time of under a hundred days should be a safe record for a long while yet. However, his time of 67 days for the Munros, though a superb attempt, was inevitably transient and served to provide the 'bait' for the next aspiring record-breaker. Symond's statistics show that his average running time per day was about eight hours, with 16 hours resting, eating or sleeping. Obviously, if any significant reduction on 67 days were to materialise, then 'running time' would need increasing to perhaps 12 hours or more. This would imply a 'gold standard' time of between 40 and 50 days, so the obvious 50-day barrier became the next hurdle to aim for.

Two determined young men named Andrew Johnstone and Rory Gibson set their hearts on meeting this challenge in the summer of 1992. A disciplined and sustained training period saw them spend much time in the Himalaya, where Rory gained a highly respectable fifth place in the famous Everest Marathon, fell running from Base Camp to Namche Bazaar. Yes, the Himalaya can be a training ground for Scotland! Andrew and Rory stuck to the 'normal' Munro round, beginning with Ben More on Mull and finishing on Ben Hope, and apart from island ferries, the self-propulsion ethic was strictly followed, using bicycles on road sections. For a nice touch, they swam across Loch Lomond to reach Ben Lomond. Although Johnstone and Gibson averaged 12-hour days, many were obviously longer; on day 15 of the trip, after climbing the awkward Munros west of Glen Etive, they cycled to Ballachulish to climb the two Munros above the village, eventually finishing at 3.00am. After eight hours' rest, they were off again to tackle the Glencoe Munros. Wisely, the following day was a rest day, the only one of the entire trip.

Johnstone and Gibson's run was blessed by superb weather until the last three weeks, when gales and rain unfortunately scuppered their chances of securing a sub-50-day time; their final result of 51 days and 10 hours was bitter-sweet, though still a monumental achievement. With the exception of Gibson spraining his ankle on day five and Johnstone suffering dysentery in Knoydart, the trip unfolded fairly smoothly. The TV and press closely followed their progress, and a Grampian Television documentary of the trip was screened in 1993.

Although Johnstone and Gibson were served by an excellent backup team providing food, rest and moral support, they used no pacers. Johnstone modestly stated that he saw Gibson and himself as among the last of the amateur athletes to attempt a continuous Munro round; they knew that their time of 51 days would easily be beaten by professional fell runners with support teams. Johnstone was partly correct, but the pair the claimed this record time for a full eight years until the close of the 20th century, when highly trained, ultra-endurance athletes began to enter the Munro arena. This record-breaking 'game' was about to get serious.

In the interim period, Mike Cudahy, a retired psychologist and legend in the world of endurance running, used his free time to compleat a Munro round in 66 days, one day faster than Hugh Symonds. This was the fastest round accomplished purely on foot, apart from the Mull and Skye ferries.

In November 1993, a young lad from Glasgow called Charlie Campbell had just watched a TV recording of Johnstone and Gibson's record run over the Munros. For Campbell, who had done a bit of running, cycling and hillwalking, but more to the point, was at a crossroads in life where he needed a challenge and a direction, the programme was a game changer. As he remarked:

> Then and there I had this feeling that I had at last
> found a purpose. Here was something that I really
> believed, from the instant I saw it, that I could achieve.[7]

Campbell had completed five West Highland Way walks by age 17 and became a fitness instructor with a growing enthusiasm for long distance endurance events. With his love of both hillwalking and running, he took up climbing Munros and some serious attempts at running the West Highland Way, which he eventually did in a respectable 30 hours.

For several years, Campbell built up his fitness levels, alternating weekends between Munro-bagging and hill races. He compleated in late 1997, and during the following two years, he pored over maps, wrote out possible daily schedules, continued hard training, organised backup teams, secured a job as a part-time postman, obtained sponsorship from Boyd Tunnock, (of biscuit fame) and above all, kept motivated with the musical assistance of Enya's theme tune from the Johnstone and Gibson documentary. Armed with the dictum, as he wrote in his book, 'Aim for the stars and you're sure to hit the moon', Campbell aimed for a time of 40 days, reasoning that with a ten-day leeway, he would surely break the 50-day barrier.

Fast forward to Sunday, 28 May 2000. A rented motor home pulls into a perfect spot below Ben More on Mull. An apprehensive but excited Charlie Campbell is poised to begin the trip of a lifetime with the help of 'Charlie's angels' – his mum, Madge, and sister, June. At 4.15am, Campbell and June make an uneventful ascent of Ben More before Campbell cycles round to Fishnish and dons a neoprene suit. He would be the first 'all-rounder' to swim the sea passages, and like Johnstone and Gibson, would even swim across Loch Lomond to Ben Lomond. Campbell had planned to ascend the three Munros north of Glenfinnan in addition to his Ben More ascent, plus cycle, swim and long cycle to Fort William; but soon he realises he has bitten off more than he can chew. The three extra Munros are postponed, and by the end of day one, Campbell is already behind schedule.

Things worsened during the first week, as a painful shin and ankle forced Campbell to visit Oban A&E and finish with a 34 Munro tally instead of the intended 55. By the end of week one, he was a depressing three days behind schedule. Plagued by poor weather and a constant game of 'catch up', Campbell ploughed on regardless, his mood lifted by a meeting with Rory Gibson the night before his Loch Lomond swim, who promised to leave him a parcel of 'goodies' at the summit of Cairn Gorm two weeks down the line. Due to further complications, this was retrieved two days after the arranged time, but Campbell's 'morale-boosting banquet' of bananas, chocolate, Coca-Cola and other tempting pieces was another mood-lifting gesture to help him on his way. Campbell then launched on his long swing back westwards, eventually reaching Skye and perhaps the highlight of the whole run. Day 35, the day of the Cuillin ridge traverse, was perfect in every sense. He ran the tricky terrain in good weather with good friends and great laughs, and finished 11 Munros on the way – surely the stuff of dreams. Arriving at the Sligachan Hotel at 11.10pm to find that the bar had stopped serving was not a problem – Campbell's friend Jim had filled a couple of two-litre water bottles with Red Cuillin ale! A monster midnight feast of mum's spaghetti bolognese fed the hungry hordes and ended a fantastic day.

Campbell was now five weeks into his quest and had averaged 39 Munros per week. To complete his run in under 50 days, he would have to 'up' his weekly tally to 44 Munros for the remaining fortnight. With fatigue and exhaustion creeping up on him, he would have to pull out all the stops. Despite more lacklustre weather, Campbell pushed on, and on day 46, he had a surprise meeting with Andrew Johnstone, the other half of the record-holding duo, at the Aultguish Inn, yet another welcome morale booster. Two days later, amongst a happy din of shouting and clapping, a kilted Charlie Campbell bounded across the rocks to reach the trig pillar of Ben Hope, exactly 48 days and 12 hours since setting off for Ben More on Mull. Hidden in the rocks of the cairn was a box wrapped in plastic. Campbell peeled it open to find a message written on the box: 'Congratulations Charlie from Andrew and Rory'. Inside was a bottle of Macallan malt whisky. Campbell felt duly honoured that the previous record-holders had made the effort to climb up here and leave it for him – a gesture that would become the norm in years to come.

If four years was a long time from a continuous round to the publication of a book, as was the case for Hamish Brown and Craig Caldwell, then 17 years was an eternity. I would surmise that the pitfalls, hurdles, setbacks and challenges of writing and publishing a book were, to Charlie Campbell, more onerous than running the Munros. However, the long-awaited literary account of his trip, *Millennial Munros – A Postman's Round* (Ringwood Publishing) appeared in 2017 and is another delightful and fascinating addition to the growing library of Munro-related books.

It was perhaps inevitable that these intervening 17 years would see at least one more serious attempt at breaking the 40-day barrier, and in fact, the second-last paragraph in Campbell's book begins:

> Since the Munro run in 2000, Stephen Pyke ran, cycled and kayaked between the Munros, and on the 3rd of June 2010, smashed the record with a fantastic 39 days, 9 hours and six minutes.[8]

Stephen Pyke, from Staffordshire, nicknamed 'Spyke' in fell running circles, was a highly experienced fell runner, having broken the Everest Base Camp to Kathmandu running record in 2007. He had also broken the record, along with Lizzy Hawker, for the traverse of Scotland's 4,000-foot mountains. With this brand of pedigree, he was the obvious candidate for a new attempt at the fastest Munro compleation. In common with his predecessor trail-breakers, Spyke had an excellent support team of helpers, friends and pacers, but his ultimate success in passing the 40-day hurdle was partly due to excellent weather, and a comparison with the miserable weather of Campbell's round is somewhat one-sided.

During his run, Spyke consumed an incredible 8,000 calories per day, carrying up to two kilograms of food, including sandwiches, trail mix, chocolate bars, malt loaf, jelly babies

> and best of all, various versions of home made flapjack that friends brought up with them.[9]

Evening meals were made by his support team. Since Hamish Brown's ground-breaking, continuous Munro round in 1974, over 20 people were known to have followed in his footsteps, and Brown himself always expressed an interest in this growing band of 'disciples'. Curious that Spyke may well pull off a new record, Brown decided to rendezvous with him at Glen Shiel, 30 days into his trip. The two men were naturally in awe of each other, for different reasons, and after sharing thoughts and laughs, they shook hands, took a few photos and parted ways. Several weeks later, following Spyke's successful round, *The Great Outdoors* magazine organised a reunion of the pair at Brown's flat in Burntisland overlooking the Fife coast. Naturally, the conversation concentrated on their respective Munro rounds and the two men's essentially different approaches to a common quest. Apart from the obvious 'hare and tortoise' comparison, there was a distinct affinity between Spyke's and Brown's take on the task at hand. As Brown relates:

> It's the same hills we're on… It's just the difference is, he's a sports car and I'm a Land Rover.[10]

There is a common and quite understandable assumption that fell runners are unreceptive to the beauty and charm of the mountain environment, but on close inspection, this view is unjustified. Mike Cawthorne, in his book *Hell of a Journey*, argues that 'racing over the hills is a kind of blasphemy', maintaining that 'enjoyment and personal fulfilment are more relevant'. Yet surely fell runners indulge in what they do for their own enjoyment and fulfilment! We all enjoy the hills in different ways, be it in winter or summer, by walking or running. Hamish Brown argues that runners who travel fast and light over the hills are more concentrated on their activity than

> the majority of people wandering around the hills who just follow a leader and bumble along.[11]

I would also add that climbing hills in large groups reduces one's 'connection' to the natural world by the very act of social interaction and conversation.

Early in Charlie Campbell's run, at Inverbeg, his mother had been on the heavy end of a vicious diatribe from the elderly male receptionist at the caravan park, who took an active dislike to the way Campbell was doing the Munros, arguing that he would not be able to appreciate them. Campbell's natural reaction would have been to present him with a 'Glasgow Kiss', but instead he made the interesting observation: 'did he think I was running blindfolded?'. This question is revealing, in the sense that hill runners often talk of being highly receptive to their surroundings in a way that even supersedes walkers. This 'flow state' or 'high' is almost akin to floating along with the body and mind in a state of transcendental composure, the legs seemingly doing their job effortlessly and unconsciously. During these periods, the mind becomes a highly receptive vessel, and the ever-changing landscape and light patterns acquire an ethereal presence, impinging on the mind with indelible intensity. Spyke comments:

> Basically we love big days out in the mountains, the same as people who go walking in them. Perhaps we're lucky because we fell run that we can attempt bigger challenges or move a bit faster, but it's basically doing the same thing: it's enjoying big days out on the hills.[12]

These were the sentiments that Spyke and Brown – the sports car and the Land Rover – shared as they basked in the memories of their respective trips. Their love for and enjoyment of the Scottish hills was the glue that held them together.

The camaraderie and fellowship of continuous Munro rounders is a recurring theme, and just as Johnstone and Gibson had left a bottle of whisky for Charlie Campbell on his last Munro, Campbell in turn buried a bottle for Spyke and subsequently added a footnote to his homepage:

> Charlie would like to offer his sincerest congratulations to Stephen on setting such a fantastic new time, and becoming the first person ever to dip below the magical 40-day barrier – brilliant.[13]

Of course, once the 40-day barrier had been broken, it ceased to be a barrier and lost its magic. The lure of 30 days now beckoned on the far horizon of the hill-running protagonist's sights... but surely there must be a natural limit to this crazy game! In *The Munro Phenomenon*, I suggested that the 'Munros in a month' may have possible ultimate challenge status, though a month could be anywhere between 28 and 31 days. Certainly, as Spyke had knocked nine days off Charlie Campbell's time, there seemed to be enough potential and momentum left for an aspiring runner to give it his best shot. It had taken a decade before Campbell's time was beaten, and it took another decade before his namesake, Donnie Campbell, finally threw himself in the ring.

Donnie Campbell, an ex-Royal Marine from Inverness, is a running coach and founder of Get Active Running. Donnie has an impeccable pedigree of long-distance running events, setting a winter record of 23 hours for the Ramsay Round (see below), breaking the record for the 53-mile Highland Fling in under seven hours and running 200 miles from Glasgow to his spiritual home of Skye. Although he had not climbed all the Munros before his run, Donnie Campbell 'had always wanted to do the round' and noted that 'it was the idea of a nonstop round that really appealed to me'. He had examined Spyke's route in great detail and made his own adjustments and changes, finally coming up with a 'good but ambitious' target of 33 days.

COVID-19 restrictions in 2020 dictated a rather late starting date of August 1. After his standard opening gambit with Ben More on Mull, Donnie crossed by kayak from Fishnish to Lochaline before the long cycle to Sgùrr Thuilm, Sgùrr nan Coireachan and Gulvain. Supported by his wife, Rachael, in a motor home, Donnie continued eastward through Lochaber and the Cairngorms, reaching the most easterly Munro of Mount Keen after only eight days. The Southern Highlands followed before he headed north again and crossed by kayak crossing from Glenelg to Kylerhea on Skye, where Donnie spent his childhood and climbed his first Munros: 'The Cuillin is my favourite place and has the best and most technical Munros'.

The second half of Donnie's run was the most demanding; on day 17, he appeared to hit the dreaded 'wall', feeling fatigued, both physically and mentally, with the unrelenting nature of his quest taking its toll on body and mind. Donnie dug deep and pulled out all the stops to keep going, focusing on a routine of eat, run and sleep. The consequences of this fatigue came to a disturbing head on day 29, having had to reascend Moruisg in Glen Carron after he made the painful discovery that the cairn he had reached was not the true summit. The last two days were a whirlwind of epic proportions, during which he climbed a staggering 28 Munros. On the penultimate day, he ascended Slioch, all nine Fannaich Munros, the Fisherfield Five and the An Teallach pair, before cycling north to finish on Ben Wyvis – a total of 18 Munros. After only 30 minutes' sleep, he then cycled westward to ascend the six Beinn Dearg Munros. He continued to the final four scattered Munros of the north, reaching the summit of Ben Hope in an incredible 31 days, 23 hours and two minutes.

Donnie was grateful for many other runners, including Spyke, who gave up their time to join him on different Munros and act as pacers. Of his wife, he said:

Rachael was amazing because she basically allowed me
to do nothing else but run, eat and sleep.[14]

His run was not without injury, however; in the first half
of the trip, he was plagued with a swollen ankle and inflamed
tendons. Reflecting on his record-breaking run, Donnie says:

It was by far the hardest challenge I have ever done,
but also the coolest and most fun. It is a dream come
true to finish a round of Munros and in record time.[15]

With Donnie Campbell's run, another eight days had been
chipped off the record. This substantial reduction seems to
indicate that the field is clear for an attempt at breaking the 30-
day barrier, but without a crystal ball, we have no guarantee that
this new hurdle will be overcome… but I have a strong hunch
that it will, though when is a different matter. Compleating the
round in 30 days would require an average of between nine and
ten Munros per day, with many days above this average. Looking
at the statistics, Donnie has the record for the most Munros
climbed in a day (18) during a Munro round attempt, but how
many Munros could conceivably be climbed in a 24-hour period?

This leads neatly to the subject of 24-hour Munro rounds,
which will conclude this chapter. Professional fell runners adopt
two specific ethical considerations when devising a 24-hour
hill run. The first is that the run must be continuous, using no
mechanical transport, to convey the runner to different groups
of hills. The second is the requirement for the run to be circular
– that is, starting and finishing in the same place. These two
'rules' necessitate the need to locate specific, concentrated groups
of hills where one's chance is maximised, of summiting a large
amount of hills over a relatively small distance.

In 1964, Philip Tranter, son of the highly acclaimed historical
novelist Nigel Tranter, the first person to compleat two Munro
rounds, saw potential in the Munros surrounding Glen Nevis. In
the same year as his second 'compleation', starting at Glen Nevis

Youth Hostel, Tranter traversed all 11 Munros of the Mamores ridge before crossing the glen to continue with the Grey Corries ridge, finishing with the Aonachs and Nevis four – a total of 19 Munros, 40 miles and 20,600 feet of ascent in a time of 23 hours. Sadly, Tranter was killed in a car accident in 1966, while returning from a climbing trip to Turkey. Considering that Tranter was essentially a hillwalker, with his 23-hour 'Tranter's Round' being undertaken as a long walk, it was obvious that his time would soon be beaten; it is now regularly completed in under 12 hours. In the 1997 Tables revisions, Sgòr an Iubhair was demoted to a Top, which reduced the round to 18 Munros.

However, the definitive 24-hour Munro challenge was the brainchild of Charlie Ramsay, who extended Tranter's Round to include five other more remote Munros around Loch Treig, bringing the total to 24 (now 23). Completing 24 Munros in 24 hours had a definite ring about it... until 1997, that is! This eastward extension necessitated pure fell running tactics, and it was not until July 1978 that Ramsay himself accomplished the feat with only two minutes to spare, following two route-finding mistakes in a thick mist. It is testimony to Ramsay's determination that two other attempts at his round were made in the next few years, both failing to meet the 24-hour deadline.

Ramsay's '24 Munros in 24 hours' record was secure until 1987, when Martin Stone acted on an idea from Jon Broxap to include the two isolated Munros south of Loch Ossian. Perfect weather accompanied him for his run, with the phosphorescent glow of the Northern Lights producing enough light to allow him to dispense with a torch, in the hours of darkness. Although drowsiness was a problem, dawn breaking on Sgùrr Èilde Mòr switched on his biological clock and gave Stone the vital impetus to traverse the Mamores ridge in only six hours. He reached Glen Nevis Youth Hostel with 36 minutes to spare, creating a new record of 26 Munros in a day.

Inevitably, the net began to be cast further afield, and the Shiel-Affric area, with its tight Munro concentration, beckoned on the horizon as a fruitful harvest of hills, ripe for the picking in a 24-hour challenge. There are 31 Munros in the area, and current record holder Jon Broxap planned to do 28 of them in 24 hours as a parting shot before emigrating to Australia! The Cluanie Inn (where else?) was chosen as the start/end point of his farewell odyssey in 1988, which began with the traverse of the South Cluanie ridge, followed by the 'Sisters and Brothers' North Shiel ridge, before the big Affric loop, ending on the North Cluanie horseshoe. His time was 23 hours and 20 minutes to climb 28 Munros over a distance of 78 miles with 33,000 feet of ascent. Though Broxap did emigrate to Australia, he has since returned – I suppose he missed the Munros too much.

Adrian Belton, who held the Ramsay's Round record, made a bold attempt in 1991 to beat the record of 28 Munros in a day by running a further extension to Martin Stone's already extended Ramsay's Round, but poor weather resulted in him only equalling the record in terms of Munro count, 37 minutes slower.

Summitting 30 Munros in a day was going to be a difficult hurdle to cross, just as surely as accomplishing a complete round of the Munros in 30 days. This 30/30 challenge would remain outstanding until its partial realisation in 2017. Concerning these matters, as I commented in *The Munro Phenomenon*, are not so much a matter of fitness as a lack of any natural extension, and the only certainty is that there are sure to be some surprises in the future. The big surprise was the shift of focus from the west coast Munros of Glen Nevis and Glen Shiel/Affric, to the sprawling, more rounded Munros of the Cairngorms and Tarf/Tilt/Mounth in the Eastern Highlands. Despite these hills being more scattered and therefore involving greater distances, the amount of ascent required, was significantly less, giving them potential to provide the prize plum of a one-day, 30-Munro round.

In 2017, Jim Mann set off from Invercauld Bridge, east of Braemar, to begin the ascent of Lochnagar and the other ten Munros forming the high plateau at the head of Glen Clova. He then crossed Glen Shee to traverse the eight Munros east of Glen Tilt before heading north to climb 11 of the 18 Cairngorm summits, then finally arriving back at Invercauld Bridge, in only 22 hours and 5 minutes! Mann had climbed 30 Munros over a total distance of 88 miles with 25,000 feet of ascent. A three-marathon-plus day, with 30 Munros to boot, was 'pure mental', as they say in Glasgow. Finally, after 29 years, the record of 28 Munros in a day had been beaten, and one half of the 30/30 challenge was realised. Examining Mann's route on a map through a pair of snail's glasses, it would appear to be a grand route for a week's backpacking, covering a leisurely 12 miles and four Munros in a day.

The challenges could not end there, of course. With nearly two hours to spare off Mann's time, someone, had to squeeze in another few Munros and usurp the 30-Munro record. That someone was Sasha Chepelin, a young and fit 23-year-old, who, together with his friend Ali Masson, decided that Ben Avon and Beinn a' Bhùird could be added, bringing the total Munro-in-a-day count to 32. Prevented by 2020 lockdown restrictions from driving to England to attempt the Bob Graham Round in the Lake District, Chepelin and Masson turned their attention to beating Jim Mann's record. Starting at Invercauld Bridge, they opted for an anti-clockwise round, beginning with Ben Avon and ending on Lochnagar, which was quite apt, as the latter had been Chepelin's first Munro. Unfortunately, due to a hamstring injury, Masson had to pull out at Glenshee, but Chepelin continued bravely on and completed the intended 32 Munros in 23 hours and 10 minutes – a truly phenomenal achievement.

The present tally of 32 Munros in a day, though a brilliant performance, still leaves wriggle room for determined runners to add on one or two further Munros. Obvious candidates for future inclusion are Braeriach, Mayar, Driesh and possibly An Sgarsoch and Càrn an Fhìdhleir. The natural upper limit seems to be 35 Munros in a day, but I am prepared to be surprised!

While one person may be limited in the number of Munros they can summit in a day, on 14 August 2021, the Carnethy Hill Running Club of Edinburgh successfully accomplished a long-held objective of many walking/running clubs and other institutions: the recorded ascent of all 282 Munros by a group of individuals within a 24 hour period. The UK charity Water Aid has attempted this challenge on several occasions and in 1988 was only two summits short, with 2,000 people taking part.

The Carnethy Club, however, had a much smaller group of people involved – 120 members ranging from highly experienced fell runners to relative newcomers. The poor weather 14 August, particularly for the West Coast Munros, made the challenge a daunting one and almost scuppered the event.

Keith Burns, a 79-year-old former president of the Carnethy Club, came out of retirement to kick off the venture by reaching the summit of remote Beinn Dearg, near Blair Atholl at 7 o'clock in the morning. Far away, at his kitchen table, Ken Fordyce was beginning his 17-hour stagnant marathon session of receiving phone calls and recording ascents from members arriving at various summits; Burns was his first call.

Sasha Chepelin, whose record ascent of 32 Munros in one day was discussed earlier in this chapter, is a Carnethy Club member. Chepelin and his companion, Ali Masson, accomplished a remarkable 40-mile round of the 12 Munros south of Glen Shiel, including the three north of Loch Quoich.

Perhaps other than the Cuillin Munros, the most ambitious and notable round of the day was Declan Valter's solo attempt on the eight Munros of Knoydart south of Loch Quoich. These are some of the most remote and demanding summits in Scotland. In the adverse weather, they were to provide a sustained and merciless challenge. Right from the start at Kinloch Hourn, chest-high, wet bracken had soaked Valter and set the scene for a long, tiring day of poor visibility and time-consuming navigational stops.

Others who had been following Valter's progress soon realised that he would not reach the final Munro of Gairich before midnight. They quickly scrambled another team, consisting of Mick James and Jonathan Marks, who had already covered 16 miles on other Munros earlier in the day. They received the call at 9.00pm and by 11.48pm had reached the summit of Gairich in shorts and T-shirts, delighted at having 'saved the day' with only 12 minutes to spare. As they waited, shivering in their wet clothes, for Valter to appear,

Sir Hugh Munro, originator of Munro's Tables. (SMC Image Archive)

Matthew Forster Heddle, a previously unsung visionary. (private collection)

The Rev AE Robertson, the first Munroist, 1901. (SMC Image Archive)

Hamish Brown, the first person to compleat a continuous round of the Munros, in 1974. (Photo courtesy Hamish Brown)

Kathy Murgatroyd, the first woman to compleat a continuous round of the Munros. (Photo courtesy Kathy Murgatroyd)

Martin Moran, the first person to compleat a winter round of the Munros. (Photo courtesy Martin Moran)

Donnie Campbell, current holder of the fastest Munro round, in under 32 days. (Photo courtesy Donnie Campbell)

Descending the Ptarmigan Ridge of Ben Lomond, the most southerly Munro.

The view northwest from Stuchd an Lochain, the Munro with the first recorded ascent in 1590.

Ben Lui, possibly the finest Munro in the Southern Highlands.

The Ben Lui group from the nearby Munro of Beinn Dorain.

The group of Munros, known collectively as the Blackmount, from Rannoch Moor, south of Glencoe.

Buachaille Etive Mòr, the guardian of Glencoe, a rock climber's and scrambler's paradise.

The sprawling mass of Ben Macdui from Beinn Bhreac in the Cairngorms.

The summit of Ben More on the island of Mull, the only island Munro outside Skye.

Ben Alder, the remotest Munro in the Central Highlands and a prized objective.

Coire Ardair of Creag Meagaidh, one of the classic Scottish corries.

An ethereal image of Ben Nevis from north of Loch Arkaig – Britain's highest peak.

The Carn Mor Dearg arête of Ben Nevis – the finest hillwalkers' route to the summit.

The most westerly mainland Munro of Ladhar Bheinn from Buidh Bheinn.

The artificial reservoir of Loch Quoich from the Munro of Spidean Mialach.

Glen Shiel and Loch Cluanie, showing the celebrated South Shiel ridge with its seven Munros.

Sgurr na Sgine, another Munro south of Glen Shiel.

The Saddle (Glen Shiel), one of the finest mountains in Scotland and with a name easy to pronounce.

The Five Sisters of Kintail, one of the most photographed and popular ridges in Scotland.

On the summit ridge of the iconic Torridon peak of Liathach. Liathach was upgraded to two Munros in 1981.

Slioch from Loch Maree, a quintessential Highland image.

A' Mhaighdean from the remote outpost of Carnmore. This Munro is commonly regarded as the remotest.

The view northwest from the summit of A' Mhaighdean – perhaps the finest view from any Munro.

On the Corrag Bhuidhe pinnacles of An Teallach, often rated as the finest mountain in Scotland.

Sgurr nan Gillean from Sligachan in the Skye Cuillin, the most viewed of the 12 Skye Munros and having the first recorded ascent.

The south ridge of Blaven rising above Camasunary, a regular haunt of the author

The author and youngsters relaxing on the south ridge of Blaven.
(Photo: Andrew Oldfield)

The Inaccessible Pinnacle, technically the hardest Munro and the conclusion of many Munro baggers' quest.

they received a message that he was sleeping out in his bivvy bag, as he was so far from a road. James and Marks cheerfully ran back to Quoich Dam to join the celebrations.

Mark Hartree, President of the Carnethy Club, ran over 9 Munros in 12 hours with his dog. At the afterparty, he commented that it was the club's audacious approach and commitment that saw them succeed in the remarkable time of 16 hours and 48 minutes between the first and last Munro summit. Congratulations to the Carnethy Hill Running Club.

Just before this book went to press, the late Martin Moran's son, Alex, and a friend, Mike Coppock, completed the first 'Island Munros Triathlon'; running, cycling and swimming in order to ascend all 13 Munros on Skye and Mull. The total distance covered was 192 miles and they accomplished the challenge in 32 hours and 22 minutes.

Alex, a geography teacher, took on the challenge in memory of his father and has stepped into his father's shoes, as a mountaineering instructor in Lochcarron. Their venture raised money for the Martin Moran Foundation, a charity encouraging youngsters from diverse backgrounds to pursue mountain adventures.

This chapter has covered much ground, in both metaphorical and literal senses. From the Ripley brothers' bold but ultimately unsuccessful attempt to round the Munros in 1967 to the nuanced perambulations of Hamish Brown through more than half a century and on to the super-charged, foot-pounding exploits of Donnie Campbell, Sasha Chepelin, and the Carnethy Hill Running Club, the complete spectrum of continuous Munro round attempts has paralleled the more relaxed methods of thousands of others who have 'compleated' in rather more manageable timescales. It is to this major group that we now turn in the next chapter, focusing largely on the why, the wonder and the fun of Munro-bagging.

CONTINUOUS MUNRO ROUNDS: A SUMMARY TABLE		
DATE	**NAME**	**TIME IN DAYS**
1974	Hamish Brown	112
1982	Kathy Murgatroyd	134
1984	George Keeping	136
1984–5	Martin Moran	83
1985–6	Craig Caldwell	377
1986	Ashley Cooper	107
1986	Mike Cawthorne	?
1988	Mark Elsegood	66
1989	Mike Wilson-Roberts	?
1989	Paul Tatersall	81
1990	Hugh Symonds	67
1990	Stuart Clements	?
1990	Kate Weyman	?
1992	Andrew Johnstone & Rory Gibson	51
1994	Mike Cudahy	66
1996	Chris Townsend	118
1995–7	Andrew Allum	?
1997–8	Peter Lincoln	?
2000	Charlie Campbell	48
2003	Steven Perry	151
2005	Lorraine McCall	?
2005–6	Steven Perry	121
2010	Stephen Pyke	39
2010	Gerry McPartlin	88
2013	Kevin Woods	?
2019–20	Kevin Woods	97
2020	Donnie Campbell	32

COMMENTS

COMMENTS
Island ferries used. Bike used.
First woman. Ferries and bike used.
Included English & Welsh 3,000ers in 29 days. No bike.
First winter round. Vehicle used.
Including the Corbetts.
Included the Furth.
Climbed 1,000-metre peaks in winter.
Fell running. Vehicle used.
First round with a mountain bike.
Included the Furth – 97 days. No bike or ferries used.
Second woman.
Fell running. Bikes & ferries used.
Fell running. No bike or ferries used.
Included Tops. Bike used.
Munros, Tops, Corbetts, Grahams, Donalds, English/Welsh 2,000ers.
Munros, Corbetts, Grahams.
Fell running. Bike used. Swam sea passages.
Part of LEJOG walk including 3,000ers of England/Wales.
Third woman.
Second winter round. No vehicle used.
Fell running. Bike used. Kayaked sea passages.
Oldest continuous Munroist at 66. Vehicle used.
Third winter round. Vehicle used.
Fell runnning. Current record. Bike & kayak used.

CHAPTER 7

The Why, the Wry and the Whimsical

AFTER A DRIVE of over two and a half hours, I finally park at the end of the old Cluanie road in Glen Shiel at 8.30am on an August morning. Even at this relatively early hour, I expect the surrounding camper vans and other parked vehicles to be alive with the smoke and smell of fried breakfasts and folk chattering and preparing for the day. The reality, however, is absolute stillness. It is as if the grey, leaden cloud, clamping the surrounding hills in a vice-like grip, has stifled and suppressed all movement and sound, other than the plaintive cry of a curlew somewhere in the distance. I guess the occupants of these vehicles have taken one look outside, then turned over to go back to sleep... and I don't blame them. For a split second, I feel like restarting the engine and driving home, but almost unconsciously I find myself lacing up my boots, grabbing my walking pole and rucksack, and sauntering southward over the bridge at the western end of Loch Cluanie.

Somewhere up in the gloom ahead are the two Munros of Druim Shionnach and Aonach air Chrith, my objectives for the day, and a small section of the seven Munros that form the serpentine crest of the fabled South Cluanie ridge. On a fine day, this switchback ridge makes a classic traverse for the determined Munro-bagger, with the enticement of seven 'easy' Munros, a lure hard to resist. However, today I am questioning my motivation to climb even just two of the seven in these mist-ridden, claggy conditions. What is really niggling me is that the forecast was for high pressure over the north-west, and my only hope is of a cloud inversion so that I might rise above the clouds higher up the hills. However, having been disappointed with such notions too many times in the past, I try not to be overly optimistic and tempt fate.

As the old road swings east above the gloomy, lifeless waters of Loch Cluanie, I search impatiently for the start of a marked stalkers' path that zigzags up the steep hillside. Eventually, a small cairn appears. I leave the road to trudge upwards on a sketchy path through the heathery tussocks. After 15 minutes, and I still have not even reached the base of the clouds, which is probably around the 1,500-foot mark. I dejectedly reason that the higher the cloud base, the less chance I have of emerging from it further up, and I almost resign myself to a day of cloud and compass work. Leaden legs take me up, finally, through cloud to a lonely lochan (Loch a' Mhaoil Dhisnich) nestled in a hollow at 1,700 feet, barely visible amid the enveloping murk.

I cross the outflow of the lochan and begin to weave up the toe of Druim Shionnach's north ridge on intermittent slabs and boggy tussocks, following my nose into the ever-thickening cloud. I stop to glance upward, hoping for the tell-tale signs of a slight brightening signalling the cloud top... but nothing. Underfoot, conditions are, at best, manageable; at worst, boggy and wet with ankle-breaking tussocks. I search for bands of rock, but even these are partially slippery in the misty, damp atmosphere. Lost in a world dominated by the few yards I can see in front of me, I plod wearily upwards for another half hour until I reckon I must be a thousand feet above the lochan. Stopping momentarily, I sense that my bubble of visibility has increased somewhat, and the surrounding atmosphere is diffused with a distinctive, more radiant light. Above, a glorious vault of deepest, ultramarine blue validates my heady expectancy. As I continue upwards on steeper terrain, I follow an eroded path snaking its way through a series of rocky bluffs which I ascend with renewed fervour and anticipation.

I stop and turn around, gazing across a vast ocean of fleecy cloud, punctuated by the sunlit summits of myriad mountains peaking above the fluff like islands. To my right, I look over the yawning gulf of a scalloped corrie, to Aonach air Chrith and waves of cloud washing over the ridge. I have emerged from a world of monochromatic monotony to a higher plane of resplendent technicolour and clarity that seemingly stretches out to infinite horizons. But I have also transformed from a sluggardly, gloomy merchant to a buoyant, revitalised hillwalker, skipping and dancing along with a fresh spring in my step.

There can be few pleasures that compare to striding out along a sun-washed ridge, slung like a tightrope above the clouds without another soul in sight. Even later in the day, as I reach the wonderfully airy summit of Aonach air Chrith, I have met not a single person; I feel intensely privileged to experience this feast of magnificence on my own. During the grand descent over the rocky, northern spur, to A Chioch, the cloud gradually disperses and the string of screeching motorbikes on the A87 knocks me back to jarring reality after my few hours in heaven.

For those fortunate hillwalkers who have experienced a cloud inversion, the preceding sentiments will no doubt resonate fondly. For those who have not, including non-hillwalkers, the account hopefully conveys a modicum of the pleasures gained by setting foot on Scotland's mountains. The religious zeal with which many hill-goers pursue their passion may require some explanation for 'non-believers', but these delights often fall on deaf ears. There is a maxim which says:

> For those who believe, no explanation is necessary. For those who do not believe, no explanation is possible.[1]

It possesses a grain of truth: if you have to ask why some people want to climb hills, and especially Munros, then you may never receive a satisfactory answer. Part of this chapter's aim, nevertheless, is to provide some sort of explanation for this phenomenon without becoming overly philosophical.

What was the real motivation for me to leave home at the ungodly hour of 6.00am, travel all the way to Glen Shiel and climb two hills? For one, I was progressing through my third round of the Munros, and I'd only ascended these two peaks twice, most recently 37 years ago. In a nutshell, the list of Munros provided the framework and challenge that inspired my early start. But was I prepared to put in all the effort of rising early, driving for several hours and climbing, just to gain the dubious pleasure of ticking off two more hills on my 'third round' list? Of course not. As Hamish Brown points out, 'Lists are a means to an end and not an end in themselves'. Chris Townsend also puts it plainly: 'Collecting summits means collecting experiences'. I would also add that those experiences, if potent enough, will form indelible, golden memories to be treasured into old age. The almost spiritual experience of that day above the clouds in Glen Shiel will remain as an enduring, precious memory in my mind, as vivid as the photographs recording the event.

Comedian and Munro-bagger Ed Byrne suggests that his attachment to climbing Munros has come about from a combination of his love of the outdoors and his nerdish enjoyment of ticking things off lists. Here again, we see the link between ticking and titillation and how a lust for lists can translate into a love of the natural world. Tickers are a bit like twitchers in that tickers will go out their way to climb an obscure summit, and a twitcher will do the same to spot a rare, feathered specimen. At heart, the enjoyment of the natural environment underpins both passions.

Imagine a scenario where no list of 3,000-foot Scottish peaks exists and the word 'Munro' is just another surname. Would hordes of hillwalkers still flock to the hills? Almost certainly not. In one sense, this is a sad indictment of hill-goers' motivations, as they seemingly require a list of hills to provide the impetus to climb them. On the other hand, the list is an inducement and encouragement to some, who perhaps would not have ventured out otherwise and who through the list become hooked on a newfound passion. The Munro list is a double-edged sword, as when the wrong edge begins to dominate, Munro-bagging verges on mindless list-ticking.

I recall an old bothy tale concerning 'the lost art of festering', where 'festering' generally translates as huddling around a roaring bothy fire with warming mugs of Irish coffee, cheerfully exchanging friendly abuse with other 'inmates' of the poor weather and listening to the wind and rain battering on the window and roof. This indeed sets the scene of resigned contentment and camaraderie... apart from one solitary, determined character in the corner, who, upon lacing up his boots, rises to his feet and proclaims, 'Well, I suppose I'd better go and get these bloody Munros out of the way.' This is no half-joking utterance said for comical effect, however – this is full-blown indignation and ill-humoured irritability. Ramming spare clothing into his rucksack, he storms off outside, his mood even more troubled than the miserable weather. In his turbulent wake, he leaves an arc of perplexed faces and bewildered expressions, all wondering, 'What strange motives affected this man?'

When the list-ticking urge becomes the overriding factor above all else, it can drive some individuals to become unthinking, unfeeling automatons, like this lonely bothy character. Yes, climbing Munros can become addictive, but like the advice on a gambling advert, 'when the fun stops, stop'. Thankfully, I have never come across such a character in all my hill travels, but I have met people who are just as hostile in their attitude to 'list-tickers'. These smug, superior beings regard 'baggers' as the lowest scum of the earth. They view such people's activities as a kind of 'train spotting' and do not appear to understand that Munro-baggers can possibly have any appreciation or sympathy for the landscape they walk on. In short, these people adopt a moral high ground by claiming not to be summit baggers, which somehow makes them more receptive to the beauty around them. I find this argument astonishing and more than a trifle elitist. They appear to be tarring all Munro climbers with the same brush – that of the solitary bothy character.

One of Scotland's finest nature writers, who shall remain nameless, is a self-professed hater of Munro-bagging, regarding members of the 'climb-every-Munro-brigade' as 'deniers of the greatest of all mountain joys – the joy of being there'. Yet surely it is the joy of being there that reels us back to the hills again and again, not just the satisfaction of another 'tick'. The joy of list-ticking and the joy of being there are not mutually exclusive pleasures, but powerful, complementary facets present in most hillwalkers. As Hamish Brown remarks, the list-ticking aspect 'brings a drive and discipline to wandering feet'. Many folk relish a framework or scheme to follow, and the Munro list provides a suitable outlet for such desires. The list brings a focus, methodology, motivation and structure to what could be viewed as an essentially aimless activity. The long-term objective of compleating the Munros is a challenge that thousands find hard to resist.

AE Robertson, the first Munroist, recalls a conversation in which he described to a friend his experiences in climbing every hill over 3,000 feet in Scotland. His friend did not see the point of this at all and flippantly commented:

Why would you want to climb every hill? No one has kissed every lamppost in Princes Street, and why should anyone want to?[2]

Robertson had never looked at the matter in this 'profane light', thus proving the notion that hillwalkers rarely explain why they climb hills or why non-hillwalkers ask the question in the first place. Kissing lampposts and climbing hills are both essentially aimless occupations, but only one offers variety, adventure, challenge, freedom and appreciation of beauty.

I once asked a group of fellow hillwalkers to summarise in just two words why they climbed hills: wonder, freedom, escape, challenge, joy, fun, peace, life, satisfaction, beauty, pleasure, camaraderie and solitude. Interestingly, but not unsurprisingly, not one reply contained the word 'exercise'. It is well-known that a healthy body implies a healthy mind and that climbing hills is an excellent way of improving cardiovascular fitness – and losing weight. Yet if exercise were the only reason to climb hills, then we may as well spend a few hours running up and down the stairs. The huge benefits of sustained exercise during a hill walk are a marvellous side effect of what is essentially an intense aesthetic and spiritual communion with the mountain landscape, which in turn feeds back positively into our mental health and well-being. On the contrary, a 'couch potato' existence can easily lead to 'death by armchair'.

There is also the argument that aesthetic appreciation is deeper and more profound if it is borne out of physical effort and toil. Flickering images of mountains from a car or coach window, while beautiful and picturesque, simply do not have the intensity and long-lasting impression that arise when fully immersed as an active participant in the landscape. The maxim 'no pain, no gain' is perhaps overrated, but again, it holds much truth. Though sometimes it may not seem so at the time, the Munro experience will always give back to the hillwalker more than the work put in... their effort is repaid a hundredfold. The mountains provide the roughage for the spiritual nourishment so essential to a truer understanding of the hills and, ultimately, ourselves.

Looking at the list of 'why' words above, four are interrelated: freedom, escape, peace and solitude. Mountaineering is often viewed as a form of escapism, and hill gangrels talk of escaping to the hills for a day or a weekend. In today's complex and ignominious world of pettiness, vanity, skewed morals, bureaucracy and contrived hysteria, the hillwalker finds escape in the simple act of putting one foot in front of the other; the 'here and now' are all that matters. In the last section of *Hamish's Mountain Walk*, called 'Aftermath – or reasons why', Brown sums up to perfection the host of reasons we climb hills:

There is a whole mixture of coloured pills: the lure of challenge and testing, the delight of achievement, the contact with our ancestral simplicity, the escape from a normal petty existence, the finding of values, of beauty, of vision. These are worth living for – and possibly dying for.[3]

Although nobody venturing into the hills has any wish to die for these noble grounds, 'the lure of challenge and testing' contains within its remit obvious elements of risk and the small but non-zero probability of serious injury or death. Non-hillwalkers and especially media pundits tend to over-emphasise and exaggerate the risk of climbing hills and mountains; annoyingly, they even equate hillwalking and rock/ice climbing as the same activity.

Hillwalkers and climbers participate in their passion in order to live more intensely, and any risk factors are minimised as much as possible. As Munro enthusiasts progress through the list, new sets of challenges present themselves, helping to maintain interest and passion and keeping adherents on their toes, both metaphorically and literally. From easier, less challenging hills through to the demanding Cuillin, from carefree summer rambles to full-on winter expeditions, from short, roadside ascents to multi-day camping or bothying backpacks – all these experiences will be met during a Munro round. Unfortunately, a few headstrong individuals will attempt to bite off more than they can chew, such as attempting a serious winter route without first gaining enough summer ascents. The old saying 'walk before you can run' remains apt. In Hamish Brown's words, 'experience is the sum of near misses'. We have all been in situations where circumstances have spiralled out of control, perhaps due to inclement weather or thick cloud, but these are rarely life-threatening hurdles unless the danger is allowed to extend too far. Reacting positively and without panic are essential traits in such situations, and the greater this bank of experience, the more prepared we will be for tackling genuinely life-threatening circumstances.

The beauty of the Munros is their universal appeal. Whether aged six or 96, a reasonable fitness level is all that is required to climb a Munro. A young lad from Glasgow, Daniel Smith, climbed his first Munro aged six years and entered the record books three years later as the youngest Munroist at only nine years of age. At the other end of the scale, an elderly gentleman (name unknown) compleated his Munros on the Inaccessible

Pinnacle on his 80th birthday. Of interest here also is Myles Hutchinson, who had been the oldest surviving Munroist until his sad death in 2020, aged 90. He was Munroist number 23, having compleated his Munros in 1955.

Crucially, 'challenge' is a subjective notion that can assume different guises for different people; young, old, male, female, fit, unfit, experienced and inexperienced. Each individual's concept of challenge is unique to them – whether it be a Cuillin ridge traverse in winter or a summer walk up the Ben Lomond tourist path. The great leveller of Munros is their infinite diversity in difficulty, enabling them to accommodate a vast range of challenges. They therefore appeal to all levels of age, ability and inclination. It seems that the Munros are a universal cure for all ills!

Those taking their first, faltering steps into the hills are usually accompanied by experienced parents or friends, and they are likely tackling the easier Munros with good paths, such as Ben Lomond, Schiehallion or Ben Lawers. Gradually, as confidence and experience grow, hillwalkers can climb longer ridges and Munro groups, such as the Creag Meagaidh group, the Mamores and the South Cluanie ridge. Perhaps, too, at this stage, an ice axe and crampons may have been purchased in order to experience the more intense challenges of winter hillwalking. At some stage, the lure of more remote groups of Munros, such as the Fisherfield Five or the Knoydart Munros, will entail the additional delights of camping and the use of remote mountain bothies.

Indeed, for some, the pleasure of bothying has almost become an end in itself; 'bothy-bagging' and 'the lost art of festering' are related bedfellows.

A simple shelter in remote country for the use and benefit of all those who love being in wild and lonely places[4]

is the lucid, nostalgic description of a bothy given in the Mountain Bothies Association handbook. The MBA has progressed much from its earlier days, when the location of bothies was the province of those 'in the know'. The 2017 publication *The Scottish Bothy Bible* by Geoff Allan is a 'no holds barred', beautifully produced handbook on bothies, and it represents a 180-degree shift from what could have been termed a secret society. A brand of cult following exists among bothy users, akin to the '30s' Craigallion Fire sitters (see chapter 3), who revel in the warm camaraderie of like-minded souls enjoying a peaty malt whilst ensconced in the cosy, wood-smoked, earthy atmosphere, indulging in chat, laughter, music and craic until the dancing flames of the bothy fire fade to dying embers, leaving only candles flickering on the stone window ledge, signalling refuge for other weary walkers. Those who have never enjoyed such intensely rich and heart-warming nights in the wild with fellow travellers are missing an essential facet of the spectrum of mountain experiences. The dual combination of a glorious day wandering the ridges followed by a cosy night's session with kindred spirits in a remote bothy is the stuff of dreams and abiding memories – a magic tonic of ancestral simplicity. The book *Mountain Days and Bothy Nights* by Dave Brown and Ian Mitchell (Luath Press) is a classic 'old school' account of first-hand experiences and well worth a perusal.

For those who like their Munros grassy and rounded, the progression from 'Mealls' to 'Sgùrrs' can be quite daunting, but for others, this added challenge provides verve and spice that can become as addictive as bothying. Mountains and ridges such as Aonach Eagach, Liathach, An Teallach and the Cuillin all inevitably enter the radar of the aspiring Munroist, and progressing through the ranks of ambler, rambler, scrambler and, ultimately, dangler, on the Inaccessible Pinnacle, is a journey which inspires both fanaticism and fear in equal measure. Scrambling and the associated exposure, certainly in my own experience, inspired little fear when I was younger, but advancing years have bestowed me with a more acute sense of self-preservation and a reluctance to indulge in the more exposed and intimidating rock routes which were the meat and drink of my youthful years. Again, the wonderful thing about Munros is that the vast majority can be ascended without ever needing to put hand on rock.

Perhaps the biggest leap from the 'comfort zone' of less demanding summer Munros is the challenge provided by the winter hills. Scotland's mountains under a blanket of snow possess an austere and awesome beauty, but are also a minefield of hidden dangers ready to trap the unwary or inexperienced. Deep snow, ice, avalanche risk, short daylight hours and biting winds all conspire to make a winter hill walk a vastly more challenging and potentially life-threatening activity than a summer outing. Cameron McNeish comments that there is no such thing as winter hillwalking, only winter mountaineering. In other words, winter mountains need tackling as serious, almost Alpine excursions, using specialist equipment, such as an ice axe and crampons. Scottish mountains can and do adopt an Alpine splendour in winter conditions, with the formation of beautifully sculpted cornices, hard *neve* and the potential for serious avalanches.

Munros should be respected at all times, but doubly so in the winter, when their potential to maim or kill is maximised. Of course, some hillwalkers prefer to remain in their comfort zone of summer ascents and never venture into the hills during the dark days of winter. However, those fortunate individuals who have felt the reassuring squeak of crampons on hard *neve* while traversing a sunlit snow ridge, or who have watched distant summits become slowly flushed fiery, salmon pink with the setting sun, will completely understand the charismatic spell of the winter mountain domain.

The down side, of course, are days of endless, wind-driven sleet and snow, when visibility is reduced to yards and white-out conditions prevail. The 'Beast from the East' cold snap can last for days and be extremely unwelcome across the country, but it also creates winter beauty. These freezing winds and associated sleet and snow are ultimately responsible for the formation of elegantly furled cornices, wind blasted furrows and fragile ice sculptures – in effect, the whole white wonderland of winter. Beauty and the Beast are inseparable, a yin and yang working in tandem. In Scotland, we have a large share of the Beast, but this also implies we have a large share of Beauty. The variability and extremes of Scottish weather contribute to its staggeringly subtle and moody landscapes – the hallmark of Highland beauty (see chapter 4). The constantly changing weather, shifting clouds, patterns of light, infinitely varied shades of green, brown and gold, wisps of delicate mist on distant ridges, fresh clarity after a storm... all these and more give Scottish mountains a dynamic vibrancy that the world's greater ranges lack.

A friend of mine once disclosed to me that he had given up bagging Munros in favour of bagging whisky distilleries. Whether this was due to advancing years and associated joint problems, a change of heart or an excessive fondness for a dram, I am not entirely sure, but I suspect it was a combination. I began to think that although Munro-bagging may be more beneficial to one's health, the two pursuits have much in common. Just as every Munro has its own distinctive character, so too does each malt whisky. Both metaphorically and literally, whisky is the quintessence, the distillation, the true spirit of Scotland; each unique whisky has its own spirit of place.

Correspondingly, the Scottish mountains, and the Munros in particular, are the kernel of Highland landscape; each Munro has its own spirit of place. 'Whisky' means 'uisge beatha' or 'water of life', but in a sense, for many avid baggers and lovers of Scottish hills, the Munros are the true water of life.

For true devotees of malt whisky, the smell, or 'nose', often conjures up the greatest pleasure. The scent of bog myrtle and crowberry wafting through soft, summer air, sweet heather pollen and vanilla gorse, or the smoky reek of winter peat... all have the potential to stir and reawaken long-distant memories. It is often smell, the most evocative of all the senses, that can also kindle and evoke past events and experiences in the hills. With whisky, the scent is followed by the core delight, the taste, so unique to each dram, like the delight of a hilltop encounter on each Munro. Finally, the pungent or sweet aftertaste translates to the fragrance of memories – all combine to produce a dizzyingly addictive passion to for whisky and Munros.

At the end of an inspirational and memorable day in the hills, what finer way of rounding off the experience than the rich, refreshing tones of a fine malt? Additionally, on those miserable days of wind and driving rain, the pleasures of a good fire, a good book and a good dram are surely the next best thing to stravaiging in the hills... indeed, some would say better!

At some point on the dedicated bagger's journey through the Munros, the act of recording ascents assumes great importance. Reliance on simply memory of which Munros one has climbed soon falters as the number increases and distinct memories become jumbled. Methods for recording summits are as numerous as the Munros themselves. For some, a simple tick in a Munro guidebook is enough; for others, a full account of the day, in the form of a diary, serves to trigger more memories. When I started climbing Munros in the late 1970s, a copy of Munro's Tables served as my guide and as a diary of ascents, on which I recorded a brief description of such things as weather and company. Irvine Butterfield's *Munroist's Log* was the first publication to cater to the growing market of Munro-baggers who wished to chronicle their experiences in a more detailed form. There are now several similar 'Munro Diaries' for sale online.

In the mid-'80s, I purchased an A4-sized hardback blank notebook and inserted all the Munros, in 50 manageable sections, such as Rannoch and Glen Lyon, the Mamores, the Cairngorms and Torridon, and left several pages blank after each listing in order to record details. Following each Munro's name, I still use a tally mark system to note the number of ascents and religiously update new ascents following a day out on the hills. The advantage of adopting such a system is my ability to keep track of all my Munro ascents and experiences, in addition to triggering fond memories upon reading past accounts from many years back.

In these days of digital technology, many people record their ascents online. Munro wall-charts are still popular, and years ago, I had one hanging on my kitchen wall with each little triangle depicting a Munro summit I had ascended shaded in red.

From a non-hillwalker's point of view, all of these elements probably point to a serious addictive personality trait disorder. Indeed, the whole obsessive game of Munro collecting and recording can be compared to a virus or disease that is difficult to eradicate. SMC member WD Brooker identified it in his article 'Rampant Munrosis: the Scottish Disease', published in a 1991 *SMC Journal*. I also touched on it in my earlier book, *The Munro Phenomenon*. The seeds of Munrosis were sown in the early days of the SMC, when two distinct, but not mutually exclusive types of hill-goers began to emerge: the 'Salvationists' and the 'Ultramontanes', already mentioned in chapter 1. In the eyes of the rock and ice 'tigers', the Ultramontanes, the peak-baggers, or Salvationists, were seen as lower-level, uncreative, soulless individuals who only ascend 3,000-foot mountains and largely by their easiest routes. The often-ridiculed list-ticking tendencies of these Salvationists were soon to grow into a new affliction that would affect vast numbers of hill-goers in future years.

The true seriousness of the disease began to make its mark in the 1980s when an exponential rise in Munro-bagging became apparent. Even *The Scotsman* newspaper contained a report by Peter McCue on 'Chronic Munrosis – a severe form of obsessional neurosis peculiar to Scotland'. A more detailed description of 'The Scottish Disease', by Dr Iain McIntosh, a Stirling GP, appeared in the *Scottish Medicine* periodical and summarises the more salient aspects of Munrosis, such as its predominance in the male, its tendency toward mad, compulsive behaviour, and its straining and often destructive influence over marital relationships. The symptoms of chronic Munrosis reach their peak at weekends and holidays, when the sufferer contracts an overwhelming and obsessive desire to elevate himself above the 3,000-foot contour. An acute and more specialised form of the disease afflicts around one in ten sufferers, who are compelled to go off in search of obscure and remote Tops. A glimmer of insight into the strange psyche of the Top-bagger can be found by reading the madcap antics of the Doctor and his companions in the chapter 'Finishing off a Top' in the book *The Ridiculous Mountains* by GJF Dutton.

Early symptoms of Munrosis include a sudden, unhealthy interest in boots, woolly hats and the latest breathable garments. This usually ends with a furtive, hen-pecked husband sneaking into the nearest climbing shop, only to emerge several minutes later with a plain carrier bag containing a pair of loop-stitch socks and a Munro guidebook. Some disgusted wives endeavour to contact support groups, such as Munro-holics Anonymous or other low altitude therapy groups, but these well-intentioned bodies rarely provide more than a temporary fix to the disease's overwhelming progress. Increasingly, many women resort to the 'if you can't beat them, join them' philosophy, and they too become afflicted. Recurrence of the disease in Secondary Munrosis (those attempting a second round of the Munros) and even Polymunrosis is increasingly prevalent. Post-Munro activities are the subject of the next chapter.

Many lesser variants of the disease are known to afflict a few individuals, and some of the more common conditions are mentioned here. Munrosis Integrale compels the sufferer to compleat the round in a single expedition (see chapter 6). The most serious associate condition is Munrosis Brevis, of which Donnie Campbell is currently the most notable survivor at 32 days. Munrosis Matrimonialis occurs when husband and wife compleat together; there are around 50 known cases of this romantic phenomenon. Several cases of Munrosis Familiaris have occurred in which whole families compleat together, such as the Morgan family in 1985. Rarer potential variants include Munrosis Incrementalis – the climbing of Munros in order of height, and Munrosis Alphabeticus – the climbing of Munros in alphabetical order… so far, no known cases of these rarities have come to light, but give it time.

One particular variant could be described as the ultimate

cure for insomniacs: Munrosis Nocturnalis. Perhaps the greatest advocate of nighttime Munro ascents is Alan Rowan, whose book *Moonwalker: Adventures of a midnight mountaineer* is a gentle nudge for daytime walkers who regard nightly ascents as daft and dangerous. Rowan's transformation from 'desk jockey to death-defying midnight mountaineer' is a unique and funny story of a 'crazy idea' to start climbing a Munro while everyone was heading to bed, seeing the sun rise from 3,000 feet and descending when everyone was getting up. Despite the predictable cries of the cosseted, comfort zone inhabitants, night walking, in the right conditions, can be safe and extremely liberating. It also opens up a whole new spectrum of wonder and beauty... the bronze sun slowly sinking behind the serrated ridges of the west, the dancing, phosphorescent colours of the Northern Lights shimmering against a starlit sky, the full moon rising, the silvery threads of mountain streams and the pale glow of dawn revealing a tangle of peaks and mist-filled glens, as yet untouched by the first rays of the sun.

Of course, the original protagonist of night climbing was Sir Hugh himself, who undertook many Munro ascents in the dark hours to avoid being seen on what he regarded as private land (see chapter 1). Landscape photographer Colin Prior (see chapter 5) must also have spent many nighttime hours on Munro summits to achieve his breathtaking dawn and early morning images.

Perhaps the ultimate in absolute freedom, escape and unhinged madness is the variant Munrosis Nudus. The 'naked rambler' who walked from Land's End to John o' Groats may have become a figure of ridicule in the popular press and spent more time in jail than walking, but he stuck to his guns to protect his high ideals. The combination of Munrosis Nocturnalis and Munrosis Nudus may well appear to be the only way forward for potential naked Munro-baggers. Hardy, cold-blooded 'nutters' need only apply!

The prolonged odyssey of peak-bagging reaches its natural termination on the ascent of the last Munro. This is a poignant moment for any Munro-bagger, an intensely sweet but profoundly sad end to a journey of many years and many experiences. The choice of the last Munro often requires some soul-searching, and many opt for a fairly easy, accessible peak, preferably within staggering distance from a decent pub. Due to its status as the only island Munro, bar the Skye Cuillin, Ben More on Mull has probably seen more champagne corks popping than most mountain summits, but other Munros, such as Ben Hope, Ladhar Bheinn, Slioch, Blaven and the Inaccessible Pinnacle all receive their fair share of summit party fame.

We now examine two 'compleations', with tongue partly in cheek. Of the following two stories, one concerns a real, pretend Hugh Munro, and the other a pretend, real Hugh Munro. One is true and the other false; the reader can decide which is which.

MUNRO MONOLOGUE I

Wee Hugh Munro of Furness was not your average God-fearing, Calvinistic, Sabbath-respecting Wee Free church minister. The fact that he had been climbing Munros for years to raise money for a complete refurbishment of the local pub kind of said it all… especially considering the church was in dire need of attention. His 'local hero' label, bestowed on him by his loyal parishioners, was certainly not shared by his formidable wife, Morag, a stereotype of the mad, battle-axe variety, who regarded Munro-bagging, like dancing and drinking, as the Devil's pastime. Wee Hugh's and 'mighty' Morag's manse was the only house where rolling pins were used to flatten more than dough.

Hugh was a great fan of Robert Burns, especially the poem 'Tam o' Shanter'. He rewrote the first verse as a special ode to both his Munros and his wife, Morag:

> When Munro machos leave the street,
> And couthy baggers, baggers meet,

> As mountain days are wearing late,
> An' sufferin' spouses wait – irate;
> While we sit dreaming at the cairn,
> Of no' hae'n a wifie and a bairn,
> We think na on the long Scots miles,
> The Tops and peat hags, bogs and stiles,
> That lie between us and our hame,
> Where sits our sulky, sullen dame,
> Gathering her brows like gathering storm,
> Nursing her wrath to keep it warm.

'Wee Hughie', as his parishioners called him, was well aware that he was the namesake of the big man himself, Sir Hugh Munro. Although he was sure that out of the thousands of 'compleaters', there must be another Hugh Munro*, his real motivation for bagging Munros was the fact that the first two compleaters were both clergymen. If a Church of Scotland minister and an Anglican minister could climb all the Munros, then he could be the first Wee Free minister!

Following his recent hip operation, Wee Hughie felt fit as a fiddle, and his experience and knowledge of the Munros was well-established. Despite being a baby boomer, the '60s revolution seemed to have passed him by. Though Wee Hughie could not tell funk from punk nor garage from grunge, he knew the difference between the top of a Munro and a Top of the Munros. He had only come across 'Rolling Stones' and 'Dire Straits' while floundering at the bottom of the 'Great Stone Chute' in the Cuillin. Wee Hughie was a paid-up member of the hip op' generation rather than the hip-hop generation.

One day, sitting and 'dreaming at the cairn' of Buachaille Etive Mòr in Glencoe, Wee Hughie began chatting with a stranger and endeavouring to put names to the various peaks around them. There was one specific 'pointy' summit on the horizon which neither of them could identify. Now, according to Muriel Gray in her book *The First Fifty*, if folk are arguing about a 'pointy' peak on the horizon, it is always Schiehallion.

No matter which Munro you happen to be on, remember that the pointy, unknown summit in the far distance is always Schiehallion – it saves a lot of time. A third walker to arrive at Wee Hughie's cairn and heard the two of them discussing the peak; he immediately divulged his superior knowledge and informed them, with a barely concealed arrogance, that the hill in question was indeed Schiehallion. To Wee Hughie, this newfound knowledge had a profound effect. Already nearing compleation, he had for some time wondered which Munro would be suitable for his last. He wanted one with striking individuality and preferably a good path most of the way up. Schiehallion perfectly fit the bill, and his mind was made up there and then.

Six months late in Furness village hall, parishioners were busy preparing for a grand Ceilidh and raffle to celebrate Wee Hughie's Munro compleation and raise more money for the pub refurbishment. Hughie himself was up a step ladder, lost in concentration, as he carefully painted large black letters on a huge poster: 'HUGH MUNRO'S LAST MUNRO: SCHIEHALLION'. Beside him on the ladder, next to his paint tin, was a bottle of 25-year-old 'Lindertis' finest malt whisky, a special treat he had saved for a very special occasion. The old adage of 'one's just right, two's one too many and three's not half enough' was not lost on Hughie; he was already on his fourth dram. He was not drinking for enjoyment, however, but to calm his nerves following a tussle with the bickering, bull-headed Morag, who could not really grasp or believe that he had climbed all his 'ridiculous mountains', as she called them.

Whilst engaged in a section of particularly awkward lettering, Hughie felt the distinct presence of someone looking up at him from below. Indeed, there was the notorious interfering village busybody, Sandy the Snoop (or Snoopy, for short). Upon meeting Hughie's gaze, Snoopy blurted out, 'Are you sure there are two Ls in Schiehallion?'.

Hughie, concealing his anger and disgust, looked disdainfully down at Snoopy and replied, 'Aye... and are there two gs in bugger off?!' Unsurprisingly, Snoopy did 'bugger off', tail firmly between legs.

Several minutes later, Hughie heard the unmistakable foghorn tones of 'mighty Morag'. In a blind panic, he grabbed the whisky bottle and sloshed it into his large paint tin while gulping back the remains of his glass with his other hand, before stuffing the glass in a pocket. Seconds later, Morag appeared below the ladder, casting a disparaging stare at Hughie and his masterpiece of calligraphy. She then accused:

I dinna' believe you've been up that Shallion or
whatever ye call it – you've probably been in that
bloody pub a' day!

Hughie, controlling his annoyance, turned round and replied coolly,

A've told you before, Morag, as a Wee Free minister,
I never drink whisky, I never swear and I never tell lies.

As he turned back triumphantly to resume his task, his elbow hit the paint tin, sending it crashing to the floor, the 25-year-old Lindertis smashing and its precious contents mixing with black paint across the floor of the hall. The hubbub was suddenly reduced to deadly silence; a dozen faces turned to Hughie and his ladder. There is no exact record of Hughie's graphic exclamation, but it is safe to assume all three of his vows were broken in that moment.

---

* The only other Hugh Munro on the list of Munroists is Hugh William Munro, from Aberdeenshire, who compleated on Slioch in 2019, one hundred years after Sir Hugh Munro's death.

MUNRO MONOLOGUE 2

Sir Hugh Munro sat pensively in the armchair, staring blankly into the middle distance, possibly contemplating his last three Tops. He 'cut a dash' in his Hunting Fraser tartan kilt, a vast improvement on the official Munro Clan's garish red and yellow tartan. Looking more closely, however, revealed that something was not quite right. No, it was not his Glengarry bonnet, or smart tweed waistcoat and jacket, nor even his sporran or woollen socks. It was his walking boots that drew the eye, oddly modern-looking, without a hint of hobnails or Tricounies.

And there was still something else strangely unreal about this 'ghost', this robotic reincarnation of a long-deceased Knight. Was this some kind of spooky apparition of Hugh Munro from beyond the grave? If you had attempted to engage in conversation with him, you would not have received even a glimmer of recognition, or indeed, consciousness. This 'being' could not be considered to be even remotely alive. It was no sentient entity, but a sedentary effigy, the grotesque Frankenstein-like creation of none other than Great Robin of Clan Campbell.

Robin was about to right a great wrong of Munro-bagging history and redeem Sir Hugh Munro's rightful place as a compleat Munroist by escorting him up his final three summits. No matter that he was a curious concoction of clay, latex, tubular bandages, coat-hangers and pillows; this ghostly essence of the great man himself was assured: Robin's visit to his grave at Lindertis did not result in any portentous omen, signalling the Knight did not actively disapprove of this hair-brained but honourable scheme.

So it came to pass that on the tenth day of November in 1991, Great Robin and his trusty companion, the Doctor (Helen Ross), together with a subdued version of Hugh Munro, battled through Glen Tilt in miserable weather to reach Tarf bothy. The good Doctor wisely decided to 'keep her powder dry' and remain in the relative comfort and shelter of the bothy, while 'Batman and Robin' continued on their glorious quest to reach the summit of Càrn an Fhìdhleir. The weather was considerably worse than that of 11 July 1908, when the living Hugh Munro had made his failed attempt on this elusive summit. Rain had turned to snow, and their arrival at the summit cairn was accompanied by howling wind and whirling, icy spindrift. Even the Knight refused to leave his cloistered, protective cocoon of plastic bin bags, and a hasty return to the bothy reunited the fearless trio before the final leg, in torrential rain and increasing darkness, returned the gallant heroes to safety.

History was made the following Sunday when Robin and the Knight successfully reached the summit of Càrn Cloich-mhuilinn, in more agreeable weather. This was, of course, Sir Hugh's intended last Munro (now a Top), and his revenant was able to finally emerge from his womb and pose for a historic summit photograph. Instead of Lindertis 25-year-old malt, Munro's posthumous compleation was celebrated with a sorry substitute of lukewarm coffee. Less than a week later, the brave Knight was smuggled into the Roxburghe Hotel in Edinburgh, where he would become the focal point and highlight of a special evening among 223 celebrants, of which 155 were compleat Munroists, gathered to celebrate the centenary of the publication of Munro's Tables. Following Robin's speech, the Knight himself, now a Munroist, was unveiled for all to see. He received a rapturous reception.

The postscript to this grand saga occurred the following year when Robin, Sir Hugh and another climber, James Kenyon, made the ascent of Sir Hugh's last Top, the Inaccessible Pinnacle of Sgùrr Dearg (now a Munro). Finally, he had climbed all 538 Tops on Munro's original list, and now the great Knight could finally rest in peace. Still no Lindertis, but a bottle of champagne was a huge improvement over lukewarm coffee. Thus ended the first and only case of Munrosis Posthumous.

And finally, a little Munro ditty, entitled 'Merry Munroing Everybody', to be sung to the tune of Slade's 'Merry Christmas Everybody'.

Are you waiting for your bagging mate to call?
Are you ticking your Munro map on the wall?
Are you dressed up for the weather?
Too wet to even speak
And the only boots you have are ones that leak.

Chorus

So here it is, Merry Munros
Everybody's having fun
Look to the future now
When all these hills are done.

Are you hoping that your marriage will survive?
That you'll get down from this mountain still alive
Are the midges trying to bite you?
When you're camping in the glen?
And you swear you won't come back this way again.

Chorus

Are you wandering round the summit in the mist?
Wondering if the cairn was passed and missed.
Have you got your map and compass?
Have you lost your GPS?
Did the clag and low cloud get you in this mess?

Chorus

Are you climbing up a mountain in the snow?
Do you think that steeper icy bit will 'go'?
Are you cursing your loose crampon
Strapped on to your boot?
And you swear you've got a blister on your foot.

Chorus

Have you only got one more Munro to go?
Before you start the encore Corbett show.
Did the thought of your 'compleation'
Put you in a spin
Did the champagne put you in the state you're in?

So there it was, many Munros
Everybody's had their fun
Treasure all these memories
Now all these hills are done.

CHAPTER 8

Below and Beyond

COMPLEATION OF THE Munros will be accompanied by a whole range of emotions… excitement, a sense of achievement, passion, pensive reflection and, yes, sadness. It is inevitable that after many years of focused planning and execution, with all the associated challenges, experiences and fond reminiscences, feelings of loss and depression at reaching the end of a happy era are destined to occur. On compleation of my last Munro, Ben More on Mull, in August 1988, my log contains the words:

> The end of an era has come. So much water has passed
> under the bridge, so many happy memories. It HAS meant
> so much for so long. The challenge now lies dormant.[1]

These sentiments will no doubt be instantly recognised by other Munroists, and it is natural to wonder what all these 'compleaters' do afterwards. Some may hang up their well-worn boots and sink contentedly into an armchair by the fireside to reminisce on past glories, but for others, Munro compleation is just a Graduate First Degree that leads on to further post-graduate lists, such as Corbetts and Grahams. The bulk of this chapter concerns itself with mountain lists under 3,000 feet. Hamish Brown, for one, advocates tackling the Munros and Corbetts simultaneously, but with the popular fixation on Munros, Corbetts are usually relegated as 'add-ons' following Munro compleation.

After my own compleation in 1988, I naturally turned to Corbetts. It was most fortuitous that in the same year, the only book describing Corbett ascents was published. Hamish Brown's

Climbing the Corbetts describes his unique experiences in ascending each and every Corbett and is, in effect, a companion volume to *Hamish's Mountain Walk*. Indeed, the two books both appeared in a single compilation volume at a later date.

Peculiarly, it was an Englishman, John Rooke Corbett, the fourth Munroist, who saw the great potential of a list of 2,500-foot peaks to rival Sir Hugh Munro's hallowed classification. Corbett was a Cambridge mathematician who became a District Valuer based in Bristol, though he was originally from Manchester. A quiet and reserved man, he had a passion for mountaineering and long-distance walking; Corbett once walked the 155 miles from Cambridge to his Manchester home. An original member of the Rucksack Club, he was not slow to note the development of

a new craze or hobby, which may be looked upon as a special form of the old passion for peakbagging,[2]

as he wrote in the *Rucksack Club Journal* of 1911. He was referring to the 2,500-foot summits of England and Wales, which he also classified, collectively known as the 'Twenty-fives'.

His focus soon changed to Scotland, and even before finishing the Munros and Tops, Corbett was actively examining the potential for a list of 2,500-foot Scottish summits. He joined the SMC in 1923, and the fifth Munroist, John Dow, another SMC member, described him as 'probably the best and most tireless hillwalker of his generation'. Corbett is generally credited with the accolade of having climbed every hill in Scotland over 2,000 feet, although there is no firm proof of this. Realising that an exhaustive list of 2,500-foot peaks would constitute too many hills for a suitable challenge, Corbett listed only those mountains with a specific amount of re-ascent on all sides. Although this was not explicitly stated in his notes, later detailed analysis concluded that the re-ascent (or drop) criteria was 500 feet, with no account taken of either distance or steepness. Sadly, Corbett never lived to see his list in print:

he suffered from a heart attack and a paralytic affliction and died in 1949, aged 72.

> Hillwalkers who concentrate their efforts entirely on the Munros will be in danger of missing many of the best of Scottish mountains.[3]

This statement appeared in the 'Introduction' of the first guidebook to the Corbetts, published in 1990. *The Corbetts and Other Scottish Hills* (SMC), edited by Hamish Brown and Rob Milne, would fast become the new 'Bible' for Munroists and the companion volume to the SMC Munro guidebook. Rob Milne, a world leader in the field of artificial intelligence, was also a high-altitude mountaineer who sadly lost his life minutes from summiting Everest in June 2005.

The strict re-ascent criterion for Corbetts ensures that they are distinct and detached summits, unlike many Munros, and prolific peak-baggers hoping for long ridges of multiple Corbetts will be disappointed. It is this isolation which arguably makes Corbetts more challenging than Munros, despite their lower altitude. The 222 Corbetts stretch from the Southern Uplands to the far north of Scotland, where Quinag, Ben Loyal and Foinaven give any Munro a run for its money. Areas such as Ardgour and Moidart, where there are no Munros, are dominated by fine peaks such as Garbh Bheinn and Rois-Bheinn, and the islands of Arran, Jura, Rum and Harris all contain Corbetts, but no Munros. In short, the Corbetts are more than a worthy and commendable post-Munro challenge, and it is therefore surprising that the current total number of Corbetteers is only around a tenth of the number of Munroists. It must be said, however, that many Corbetteers, including myself, have not informed the SMC Clerk of the List of their completion, or are not aware that an official list exists.

Corbett's list of 2,500-foot hills was readily accepted by the SMC and soon began to appear in the book of Munro's Tables, which subsequently was called *Munro's Tables and other Tables of Lesser Heights*. Also included was a third list of hills, known as the Donalds. Percy Donald, the compiler, climbed every hill over 2,000 feet in the Scottish Lowlands over five months, using mainly public transport and wearing a kilt. The result of this dedicated foray was a list of 140 hills comprised of 89 Donalds and 51 Donald Tops, compiled in 1935, well before the appearance of Corbett's list. Donald used an archaic and convoluted rule, based on units of one-twelfth of a mile, to distinguish between 'Hills' and 'Tops', although his methodology will not be pursued here.

The obvious question, of course, is why did Donald restrict his list to the Scottish Lowlands? It would appear that Donald, who was not a Munroist, did not have the necessary knowledge, time or inclination to widen his scope to the Highlands, which would have been an incredible task. Another man not only realised the enormity of such a task, but positively thrived on it: William McKnight Docharty, the 13th Munroist in 1948, who also completed the Furths in 1949. Docharty was a latecomer to the Scottish hills, having only ascended Ben Lomond in 1916 during Army leave. He also enjoyed numerous trips to the Alps, delighting in their 'crystal atmosphere and virgin snow'. Finally, in the autumn of 1933, he met a John Thomson, who awakened in him an enthusiasm for the Scottish hills that would occupy the rest of his life.

A year before his Munro compleation, he became aware of a choice between two contrasting alternatives, one that many modern Munroists will also have to make:

> To devote myself to a second series of excursions, with the Munros and their 3,000-foot subsidiaries once more as principal objectives, or to open up a new series on fresh ground with these no more than incidental.[4]

Two post-Munro trips to Rum and Knoydart clinched the deal and

> left a profound impression upon me as to the latent possibilities of excursions on hills of sub-Munro standard.[5]

Unsurprisingly, Docharty followed the second course of action and conceived the idea of producing detailed lists of British mountains under 3,000 feet.

Unlike Corbett, who only listed principal mountains over 2,500 feet, Docharty included lesser, subsidiary summits in this height range with a classification that extended down to 2,000 feet and included England, Wales and Ireland. Over the course of the 14 years directly following the Second World War, Docharty spent all his free time climbing and classifying British mountains. In 1954, he published the first of three volumes, entitled *A Selection of Some 900 British and Irish Mountain Tops*, which essentially covered the mountains between 2,500 feet and 3,000 feet. The following eight years were spent climbing and classifying all the 2,000-foot summits, including many under that height, and in 1962, his second volume was published, bringing the grand total of listed mountains to 2,801. Docharty brushed aside the monumental effort of such a self-imposed task, who claimed he spent 14 years of intense pleasure

to share with friends who have given me of their
comradeship on lofty ridge and high plateau.[6]

In Scotland alone, Docharty recorded 541 excursions, covering 8,000 miles and climbing 1,628 mountain tops.

It is almost certain that Docharty was aware of Corbett's list; he too used the 500-foot drop criterion for independent mountain status. However, he forsook, or at least relaxed, the rule in certain circumstances, particularly in England, where it was replaced by a 250-foot drop, arguing that a 500-foot drop would exclude too many individualistic summits. In Scotland, he also relaxed the rule in many rolling tableland areas, such as the Monadhliath and Atholl, where a 50-foot drop was seen to suffice. He also included borderline cases but did not include 2,500-foot Tops of Munros – a strange omission.

Docharty's volumes were not only extensive mountain listings, but also included a series of superb, panoramic, monochrome photographs, each constructed from several component prints and of remarkable quality and clarity. His 'list-ticking' and 'being there' mentalities are perfectly combined, along with the inclusion of beautifully crafted prose that tugs the heartstrings of all mountain lovers. A small sample from his first volume:

> And if I may leave a good wish with you on behalf of our Scottish hills, I should like it to be a crisp north-west breeze on your face before which the mists are reeling to disclose the vast blue firmament, in which not far above your head sail scattered squadrons of lofty snow-white spinnakers of fleecy Cumulus, whose dark shadows stride swiftly athwart the course you have set on the ridges.[7]

Docharty's labour of love continued to a third volume devoted entirely to his British and Alpine experiences; this too contained marvellous panoramic photographs. This 'man with a mission' brilliantly portrays across his three volumes the tenacity and perseverance he put forth to compile his lists, but perhaps above all, Docharty highlights his intense love for mountain landscapes. That Docharty had produced, from the head and heart, such a comprehensive and unique series of Scottish mountain listings – and that he was a well-respected SMC member – seemed like an assurance that his sub-2,500-foot list would be published in the Munro's Tables book, yet it was not to be – the SMC's likely justification being the sheer complexity, quantity and subjectivity of the lists. In my opinion, this omission was a huge injustice and a missed opportunity to secure a reliable classification of 2,000-foot summits, which would not come about for several more decades.

Docharty's three volumes had a private and limited publication; only 500 were produced. This regrettably ensured that they made little impact on the popular hillwalking fraternity of the time, and his work rarely extended beyond a tight inner circle of individuals and interested parties. I was lucky enough to borrow copies from Hamish Brown and was grateful for the opportunity to glimpse into the psyche of a man who, like Matthew Heddle and Ronald Burn, deserves more recognition in the story of Munro-bagging and Scottish mountains in general.

It was not until 1997 that the now definitive list of 2,000-foot Scottish hills, known as the Grahams, was finally included in the book of Munro's Tables. The creation and development of the list has an interesting and involved history, which will be briefly outlined here. In 1992, two key publications led directly to today's list of Grahams. The first was Alan Dawson's book *The Relative Hills of Britain* (Cicerone), which lists every summit in Britain with a re-ascent of 150 metres. The 150-metre criterion is the rough metric equivalent of Corbett's 500-foot guideline (500 feet equals 152.4 metres). Thus, Dawson applied a metric Corbett criterion to all the hills of Britain, regardless of their height above sea-level (hence the title 'relative hills'). Numbering over 1,500, these hills were named, somewhat whimsically, 'the Marilyns', a whimsical spin off the surname of actress Marilyn Monroe. Since 150 metres is actually 492 feet, all the Corbetts have at least this amount of re-ascent, or drop, and so are a subdivision of the Marilyns. However, not all of the Munros are Marilyns, since many Munros do not have a 150-metre drop on all sides. Of interest here, however, is the distinct subgroup of Scottish Marilyns between 2,000 feet and 2,499 feet, which Alan called Lesser Corbetts, abbreviated to LCs or 'Elsies'.

The second key publication in the autumn of 1992 was an article in *The Great Outdoors* (TGO) magazine by Fiona Torbet (née Graham). Torbet had spent a two-month spell in hospital recovering from a skiing accident, and with nothing else to do, she used the time to compile a list of Highland hills between 2,000 feet and 2,500 feet. Her chosen criteria for inclusion was

having a descent all round of about 150 metres, or being the highest point all round for about two miles.[8]

The double inclusion of 'about' introduced an element of ambiguity into her list that was not present in the list of Alan Dawson's 'Elsies'. Obviously, having two separate but broadly comparable lists of hills was confusing, so wisely, Torbet and Dawson got together to thrash out a common solution, which resulted in the inclusion of southern Scotland and the exclusion of some of the hills on Fiona's list. The collaboration brought the total to 222 hills, which, by mutual agreement, would be known as the 'Grahams' for Fiona Torbet's maiden name – while 'Torbet' could have been used for this class of hills, it would no doubt have produced a Corbett–Torbet confusion.

The history of the Graham list has rather a sad finale. While on a walking holiday in the West Highlands, Torbet disappeared and was a missing person for almost a year. Her body was eventually recovered; tragically, she had been murdered. It is appropriate and fitting that the generic name of the Scottish 2,000-foot peaks reflect her memory.

The SMC were sluggish in their acceptance of this new list; it was rejected in December 1992 on the basis that 'the last thing we need is a proliferation of lists'. Little did they know what lay in the future! Published in the form of a small booklet in the 'Tacit Tables' series in 1995, it finally gained 'official' recognition by the SMC in 1997 when it appeared in that year's edition of Munro's Tables. At that time, there were 224 Grahams, which have now been reduced to 219 after subsequent resurveying.

Judging by the amount of mail received, regarding Fiona's classification in *TGO* magazine, many hillwalkers are fascinated and inspired by lists of hills; I was certainly one of them. Following on from my own two successes in the book publishing sphere (*Classic Mountain Scrambles in Scotland* in 1992 and *The Munro Phenomenon* in 1995 – both Mainstream), I was actively seeking inspiration for a third book. Fiona's article, Alan Dawson's book and the Tacit list of Grahams, all hinted that a guidebook to the Grahams was the obvious answer. So despite being halfway through a Corbett round, I decided to change tack and pursue the Grahams with great relish, especially since Mainstream Publishing had signalled a 'thumbs up' for the idea. So between late 1994 and 1997, I ploughed my way through the Grahams, writing the book as I went along – the final result, *The Grahams – A Guide to Scotland's 2000-foot Peaks*, was so successful that it went on from hardback to two paperback editions.

I reckon that I am probably one of only two people known to have climbed the Grahams before finishing the Corbetts, as the latter are normally the first challenge on the radar of a post-Munroists. The other person holds a special claim to fame for having completing the Munros, Tops, Corbetts and Grahams all on the same day. Brian Ringland, a retired mechanical engineer from Balinode, in County Monaghan, climbed Beinn a' Chapuill (a Graham), then ascended Beinn Sgritheall's subsidiary Top, followed by the Munro Beinn Sgritheall itself, before finally climbing the Corbett of Beinn na h-Eaglaise. Interestingly, this Corbett was my own last Corbett, which I climbed in 2004 with my great friend Ken Black just two months after Brian's multiple compleation! Brian may also be the only person to have completed the Grahams before the Munros, though by only around an hour. Brian became hooked on Munros during a holiday in October 1990, after which he regularly visited Scotland on a couple of annual three-week trips for the next 14 years. He spent those journeys climbing Munros, Tops, Grahams and Corbetts in long, continuous walks. Because of this mixing of hill categories, he never used a guidebook and enjoyed creating his own routes through the hills. Brian's approach to hillwalking is among the purest and most natural I've witnessed. Between his Scottish trips, he climbed all the Irish hills over 500 metres and visited every Irish lake above 300 metres. Brian is a truly unique hill gangrel who certainly has not wasted his retirement.

Finally, in 2015, 18 years after my own guide to the Grahams was published, the SMC launched *The Grahams and the Donalds*, essentially Volume 3 of its hillwalking guides, following on from *The Munros* and *The Corbetts* guidebooks. This publication was certainly a step up from my own guidebook; it featured full-colour contoured maps and included the Donalds. It is a beautifully produced volume on good quality paper and a must-have for Munroists and Corbetteers looking to extend their repertoire. I still have to climb over half the Donalds, so my copy has much use left in it.

A summary, so far, of post-Munro challenges includes Munro Tops, Corbetts, Grahams, Donalds and the Furth (3,000-foot summits in England, Wales and Ireland). This set of lists, including the Munros, has become collectively known as a 'Full House'; for a few dedicated hill-goers, it represents the ultimate hillwalking challenge in the UK. The title 'Full House' is rather a misnomer, however, as it gives the impression that there are no challenges or lists beyond these. As we shall see, nothing could be further from the truth.

More than 70 people are known to be 'Full Housers' and I am not one of them, as many Donalds and a few of the Furth remain outstanding on my list. I consider Donalds particularly awkward among the other lists, as their localised nature, antiquated definitions and overlap with Corbetts and Grahams contribute to their unsatisfactory nature and lack of appeal. However, this is simply my opinion; similarly, I know that many Munroists have negative feelings towards Munro Tops, and only around one in ten Munroists bother to 'Top up'. There is a parallel here to the two highest mountains in the world: if you have climbed Everest, you have earned bragging rights, but if you have climbed the considerably more challenging K2, you have earned respect. The same could be applied to Munros and Tops, in the sense that the more serious and dedicated Munroists will graduate to the Tops.

So what further challenges lie beyond the Full House, or indeed, apart from the Full House? Staying initially with hills over 2,000 feet and mainly with Scotland, the reader will probably realise that there has been no discussion of subsidiary Tops of Corbetts and Grahams apart from Docharty's listings. Following on from Alan Dawson's creation of the 'Murdos' – Scottish mountains over 3,000 feet with a re-ascent of at least 30 metres (see chapter 4) – Alan Dawson and Dave Hewitt used the same drop criterion to produce a list of nearly 700 Corbetts and Corbett Tops and almost 1,000 Grahams and Graham Tops. The second listing drew on earlier work by ED Clements and James Gordon. The sheer numbers involved here are an indication that the popularity of these Tops remains small, and indeed, if Munro Tops are anything to go by, that assumption is justified.

It is beyond the scope of this book to give a detailed discussion of the classification of 2,000-foot summits outwith Scotland, but the mere mention of such lists as Bridges, Nuttalls, Deweys, Hewitts and Wainwrights give an indication of the enormous interest and complexities involved. All these lists (except Wainwrights) and the Scottish subsidiary Tops lists were finally superseded in 2010 by Alan Dawson's creation of the Sims (or Simms), a mega-list of all British hills over 600 metres (1,968 feet) with at least 30 metres of re-ascent. This huge, unifying list of over 2,500 hills was the first to adopt metric measurements for both absolute and relative height (other than Marilyns, which are only defined by relative height); as yet, only a handful of people have climbed them all. 'Sims' is a loose acronym for Six hundred Metre Summits. 'The 'Wainwrights' are not all Sims, as they are a personal selection of 214 summits of varying heights – including many below 2,000 feet – in the Lake District. For a detailed analysis of these other lists, see *Scaling the Heights* from The Munro Society.

Clearly, the more prominent and distinctive summits, such as the Corbetts and Grahams, are more appealing to hillwalkers than subsidiary Tops. Also, the list of Marilyns, with their 150 metres of relative height, is an obvious target for many Munroists, regardless of whether they had completed the Corbetts and Grahams. For those who had ascended all the Corbetts and Grahams, the next logical step was to climb the Marilyns under 2,000 feet. The 2,000-foot contour is regarded by some misinformed souls as the division between mountains and mere hills, or between what is worth climbing and what is not, though the flaws in this viewpoint are numerous.

Bulk and height are important elements in mountain

grandeur, but outline and features are, as with human beings, even more important[9]

wrote Sheriff Alexander Nicolson of Skye. Perhaps AW Wainwright put it best when he observed:

Some misinformed sources have defined a mountain as a hill which exceeds 2,000 feet in height. Of course they are wrong. The status of a mountain is not determined by any arbitrary level of altitude but by appearance. Rocks and ruggedness, roughness of terrain and a commanding presence are the essential qualifications.[10]

Roughly 1,200 of the 1,500-plus Marilyns are Scottish hills, with almost half of these 1,200, below 2,000 feet. It is this smaller subset of hills that hillwalkers are generally referring to when they talk of the 'Scottish Marilyns', since the higher ones are still commonly known as Munros, Corbetts and Grahams. The popularity of Marilyns is gradually increasing, with around 400 people having climbed at least 600 Marilyns, and nearly 200 having reached 1,000. However, only ten people have climbed the lot (at the time of writing), mainly due to the relative inaccessibility and highly technical climbing demands of the remote and hard to reach St Kilda sea stacks on the list.

I was an avid bagger of Marilyns, reaching the 1,000 mark some years back, but increasingly, a growing dissatisfaction seemed to creep in. Despite the generous 150-metre drop, I still found many of the hills lacking in charisma and presence, and driving increasingly long distances to climb a few obscure hills just did not hit the spot. I was also unhappy that one of my favourite wee hills, Ben A'n in the Trossachs, is not listed as a Marilyn despite its commanding presence. These considerations, along with the fact that nearly 600 hills under 2,000 feet was too large a list for most people, persuaded me to create my own smaller list of 'Hughs', an acronym for 'Hills Under Graham Height in Scotland'. Hughs are essentially hills with attitude, not altitude, meaning they have a distinctive prominence, position and summit panorama. At the time of writing, the Hughs are still an ongoing project, and only one of a two-volume series is presently available: *The Hughs – Scotland's best wee hills under 2,000 feet – Volume 1: The Mainland* (Luath Press). Volume 2, covering the Scottish islands, has been delayed, mainly due to the COVID-19 chaos, but watch this space!

When I was researching into possible contenders for Hugh status, my tentative list seemed to converge on roughly 200 hills, so I decided that a total of 200 Hughs would constitute a reasonable challenge: 100 mainland Hughs and 100 island Hughs. This number was also comparable with the number of Munros, Corbetts and Grahams, each list being over 200. It is perhaps fitting that the acronym 'Hugh' is also the first name of the great man himself, and as the Hughs are a subjective list, there is a sense of coming full circle from Munros to Hughs. I certainly do not expect the Hughs to gain a massive following and in no way can they be considered an official list, but I know a fair number of people who are interested in them and actively climbing them – and they aren't all over 60!

For a while, there existed only one list of hills with a drop criterion and no height criterion – the Marilyns. With predictable inevitability, however, this situation did not last: in 2007, Mark Jackson produced the list of 'Humps', which extended the 150-metre drop down to 100 metres. The name is derived from 'Hundred Metre Prominence', but suffers in many respects from its rather lowly association with insignificant 'bumps'! The list, which obviously includes all the Marilyns, stands at almost 3,000 hills, double the number of Marilyns, with well over 2,000 of them in Scotland. In the introduction to my Hughs book, I described the Humps as a 'list too far'.

However, if the Humps were a list too far, the next development could be described as a list totally off the scale. The small 30-metre drop, forming the basis for classifications such as Corbett Tops, Graham Tops and Sims, all over 600 metres, could in theory be extended down to, well, 30 metres. The sheer number of 'hills' thus produced would be unimaginably high, and the enormous effort and time required in research would be of dubious value. Yet, in 2009, Mark Jackson published the list of 'Tumps' (Thirty and Upward Metre Prominences), spending three years researching hills below 300 metres in height alone. The current total is over 17,000 and is, in effect, an all-encompassing list of hills in Britain, which includes all principal lists previously mentioned. The word 'ultimate' may be overused, but this mega-list is without a doubt the ultimate list of hills in Britain and could be considered a lifetime challenge for hillwalkers. Incredibly, it is known that a couple of people are already over halfway to completion. The word 'hillwalking' is perhaps a misnomer for a large proportion of these 'hills', given that many of them appear within city boundaries – Edinburgh alone has 27, and both Glasgow and Dundee contain a handful each. At the other end of the difficulty scale, the list contains a multitude of vertiginous, inaccessible sea stacks. The sheer number, scope and quality of experience gained in tackling this challenge, from high points of obscure Buckinghamshire fields to Edinburgh housing estates to the intimidating verticality of Am Buachaille sea stack off Sandwood Bay, makes the kissing of every lamppost in Princes Street seem like a normal activity!

On a more practical angle, the list is best seen as a comprehensive database of British hills, allowing users to construct their own specific, manageable list relating to an explicit locality or criterion. In this respect, the complete classification is the ultimate source for setting achievable goals specific to any level of challenge. I have read that this list is unlikely to ever be completed by a single person, but this assumption severely underestimates the power of motivation and plain bloody-mindedness among the crazy, driven individuals who cannot resist a challenge!

Before turning to post-Munro challenges beyond hills, one unique, personal hill list deserves a special mention. A couple of years after publication of *The Munro Phenomenon*, I received a letter from an individual named Bernard Beal, who claimed that

it does not seem to have occurred to anyone else that
all mountains have a second measurable attribute
besides height.[11]

Beal was not referring to relative height, but to the distance to
the nearest higher summit; in other words, a summit which is
higher than everything else in its neighbourhood. To qualify
for inclusion on his list, the hill must be at least ten miles away
from a higher summit. This was essentially the only criterion,
apart from his stipulation of a minimum height of 1,000 feet,
in order to remove dross and accentuate more moorland and
mountain character.

Beal had begun his project many years before and returned
to complete it in later life. The result was a list of 110
'Supersummits', arranged not in order of height, but in order
of remoteness from higher ground. Thus, Ben Nevis rightfully
heads the list, being some 480 miles from Norway, the nearest
higher point. On a 'normal' mountain list, based on height, Ben
Macdui would appear second, but it is a mere 54 miles away,
so it ends up in eighth place. Second place goes to Snowdon,
in Wales, which is 227 miles away from anything bigger, and
Ronas Hill, in Shetland, 132 miles from Ward Hill in Orkney,
sits at third place. At the other end of the scale, the 110th and
final hill is Ben Griam Mor in Sutherland, which is just ten miles
from Ben Armine. Ben Armine itself is not on the list.

Scotland accounts for 71 of the summits, but interestingly,
only 25 are Munros, including the likes of Ben Lawers, Ben
Alder, Ben Cruachan, Creag Meagaidh and Bidean nam Bian.
Islands, being generally remote, account for 16 spots on the list,
including Goat Fell (Arran), Sgùrr Alasdair (Skye) and Snae Fell
(Isle of Man). The most remote is seventh on the list, Conachair
on St Kilda, 58 miles from any higher ground. Beal went one
step further and included nine 'optional extras', satisfying a
metric version, with qualifications based on 15 kilometres and
300 metres.

In his letter, Beal enquired as to how he might go about

getting the list published. I replied with some advice, and the list, together with a short article, appeared in *TGO* magazine some time later entitled 'Super Summits – Britain's backyard Everests'. The idea of classifying peaks according to their distance from higher ground is both logical and fascinating, and it is surprising that the notion has not been taken further, for instance, by reducing the distance to five miles, or even five kilometres.

We now move on to other post-Munro challenges beginning with the maritime equivalent of Munro-bagging: the bagging of islands. Scotland's contorted and complex western coastline supports a staggering array of over a thousand islands, ranging in size from tiny rock skerries to large bodies of land such as Mull and Skye. The special magic and thrill of being on a small, possibly uninhabited island has a fascination as addictive as mounting the summit of a remote hill – in some respects, the thrill is even greater. Not surprisingly, recent years have seen a surge in the popularity of visiting isolated, offshore havens, and the islands themselves have been subject to various rigid classifications. A cursory scan might suggest that it should be relatively easy to compile a list of islands, considering that they are clear-cut pieces of land surrounded by water. However, apart from the obvious question of when a piece of land (or rock) surrounded by water becomes big enough to qualify as an island, what about tidal islands, bridged islands and islands connected by causeways? All these 'grey areas' were partly the reason that in my previous book, *The Munro Phenomenon*, I commented that 'no authoritative list of Scottish islands exists'.

Yet by 1996, Hamish Haswell-Smith came to the rescue with his magnificent tome, *The Scottish Islands*, subtitled 'The Bestselling Guide to every Scottish island' (Canongate). The book was certainly a beautifully produced compendium, including the author's own sketches and watercolours, with a wealth of information on Scottish islands, including access points and nautical details relevant to sailors and yachtsmen. The book fast became the island-baggers' equivalent of the SMC's Munros guidebook; it is an 'islandeer's Bible'. From a practical user's point of view, it would have benefited from being dustcover-less, like the SMC guides, particularly considering the damage-inducing barrage of salty sea spray and winds.

However, the book's seemingly grand subtitle was in fact hugely misleading. The 168 'Haswells' listed in the latest edition of the book are only a tiny fraction of the 1,000 or so Scottish islands, which begs the question of what criteria Haswell-Smith used to construct his list. He only listed islands with an area of 40 hectares or more (roughly 100 acres) and excluded tidal and bridged islands, and with causeway linked islands treated as one entity. In my own opinion, these exclusions are unnecessary; most crucially, the omission of Skye because of its bridge is plain daft. Despite these omissions, Haswell-Smith does describe some 'excluded' islands, such as Skye and Staffa (area 33 hectares) in an appendix, but I maintain that placing the finest Scottish island in an appendix is more than a trifle contrary.

In the first edition of his book, Haswell-Smith used the time-consuming and inexact method of planimeter readings to estimate island areas. In 2013, he met with Marilyn-bagger Jon Metcalf, who had devised a more accurate, digitised method of area computation. Their collaboration resulted in seven extra islands and one demotion, which appeared in the latest 2015 edition. Metcalf's efforts were thoroughly checked by his friend, Alan Holmes, another Marilyn-bagger and a keen island advocate, who had already compiled his own list of British islands using stricter criteria. Holmes' conditions for inclusion were both area- and height-based, stipulating that contenders had to have an area of at least 30 hectares *or* have a highest point of at least 30 metres in elevation. However, in order to exclude problematic sea stacks, he cunningly insisted that high points had to be climbable by nothing harder than a grade 1 (easy) scramble. This ensured that all island summits were accessible to reasonably fit and agile walkers, with no requirement for technical equipment. However, the main problem with islands is not generally climbing to their high points but reaching them in the first place, and kayaking, yachtsmen or friendly boatmen, are obviously required. In fact, landing on many of the islands is notoriously tricky, even with a boat, and some of Holmes' 566 'Sibs' have no recorded landings. The name 'Sib' is an acronym for 'Significant Island in Britain', and Holmes' classification is the most detailed and serious attempt yet of compiling a definitive list of islands in the UK.

The 30-metre height condition ensures that many of the Sibs are contained within the 'Tump' definition – but not all, as a Sib may have an area exceeding 30 hectares but have a high point less than 30 metres. If all this is beginning to sound slightly nerdish, we should not lose track of why we wish to visit these far-flung places. As Hamish Haswell-Smith remarks,

> I am taking a calculated risk that newcomers will
> visit these secret places, not just to chalk up another
> conquest, but because they have poetry in their souls
> and a true love of islands.[12]

This sentiment obviously also applies to hills, like Hamish Brown's observation that 'a list is a means to an end and not an end in itself'.

Before taking our leave of lists, a mention must be made of a worldwide list of mountains that could be regarded as truly ultimate. Named aptly as the 'Ultras', these are peaks of the world with at least 1,500 metres of relative height – or drop. Presently, the exact number of these is indeterminate, but it hovers around the 1,540 mark, with about 40 in each of Greenland and Antarctica, many as yet unclimbed. In terms of relative height, the top three on the list are Everest, Aconcagua (South America) and Denali (Alaska), all of which are on the 'Seven Summits' list of the highest peaks in each of the world's seven continents and have over 6,000 metres of relative height.

There are 98 Ultras in Europe. Richard Mclellan was the first British and second overall person to climb all 98, after Norwegian climber, Petter Bjorstad, was the first. Top Marilyn-bagger Rob Woodall is in the running to be third, but political unrest is preventing his completion. Both Woodall and Mclellan are among the few who have completed all the Marilyns. Mclellan's wife, Denise, would have been the fourth, but she has been unable to complete, because her last summit, Atos, lies within a Greek Orthodox monastery area, which allows access only to men! Only about 650 Ultras have had recorded ascents, and these three Brits are in the top four of the Ultra-bagging league table, each having climbed over 200. The chances of anyone ever completing all the mountains on this list to end all lists are slim, to say the least, but I suspect that in the far future, some rich, crazy, passionate and truly dedicated individual will give it a try. I have done three – Mont Blanc, Kilimanjaro and Mount Whitney... so only another 1,537 to go! I find it both salutary and gratifying that there are still major challenges left in a world which is shrinking, tamed and subdued by the hand of man. For more information on Sims, Marilyns, Humps, Tumps and Ultras, contact the 'Relative Hills Society' online.

Many post-Munro activities do not entail ticking off lists of summits or islands. Some, through the joys of scrambling, may move naturally into rock climbing, whilst others will develop an interest in full-blown mountaineering, perhaps tackling some of the easier Alpine summits. In my own particular case, I felt the need for a long and sustained encounter with the Scottish Highlands, so the idea of a continuous walk from Ben Lomond to Ben Hope, traversing other Munros en route, lurked in my mind. This notion was eventually modified to a walk connecting the two extremities of the Mull of Kintyre lighthouse and the Cape Wrath lighthouse, named for charity purposes as 'Scotwalk '89 : Kintyre to Cape Wrath', which had a ring about it. Climbing mountains was not the aim of the trip; rather, it was the simple, escapist pleasure of solitary wayfaring, of rising with the sun and setting off in the exhilarating freshness of a mountain morning. I was to discover that total immersion in Scotland's wildest country for four glorious weeks bred a truer and stronger communion with the land than any weekend or day trips. Also, route planning, the detailed study of maps, the checking of times and distances and the booking of the odd hotel for rare moments of luxury were all part of the satisfaction.

The route itself was designed to pass through some of Scotland's finest wilderness areas, including Ardgour, Knoydart, Kintail, Monar, Fisherfield and Assynt, and I widely used both bothies and a tent. The only real centre of population I encountered was Ullapool, and for the middle fortnight of the month's walk, I was completely on my own – the most satisfying and pleasurable part of the trip. In retrospect, I look upon July 1989, as one of the most contented and fulfilling periods of my life, 'halcyon days, when youth, vigour and enthusiasm were at a peak'. Walking 350 miles through the Highland Heartland of western Scotland was a unique and memorable experience, and raising over £1,000 for the Save the Children Fund was an added bonus. In a small way, I sampled some of the satisfaction that ultra-long-distance backpacker Chris Townsend attains on his epic journeys.

Naturally, I undertook other long-distance walks in the ensuing years, but the only one to rival 'Scotwalk '89' in terms of intense satisfaction and contentment was a month's walk around the entire coastline of Skye in the summer of 1998. I wrote a book describing the walk, entitled *Skye 360*, published in 2003 by Luath Press. My passion for coastal walking grew during this trip and resulted in a desire to complete what I regarded as the best coastal walks in Scotland. The ultimate conclusion of this ideal was the publication of *100 Classic Coastal Walks in Scotland* (Mainstream) in 2011.

In the early years of the new millennium, I began a coastal walk at John o' Groats, heading south to arrive at Inverness, over the course of two separate walking holidays. Many years later, I resumed the walk, and again, over the course of several multi-day stints, plus day walks, eventually reached Whitley Bay, near Newcastle. The idea, if it ever materialises, is to complete a round Britain coastal walk, but realistically, I have an inkling that time is not on my side. I have at least walked from Land's End to Barnstaple, following the South West Coastal Path, before taking an inland route to Bristol, so I will skip that section if I ever reach as far as Land's End!

Most people's introduction to long-distance walking is the completion of 'official' routes, such as the West Highland Way or Pennine Way, neither of which I have done, preferring to create my own itineraries. Having said that, I have walked both the Southern Upland Way and Wainwright's Coast to Coast route, both of which I highly recommend. Of course, the 'collection' of official long-distance routes constitutes yet another list of challenges for the avid walker, and indeed, many individuals are working their way through these.

Another course of action, beyond Munro compleation, is perhaps too obvious to mention – embarking on a second round. It is unlikely that anyone having accomplished a round of the Munros will have climbed each Munro exactly once. Many of the classic Munros or Munro groups, such as Liathach, An Teallach, Ben Nevis and the Cuillin, will likely have seen several ascents, as will the more accessible Munros. So, on compleation of a round, the individual may discover that they are at least part way into a second round, even if it is only by a dozen Munros. Some purists maintain that any new round of Munros must be started from scratch, discounting any previous re-ascents. If 'Polymunrosis' relates to the condition of compleation of two or more Munro rounds, then 'Pure Polymunrosis' could relate to this stricter condition. Dave Hewitt has described Polymunrosis as 'banker's rounds' and Pure Polymunrosis as 'golfer's rounds'. Just as a golfer completes one round of golf before starting another, so too does a Pure Polymunroist have to compleat one Munro round before starting another… from scratch. (Please excuse the golfing pun.) On the other hand, a banker can 'bank' his ascents to save them for the next round.

Frankly, I find this stricter condition rather silly. If you have climbed a Munro twice, or three times, then it should not matter when it was achieved, and any ascent should contribute to another round. Of course, some people treat these and related notions extremely seriously, and they no doubt adopt a whole gamut of Munro-bagging ethics. The fact is that there are no hard and fast 'rules' governing these subjective areas, and individuals will and should, do things in their own individual way. On my own compleation in 1988, I was already over 90 Munros into a second round, and I certainly was not going to dismiss them to start all over again.

In a pub conversation many years ago, I was informing a friend about my intention to climb a certain Munro for the second time. His look of astonishment was followed by the question, 'Why?'. He could not fathom why I would want to ascend the same Munro again. Nor could I fathom why he was asking the question. My reply firstly stressed the point that if a Munro is worth climbing once, then surely it is worth climbing again. Secondly, I emphasised the excitement of climbing the Munro by a completely different route and possibly in different weather conditions, which would be almost equivalent to ascending a different Munro and therefore be a different experience. His reaction reflected a grudging acceptance of my arguments, but I still had the feeling that attaining the summit was, to him, the only thing that mattered; he viewed the entire package of experiences and emotions involved in a day's hillwalking as somehow redundant and of no consequence. The old adage concerning lists could be recast to say that the summit is not an end in itself, but only a means to an end. The reason we climb a hill for a second or third time is exactly the same reason we climbed it for the first time – because the whole experience is fun, enjoyable and memorable.

I often compare Munros to old friends, and in some respects they are more reliable! Posing the question, as my friend did above, is rather akin to meeting someone for the first time, liking them, and then questioning why you would ever see them again because you have already met them once. Just as people reveal different facets of their personality over the course of subsequent meetings, so too do Munros reveal contrasting facets of their character. It has been said that to truly know the character of a mountain, you must have slept on its summit. I do not know if I would go that far, but experiencing a mountain in its many moods and weathers over the course of several ascents gives a deeper and more intimate connection with the landscape than a single 'up and down' by the same path.

The first person to accomplish two rounds of the Munros was the 45th Munroist, Philip Tranter, in 1964, followed by a further three people in the '60s and '70s. However, it was Munroist number 62, Hamish Brown, who really kicked off the trend of multiple rounds; by the end of the 1970s, he had already chalked up a remarkable six rounds, including his famous continuous round in 1974. Brown is now known to have compleated at least seven rounds. His two dogs, Storm and Kitchy, have also climbed all the Munros, and Brown himself has compleated a so-called 'Calendar Round', having ascended a Munro on every day of the year. The only other person from this era to come close to Brown's record was Matthew Moulton (Munroist 76), who had compleated five rounds by 1982.

A year before this, in 1981, a man called Stewart Logan finished his first round of Munros. Over the course of the next 20 or so years, he managed to notch up an amazing ten rounds, a record which remained so for several years. Not only that, but each of his rounds also included all the subsidiary Tops; Logan has definitely earned the honour for the most 'compleations' of 'Munros plus Tops'. Despite hailing from Kirriemuir (Sir Hugh Munro's home), Logan only became aware of Munros later in life; he was in his early 40s when he compleated his first round. His enthusiasm for hills is legendary, and his friends recognise a weather condition known as 'Logan's Blue Sky', referring to his unbridled optimism for always looking on the bright side on even the most miserable days. Logan often wears a kilt on his hill excursions, but this has led, on more than one occasion, to some memorable incidents. While abseiling from the Inaccessible Pinnacle in his kilt, a shout came up from below... 'Ladies, avert your eyes!' To save Logan's embarrassment, I will not amplify another story, concerning a wobbly deer fence and a group of lady walkers from Fife! Logan's Blue Sky maxim perhaps needs some amendment, however, as his ambition to enjoy a clear view from the top of every Munro was only achieved well into his tenth round. So why does he climb Munros? 'Because they are there', he says. And why has he climbed them so often? 'Because I'm still here and they're still there'. Amen to that.

Multiple rounds have not been confined to men. Also compleating her first round in 1981 was Geraldine Guestsmith (Munroist 260), who had proceeded to her sixth round by 1995, also accomplishing three rounds of Munro Tops. The most prolific current female bagger is Hazel Strachan who, in 2018, became the fifth person to reach the gold star of ten rounds. Hazel revels in long, solo sojourns across groups of hills and takes huge delight in camping and bivvying, sometimes on mountain summits. 'Walking by myself has made me into a happy and confident woman', she remarked. Considering that she has clocked around 2,600 Munros solo, out of her 2,800 total, she has certainly had opportunity to be happy and confident. Anne Butler, current president of The Munro Society, has compleated six rounds and recently became the 53rd 'Full Houser'. Unlike Hazel, she prefers day walks rather than multi-day trips with a tent.

Way ahead of the league is current record holder for most Munro rounds, Steven Fallon, a mountain guide based in Edinburgh who is on his 16th round. Fallon's first Munro was Ben More at age ten, and he reckons the views that particular day, plus Irvine Butterfield's book *The High Mountains*, got him hooked. Seeing Hamish Brown's seven rounds, Fallon thought, 'I could do that', and following compleation of his first round in 1992, he began to average roughly one round per year throughout the '90s. Unsurprisingly, Fallon is a keen hill runner and wrote the book *Classic Hill Runs and Races in Scotland*. Of Sir Hugh Munro he remarks:

> He's opened our eyes to the magnificent scenery that our little country has to offer, and the list has had the effect of attracting people from all walks of life and all corners of the globe.[13]

The preceding discourse may appear to indicate that engaging in further Munro rounds is a common activity, but it is reckoned that less than one in 20 Munroists compleat a second round, giving a total of around 350 'second-rounders'. Climbing a single Munro many times may appear to be an unimaginative use of time, especially given the old adage that 'familiarity breeds contempt', but this is certainly not the case according to the experiences of many hillwalkers. Jock Nimlin's 100 ascents of Ben Lomond (see chapter 3) were accomplished partly through ease of access from his native Glasgow, but more due to his deep affinity and love for the outdoors and for that particular mountain. My two most climbed Munros are both within an hour's drive from my Perthshire home – Ben Chonzie and Ben Vorlich, both of which I have ascended around 30 times. On days when the thought of driving for hours in order to climb a hill is off-putting, these two summits and other nearby Corbetts, such as Ben Vrackie and Ben Ledi, provide wonderfully relaxed and intimate unions with hills that have become my firm favourites over the years.

Many years ago, when teaching at Fort Augustus, I reached the summit of a local Munro, Sròn a' Choire Ghairbh above Loch Lochy, when I met another local walker, Richard Wood. It transpired that he was Munroist number 88, compleating in 1969, but more memorable was the fact that he would go on to ascend this same Munro 1,000 times. He would also climb the nearby Corbett, Ben Tee (my first Corbett) 1,000 times! This obsessive level of commitment to two hills is borne out of a love of the landscape on your doorstep and a desire to commune with that landscape in all weathers and moods. Over the top? Possibly. Other Munros and smaller hills have also seen a thousand ascents by one individual, including Ben Lomond by Alan Douglas and Ben Cleuch, in the Ochils, by Dave Hewitt, the latter allegedly having received 1,500 ascents by another individual.

This chapter has explored the myriad activities and challenges available to the newly 'compleated' Munroist. But once the champagne bubbles have fizzed and fizzled out and the euphoria of compleation fades to quiet reflection, the first action of the majority of new Munroists is to inform the SMC of their achievement in order for their name to be added to the list of the thousands who have gone before. Following this is the delivery of a small package: either a Munroist tie or brooch, each sporting the Munro Crest and the number '3,000'. The package will likely also contain a 'flyer' advertising 'The Munro Society' (TMS), presenting an opportunity for membership.

Back in 2001, I received a letter from fellow Munroist, Iain Robertson, who proffered the idea of creating a kind of club, or society, for those who had climbed all the Munros. With the fast-growing number of compleaters already numbering more than 2,000, the idea seemed sound and to have enormous potential. I affirmed Robertson's request for assistance in the possible formation of such a society despite my natural disinclination to clubs and societies. I was never a member of a hillwalking or mountaineering club, preferring to 'plough my own furrow', so to speak. Yet I found myself attending a preliminary meeting with Iain Robertson and other such luminaries as Irvine Butterfield and Robin Campbell to thrash out the rationale and core motivations and ambitions of such a society. A date was set for a follow-up meeting to form a 'steering committee' on 22 September 2001. When the day of the meeting dawned, a ridge of high pressure attached itself over Scotland. The thought of sitting in a stuffy committee room discussing policies, people and proceedings, was not greatly enticing, so my heart ruled over my head. I 'escaped' to the Cairngorms to climb Beinn Mheadhoin and three Tops I had not previously bagged. The Munros had upstaged The Munro Society. My conscience told me that day that I was not committed or cut out to be a midwife during the birth throes of The Munro Society, and I declined my services to the cause. However, I retained membership and attended the inaugural dinner at the Atholl Palace Hotel in Pitlochry in 2002, the true launch of the Society.

A main aim of TMS was to 'give something back to the mountains', and this noble cause was initially partly addressed, by the creation of a system to assess the quality of hills and paths and the quantity and extent of erosion and other factors. The secretary, John Burdin, devised a Mountain Quality Indicator (MQI) system of seven indicators concerning factors such as access, human influence and flora. The idea for quality indicators no doubt derived from business, industry and education sectors, where such tools are widely used to assess the attributes of specific departments and offices. Similar quality indicators were used in the school where I taught, and indeed, throughout the whole educational system. In my opinion, they were a bureaucratic, time-wasting nod to supposed 'curricular development', and I had a somewhat negative reaction to their use in The Munro Society. I was effectively allowing my ingrained dislike of quality indicators in the educational setting to cloud my vision of their potential validity in an outdoor setting. Whether it was this extra layer of officialdom or my inherent anti-club/society nature, I eventually lost ties with TMS.

Despite my own disinterest, in the 20 or so years since its inception, The Munro Society has evolved and matured into a highly credible and respected body, not only operating as a club and social network, but also as an authoritative and influential vehicle for the protection of, and access to, Scotland's mountain landscape. TMS holds regular 'meets', issues newsletters and produces a substantial journal every few years. The AGM in April and formal dinner in October are supplemented with both internal and outside speakers. In 2019, an exhibition of Munro-related material was held in the AK Bell library in Perth for the centenary of Sir Hugh Munro's death. This exhibition had subsequent venues throughout Scotland. An archive of relevant material is also stored in Perth Library.

Current TMS membership is around 300, but only a relatively small percentage of these are actively involved in Society matters, with about 80 attending the annual dinner. Less than one in ten 'compleaters' join TMS, and there has been some enquiry and discussion as to why uptake is so low. The Munro Society often has to defend itself on grounds of elitism. TMS strongly rejects these accusations and insists that new members are welcomed with open arms. However, the stringent entry condition of Munro compleation surely creates at least a modicum of exclusivity, perceived or otherwise. The prerequisite of Munro compleation in order to gain membership was justified using the argument that the accomplishment of all members would be 'a real strength in terms of credibility and substance', effectively implying that the views of non-Munroists on mountain matters would not possess the same clout, relevance or authority. The flaws in this implication are not difficult to identify. My conclusion here may be partly unjustified, but it surely indicates an argument for the admission of non-Munroists. In its present form, The Munro Society could well be renamed The Munroist Society.

But perhaps I am being too harsh here, as it ought to the Munros themselves, not Munroists, that are the real 'stars of the show'. I know that the essential reason The Munro Society exists is to foster and protect the Munros, and indeed, the wider landscape of Highland Scotland. The whole issue of landscape protection, conservation, ecology and access is covered in chapter 10, but the penultimate chapter concentrates purely on the core attraction – the Munros themselves.

CHAPTER 9

Memorable Munros

SOME YEARS AFTER publication of *The Munro Phenomenon*, I regretted the omission of a chapter concentrating purely on the Munros themselves, or at least on a small selection of them. After all, in the great drama 'where men and mountains meet', the real star players are the hills and mountains. They are more than just the stage and background scenery, but the very reason for the unfolding drama; the heart and heroine of our experience.

This chapter aims to remedy that omission by providing a personal 'mountain monologue' for a choice selection of 'memorable Munros'.

The mountains have been chosen not necessarily on the basis that they are particularly memorable for me, though many of them are; rather, they each possess a unique quality, presence or popularity which may even have touched on the general public. Munros from this chapter such as Ben Nevis, Ben Lomond and the Inaccessible Pinnacle are well-known, but others may not be. The Munro Monologues, a series of essays on each Munro, proceed in a general south to north direction, concluding with the islands. I once came across the following quotation, although I am ignorant of the source:

> Hills are your lifetime's companions when doing them
> and your lifetime's memories when you're done.[1]

For those who know the hills, all Munros are memorable, not just the ones in this chapter. And where better to begin than with the most southerly Munro?

BEN LOMOND

Despite standing proudly above the 'bonnie, bonnie banks of Loch Lomond', if Ben Lomond had a voice, it probably would not sing this ancient Scottish air, but 'I belong to Glasgow' instead. Surely, homely Ben Lomond is Glasgow's own cherished hill, its bold outline visible from higher parts of the city. Its name, meaning Beacon Hill, from the Cumbric 'llumon', is an apt description of this watching sentinel proclaiming its presence on the southern edge of the Highlands, beckoning Clydesiders and other Lowlanders to venture forth, stand on its lofty summit and gaze northwards to greater things.

With its ease of access from the urban sprawl of Clydeside, it is not surprising that this, the most southerly Munro, has adopted the honour of the most common first Munro and one of the most climbed mountains of Scotland. It was my own introduction to the Munros, and I had ascended it twice in the space of a few months before climbing any other Munros.

Its named link with the Lomond Hills in Fife is made more remarkable by the fact that Loch Lomond was once called Loch Leven, which is the loch at the foot of the Lomond Hills. The river flowing from the south of Loch Lomond is none other than the River Leven.

Of the ten occasions I have climbed this hill, only three have been solo excursions, and even these have been enlivened by chance encounters with the inevitable Glaswegians and their welcome wit and earthy humour. Ben Lomond is the peoples' hill. On 17 October 1996, I was invited to join Cameron McNeish and a large crowd of around 40 souls for a special ascent of Ben Lomond. Photos, speeches and interviews all took place at the summit for the launch of his new book, *The Munros*. What better mountain on which to perform a book launch than Ben Lomond? The social event theme continued on my ninth ascent in July 2013, when a crowd of 11 'men behaving badly' climbed the hill, complete with four bottles of champagne, one bottle of Glenmorangie and a bottle of Glayva. During the hot, sweaty ascent, a leaking rucksack was discovered; the result of someone's bright idea to have ice with our champagne. The descent was made with six empty bottles, no leaks and 11 jolly faces! Hendrie Barbour's 'stag-do' was certainly one to remember.

The ascent of Ben Lomond from Rowardennan, by the tourist path, is the trade route to the summit and an alternative descent route follows the Ptarmigan ridge, making a fine horseshoe. However, on one occasion, I approached the hill from the north, leaving Comer farm to climb the north-east ridge and subsequently traversing Ben Lomond to reach the Graham of Cruinn a' Bheinn. This is a fine route and samples the northern corrie, a delight most will miss by the tourist path.

The view south from the summit draws the eye down to the placid waters of Loch Lomond, past its scattering of wooded islands and eventually to the distant smog of Scotland's industrial heartland. The view north, however, is of a jostling array of peaks and ridges stretching to distant, beckoning horizons, Scotland's Highland heartland. Ben Lomond's spectacular position on the Highland Boundary line is undeniable, a frontier between work and play. For those working-class stalwarts of the 1930s (see chapter 3), it was a frontier between despair and desire. Ben Lomond was and is the gateway to freedom; the portal to truth.

BEN VORLICH (AND STÙC A' CHRÒIN)

Like Ben Lomond and Ben Ledi, Ben Vorlich and its squat neighbour, Stùc a' Chròin, are frontier mountains standing boldly on the Highland Line, separated by the high Bealach an Dubh Chorein. The tantalising skyline containing these summits is prominent from the Forth valley, and the 'Vorlich-Stuc' pair dominate the western skyline from the Earn valley. The latter was my first view of the pair when I relocated near Perth in 1985, and these are two of only three Munros visible from the vicinity of my home – the other is Ben Chonzie. That skyline vista so controlled my thoughts and captured my imagination that, unsurprisingly, it earned the honour of being the first Munro I climbed after moving to Strathearn. Since then, it has seen nearly one ascent every year and is now my most climbed Munro at 30 ascents.

Nan Shepherd, author of *The Living Mountain*, wrote, 'The thing to be known grows with the knowing', and my knowledge and experience of Ben Vorlich, in all weathers and moods, has grown and continues to grow. Like a faithful and reliable friend, Ben Vorlich is always there when needed; its relatively close proximity to my home is an added blessing. Friendly, familiar and commodious, like a favourite armchair, its homeliness never jades or palls. Familiarity with Ben Vorlich has never bred contempt.

Most guidebooks confidently assert the meaning of 'Vorlich' as 'sea-bay', from the Gaelic 'Mur-Bhalg', referring to the small bay in Loch Earn at the foot of the mountain. This would also apply to the other Ben Vorlich standing above the west shore of Loch Lomond. However, Peter Drummond, in his goldmine book *Scottish Hill Names*, offers several just as plausible derivations, including Beinn Mhòr-Luig, meaning mountain of the big corrie or hollow, which could apply to any three of the hill's scooped-out corries. The Reverend Burn (the second Munroist), in a 1918 diary, declared that a local shepherd had informed him the name meant 'Beinn mhor lic', or hill of the big stone.

Whatever the meaning, its attraction is assured on whichever route is taken. The 'via normale' or northerly approach from Ardvorlich and Loch Earn can become congested, so the best line of attack begins at Braeleny, north of Callander, or from the longer Glen Artney approach by the exquisitely tranquil Gleannan Dubh Choirein. Both of these less busy options give a good opportunity to include Stùc a' Chròin in a fine, natural horseshoe route. A traverse of both Munros, beginning in Callander and ending at Lochearnhead, was a classic high level mountain day when the railway still connected the two places, but with increased car use, this long expedition has fallen out of favour.

I have been blessed with many diverse experiences on this mountain. One of the most memorable was an autumn Glen Artney approach, complete with golden sun, russet tones and bellowing stags... and not another soul to be seen. At the opposite end of the spectrum, one winter ascent of the north ridge, by the normal route, saw my glasses blown clean off my face by an almost gale-force cross wind. My vain attempt to find them in the deep snow and near white-out conditions was a lost cause, and I took it as a sign to retreat. Ben Vorlich was also my son, Ruaraidh's, first Munro and the beginning of a lifetime's adventuring.

The bold and dramatic outline of Ben Vorlich and Stùc a' Chròin is a permanent fixture on the horizon from my home in Perthshire; it is also a permanent fixture in my mind and memory.

BEN LUI (BEINN LAOIGH)

On the scenic drive north and west from Stirling to Tyndrum, several mountains grab the attention – friendly Ben Ledi, above Callander, the lofty magnificence of Ben Lawers and its satellites from the top of Glen Ogle, the conical simplicity of mighty Ben More and its sawn-off twin, Stob Binnein, the Castor and Pollux of the Southern Highlands. But the real head-turner makes its late appearance just before Tyndrum itself. A glance left, to the west, reveals a mountain whose might, majesty and elegance of form combine into a literal show-stopper, especially when adorned in a mantle of snow that creates a truly Alpine character. Many mountains are loathe to reveal their true splendour to the casual observer, but Ben Lui flaunts her wares in unrestrained abandon. Two soaring spurs leading to the mountain's twin summits enclose a vast central corrie, Coire Gaothaich (Corrie of the Winds), the mountain's finest feature. The twin summits, likened to the horns of a calf, are likely the likely origin of the name of Beinn Laoigh: 'Calf Hill'.

Assigning a mountain as either male or female is a fairly

common notion, and Ben Lui is definitely female. She has, in fact, been christened in some quarters as the Queen of Scottish mountains, though that accolade has also been bestowed upon Ben Loyal in the far north. Ben Lui is a truly beautiful peak and a queen in every sense. She possesses an array of 'attendant' hills, such as Beinn Dubhchraig, Ben Oss and Beinn a' Chlèibh, but these loyal subjects pale in her supreme presence.

Like any woman, her character is complex and full of surprises. She tempts and teases with more than a handful of possible routes, of varying standards of difficulty, to her twin summits. For the winter mountaineer, the classic challenge, is the direct ascent up the headwall of the central corrie, the so-called 'Centre Gully', a route pioneered in the early 1890s when Tyndrum was a meeting point for the early Scottish mountaineers. While the hillwalker has a tantalising choice of routes, the finest two involve the ascent of each curving spur enclosing the central corrie. The left spur involves some scrambling in small sections while the right is a much easier climb.

The classic approach to Ben Lui is via Glen Cononish, from which the great north-eastern corrie is seen to perfection and the mountain draws the walker in to her Alpine-like realm. Having only climbed the mountain on three occasions, twice by this approach followed by the left spur and once from Glen Lochy, I feel that I still do not 'know' Ben Lui in the way that I do Ben Vorlich or Ben Lomond. Cocooned in her winter garb of white ermine, she espouses an unparalleled splendour that still clutches me in her thrall. The righthand spur of the central corrie is ripe yet for an ascent. It is a blessing that mountains such as Ben Lui have the charisma to stir passions well into advancing years and entice the walker in, to worship at her shrine. Ben Lui is simply the finest mountain in the Southern Highlands.

SCHIEHALLION

Perthshire is often credited as being the 'heart of Scotland', and the grand, popular vantage point of Schiehallion could claim to be the heart of Perthshire. The patriotic toast of the Rannoch Highlanders, 'Here's to the back o' Schiehallion', mirrors this claim. The generally acknowledged meaning of Schiehallion is 'the fairy hill of the Caledonians', from 'sithean chailleann', although 'sine chailinn', meaning 'breast of the maiden', has also been suggested, and the mountain's smooth, cone-like appearance from east and west justifies this claim. However, its true nature is of a long, whaleback ridge when viewed from the south or north. The classic view of the hill is from the eastern end of Loch Tummel, known as the Queen's View, from which the long, easy-angled east ridge rises in a single sweep, to the rocky summit.

As already mentioned in chapter 1, the isolation and uniformity of Schiehallion made it ideal for the Astronomer Royal, Nevil Maskeleyne, to spend four months on the mountain in 1774, where he used plumb lines to ascertain the mass of the earth. Not so well-known are the events surrounding the celebratory ceilidh at the end of his study. Copious supplies of whisky were secured from Kinloch Rannoch by a certain Duncan Robertson, who also supplied the lively fiddle music. In the midst of the raucous celebrations, the hut caught fire and the fiddle was destroyed. Maskeleyne, feeling duly responsible, assured Robertson that upon his return to London, he would seek out a new fiddle and send it to him – and he did, in style. A Stradivarius arrived, on which the delighted Robertson composed an air, 'A' Bhan Lunnainneach Bhuidhe', the Yellow London Lady, in thanks for and honour of the extravagant instrument.

Such is Schiehallion's popularity that the original path up the east ridge had degenerated into an ankle-sucking, boggy morass. The John Muir Trust stepped in to save the day in 1999 and built a new path of compacted gravel, with properly engineered rock steps and drainage facilities, which zigzags its way up to the shoulder at a cairn. Whether the money ran out – the cost was £817,000 – or the terrain just became too difficult, is uncertain, but the final section to the summit is an awkward jumble and stumble of quartzite blocks, with a few false summits thrown in for good measure. For a quieter and more satisfying, circular route, follow the lower track south into Gleann Mor and head west along the glen, before the steeper, south-west flank, to gain the summit, then descend by the east ridge. Schiehallion, like Ben Lomond, is a peoples' hill. I have made 14 ascents, many with school kids, teachers and even nuns. If a 72-year-old nun called Sister Quilty can climb Schiehallion in skirt and ordinary shoes, then anyone can!

BEN MACDUI

Probably more has been written about the Cairngorms than any other upland area of Britain, and for good reason. They contain the highest and most extensive area of sub-Arctic wilderness in these islands, along with five out of the six highest mountains in Scotland, Ben Macdui being the second highest. Nowhere else in Scotland, apart from the Monadhliath range, is the notion of a dissected plateau more fitting than in the Cairngorms – or Monadh Ruadh (red hills). The Monadhliath (grey hills), to the north-west, are lower in altitude and of less grandeur. But the Cairngorms are not a mountain range in the accepted sense. The summits of this 'brindled upland' do not proclaim their individuality like the sharp summits of the west. The Cuillin shout their verticalities, but the Cairngorms whisper their wide, open spaces. Here, listening is an art. In the Monadh Ruadh, there are mountains of the mind, not mountains of the moment.

It is the vast scale of the Cairngorms, one of their most notable and noble features, that all walkers and climbers contend with. Hamish Brown remarked,

Nowhere else among our hills is one forced to put in the miles to gain any reward. That is the reward.[2]

In the Cairngorms, the journey is more important than the destination. The whole area is essentially formed from secret corries, boundless, boulder-strewn plateaux and vast skies. In many respects, the corries are the essence of Cairngorm wildness; these scalloped, ice-scoured sanctuaries perfectly complement the immense, lonely majesty of the high sub-Arctic plateaux.

Of the 18 Munros contained in the main massif, Ben Macdui is the most central. It lies at the heart of the range, and consequently requires many miles to claim its stony summit... and Cairngorm miles at that. Ben Macdui (or Macduff's hill) can be ascended from so many different directions and combined with so many other hills that several pages would be needed to outline all the possibilities. That is not the aim here.

Ben Macdui stands 2,000 feet above the dark cleft of the Lairig Ghru, the finest pass in Scotland. Dramatic corries bite into its southern and eastern flanks, including Coire Sputan Dearg, with its grand precipices, 'green lochan' and the lonely, elemental Coire Etchachan, its yawning depths holding the highest, large loch of this size in Britain: Loch Etchachan, an entrancing spot far from the madding crowd. Below and to the north is Loch Avon, the true heart of the Cairngorms, nestled in a deep, cliff-girt trough; the epitome of wildness. I often compare Loch Avon with Loch Coruisk, in the Cuillin, as both are atmospheric, primordial jewels in the crown of their surroundings.

Yet the Cuillin and the Cairngorms could not be more different in terms of form and feeling, although they both have challenges unique to their topography. For the walker, the Cuillin intimidate by their difficulty; the Cairngorms intimidate by their distance. Many accidents, incidents and benightments in the Cairngorms have their root cause in an underestimation of the sheer distances involved. In the Cuillin, the dangers are immediate; in the Cairngorms, they creep up, unawares. Enjoy the long and lonely miles, stay safe – and listen to the silence.

There is no haste, no frenzy in the majestic flow of days, and solitude re-echoes the tread of passing time. – Axel Firsoff.[3]

BUACHAILLE ETIVE MÒR

North of Loch Tulla, the A82 bends sharply left before swinging back right, moving uphill in a wide arc, past the piper's lay-by and the Rannoch rowan and onto the vast, watery wilderness of Rannoch Moor. Driving north, there is the feeling of entering another domain... the Highland Heartland. Somewhere around Loch Ba I usually sample Runrig's 'Alba', the first track from their *The Cutter and the Clan* album, its soaring, Gaelic-rock rift at full volume, the perfect musical embodiment of the wild landscape beyond the windscreen. Then, suddenly, it appears. A colossal, majestic pyramid of naked rock, split by deep gullies into soaring buttresses, ridges and pinnacles, tapering to a grand, pointed summit. The Celtic rock legends, Runrig, have been upstaged by another rock legend: Buachaille Etive Mòr, the big shepherd of Etive, the guardian at the gates of Glencoe. Its presence even upstaged 007 himself, Daniel Craig, in the film *Skyfall*. Some mountains reel you in slowly and subtly, but 'the Buachaille' knocks you out at first glance.

In the eyes of the uninitiated, the mountain appears impregnable to all except perhaps adventurous rock climbers, and indeed for over a century it has been the playground for connoisseurs of the game who revel in the rough and reliable porphyry endowed with in-cut holds. The mountain has a star cast of classic and cult routes, such as Crowberry Ridge, Agag's Groove, January Jigsaw and Raven's Gully. For determined scramblers, however, the classic Curved Ridge gives a ringside view of the notorious Rannoch Wall, a rock climber's dream.

As you drive on further, to the north of the mountain at Altnafeadh, a chink in the armour of this rock giant appears in the form of Coire na Tulaich (Corrie of the Knoll), where a rocky path forms the Munro-baggers' trade route to the top. Considering the immense popularity of the peak, it is incomprehensible why a decent car park has never been constructed at Altnafeadh. On any day of the year, parked vehicles clutter lay-bys, tracks, pot-holed waste ground and every conceivable scrap of land. Yet just two miles further up the road, the less popular Buachaille Etive Beag is afforded a fine, artificially surfaced car park.

The name 'Buachaille Etive Mòr' applies to the whole three-mile-long ridge, extending from Stob Dearg (the peak itself) to the other lonely Munro of Stob na Bròige. The argument for the promotion of the intermediate summit of Stob na Doire to full Munro status was discussed in chapter 4.

A dozen ascents of this imposing mountain by a host of routes, including Lagangarbh Buttress, Broad Buttress, North Buttress, Curved Ridge and Coire na Tulaich, have partially quenched my thirst for the mountain's allure, and a recent ascent of the Curved Ridge, with my son, Ruaraidh, opened younger eyes to the addictive raptures of rough rock and mountain magic. A classic mountain day begins with a romp up the Curved Ridge, including the airy Crowberry Tower, to the summit, followed by a wonderful ridge traverse out to Stob na Bròige and a return by Lairig Gartain. On a clear spring day, such is the stuff of dreams.

BEN ALDER

The vast, sprawling mass of Ben Alder is the great, unsung monolith of the Central Highlands. Remote, solitary, aloof and with an air of mystery to match its complex topography, it holds cult status as one of Scotland's grandest isolated mountains. With its extensive summit plateau and retinue of fine corries, it is almost as if part of the Cairngorms has been removed and relocated far to the south-west. Situated in the remote hinterland between Loch Ericht and Loch Laggan, it is a hill which will 'reel you in slowly and subtly', unlike 'the Buachaille'.

All this would suggest that the ascent of Ben Alder is probably not accomplished, until well into the Munro-bagger's hillwalking career. So for it to have been my second Munro is something of an oddity. The explanation was outlined in chapter 5, when I briefly described my experiences on a Ben Alder–to–Ben Nevis backpacking expedition organised by Glenmore Lodge, back in 1978, my 'rookie' days.

Despite its remoteness, there is a distant view of the hill from Dalwhinnie, a full 12 miles away, down the long, lonely miles of Loch Ericht, one of the lengthiest and narrowest lochs in Scotland. Pony carts once plied the track on the north side of the loch all the way from Dalwhinnie to what used to be a small hamlet, including Benalder Cottage – now a bothy. With the raising of the water level by the Dalwhinnie dam, the track was partially drowned, and the marked path is either sketchy or non-existent. On completion of the dam in the 1930s, the Grampian Electricity Supply Company became the first Scottish producer of public use hydro-electric power. This 'opened the floodgates' for subsequent, more ambitious hydro schemes in the 1940s and 1950s.

Not surprisingly, all routes to Ben Alder are long, and of my three ascents, only one was accomplished as a day trip, using a bike from Dalwhinnie to Culra bothy. A fine scramble on the Long Leachas led to Ben Alder's summit plateau, followed by a traverse of Ben Alder's wee brother, Beinn Bheoil, another Munro. This forms the classic high-level circuit; including the bike run, it is a lengthy ten-hour day – another memorable Munro experience. Overnight expeditions are simplified by the use of two conveniently placed bothies – Benalder Cottage to the south and Culra bothy to the north, though use of the latter is currently discouraged due to asbestos issues.

Ben Alder literally means 'mountain of rock and water', and its northern and eastern cliffs and buttresses still have much unexplored rock-climbing potential. Between the two Munros is the lonely, atmospheric Loch a' Bhealaich Bheithe and the shores of Loch Pattack to the north-east, favourite haunts of garron (white ponies). The environs of Ben Alder are a prized wild area, and the air of inaccessibility exuded by this unique mountain will always be an attraction for the true connoisseur of the Scottish Highlands.

BEN NEVIS

Ben Nevis is a mountain of superlatives: the highest peak, the highest rainfall, the windiest weather, the highest cliffs, the longest climbing routes… but not the most beautiful. 'Attractive' is not a word generally used to describe 'The Ben' – grand, awesome and bold, yes, but not beautiful. From most vantage points, it appears as a colossal, sawn-off whaleback; a great hulking, skulking brute… that is, if you are given the privilege of seeing it at all, for it is said that the summit is obscured by clouds for at least half the days in a year. Indeed, the name 'Ben Nevis', among its multitude of other interpretations, could be construed as 'mountain with its head in the clouds', though current thinking points more to 'evil' or 'venomous mountain', from 'nimheil', or 'nibheis'.

Perhaps the mysterious derivation of the name is apt, in the sense that the mountain itself displays various facets of its character. It is certainly a mountain with a split personality; a mountain of two halves. Its uniform, western flanks, facing Fort William, are in stark contrast to the hidden grandeur of its northern cliffs and buttresses, a secret hidden from the standard pedestrian but well-known to adventurous ramblers, scramblers and rock climbers. This 'Jekyll and Hyde' – or should it be 'hide' – nature is part of the charm of Britain's highest peak.

Of the 150,000 people who climb Ben Nevis each year, the vast majority trudge up the 'Tourist Path' starting at the Glen Nevis Visitor Centre. The tourist path is a trail of trial and trauchle in equal measures. The 'trial' aspect does not refer to the path itself, but to the trail of usually noisy, colourfully clad and ill-equipped trippers jostling along, many oblivious to the fact that the weather conditions 4,000 feet above them would test even the hardiest polar bear. Additionally and crucially, the vast, featureless expanse of the summit plateau, under the usual cloud blanket, can be a navigational nightmare even for the experienced, and it is the root cause of many fatalities. A woman once approached me near the summit, in misty conditions, enquiring as to the route down. She was carrying only a plastic carrier bag and wore a skimpy top with a pair of scuffed kitten heels!

Of my nine Ben Nevis ascents, only one was via the tourist path; the rest almost exclusively followed classic north face routes, such as Tower ridge, Castle ridge, Ledge route and the fabled Càrn Mòr Dearg arête. The latter, often shortened to the CMD arête, is the hillwalker's finest hour – a narrow, rocky, curving highway in the sky, with jaw-dropping views of the magnificent north face in its entirety. I have not been along it in years, but maybe on my tenth ascent?

My most memorable experience of Ben Nevis was a night spent in the small summit shelter built on the remains of the old observatory. Myself and a friend, John Burgess, had completed an epic ascent of Tower ridge, going off route on steep, slabby and greasy rock, carrying enormous rucksacks, finally reaching the summit shelter at 11.00pm. The low cloud, which had enveloped us during our ascent, cleared by the 'wee hours' to reveal a staggeringly beautiful dawn. Fleecy Cumulus cloud below us stretched to distant horizons, with blue sky above. The chirping of a tiny, white snow-bunting welcomed the new day, and it too seemed appreciative of the remarkable cloud inversion. Several hours later, we were joined by another friend, Simon Pengelley, who had slogged up by the tourist path and with whom I would then embark on a challenging four-day traverse of all eight 4,000-foot peaks in Scotland, covering 85 miles and 17,000 feet of ascent. With the promotion of Sgùrr an Lochain Uaine in the Cairngorms, the current number of 4,000ers is nine (five in the Cairngorms and four around and including Ben Nevis).

Ben Nevis will always remain a mountain of extremes, whether that be weather, technical difficulty or rapid ascents... the current 'up and down' record is an astounding one hour and 25 minutes. Many who scale the Ben will never climb another mountain in their lives, but equally, for many, it will be their first Munro that begins a long and lasting relationship with 281 other mountains.

CREAG MEAGAIDH

This huge, sprawling, complex mountain has many similarities with Ben Alder to the south. An extensive summit plateau throws out a radial array of superb spurs and buttresses enclosing some of the finest corries in Scotland. Yet again, the Cairngorms have extended their influence to far-flung corners. A full exploration of this grand mountain, four attendant Tops and half-dozen corries takes more than the three ascents that I have made over the last 40-plus years. Creag Meagaidh still retains an air of mystery, with many hidden nooks and crannies awaiting exploration.

The jewel in the crown of this majestic massif is what some regard as the finest corrie in Scotland – Coire Àrdair. Completely hidden from the Loch Laggan road by the spur of Sròn a' Ghoire, this secret sanctuary can only be reached by a four-mile walk from Aberarder, in itself a rewarding excursion. The corrie contains a fine lochan and is backed by enormous cliffs of mica schist, riven with gullies, ledges and undercut holds, a major venue for serious winter climbing. Higher up and to the right of the corrie is a feature known as 'The Window', a narrow gap in the terrain through which a jet plane flew as I ascended. Looking down to the jet from only a few hundred metres away, I could see the pilot in the seat.

Creag Meagaidh has a special place in my heart, as it was one of the first Munros I climbed upon relocation to Fort Augustus in 1978. On the ascent by the long, south ridge, I was accompanied by several pupils from the Abbey school and history master Mike Haines, a true lover of the hills and the definitive 'to serve them all my days' public school pillar of silent strength who had dedicated his life to teaching and moulding young lives. His hillwalking trips had an almost cult following of a select few, and for some, the rapid descent method of glissading in winter became the highlight of an outing. Mike's unique character and wit is summed up to perfection in a splendid snippet from the school's March 1979 newsletter:

A much favoured ploy on descents is to glissade on
one's seat for a time, riding a mass of snow blocks
yet gradually being engulfed by them. Great skill was
shown by all, particularly Hell-Diver Dempster, Flying
Bedstead MacCallum and the original Avalanche,
Keegan, while King, Queen and O'Donoghue added
their more sober cries to the general racket.[4]

Life-long friendships were forged and fostered in these heady
and formative years at Fort Augustus, and indeed, ex-pupil
Gavin Queen has become a true friend and regular hillwalking
companion of mine. Of course, I also made life-long attachments
to the hills, including Creag Meagaidh.

LADHAR BHEINN

The great linear trough of Glen Albyn, the Great Glen Fault
line, is a divide between areas of strikingly different geology
and form. The area west of the Great Glen is dominated by
east-west glens, inland lochs, sea lochs and long, undulating,
narrow ridges. These physical changes however, are only one
side of the coin.

Leaving Invergarry in the Great Glen and driving west,
there is a quickening of the pulse, a spring in the proverbial
step, a feeling of returning home, far in the west – 'west, where
all dreams lie'. Like old friends, mountains jostle and clamour
for attention, distant sea lochs glitter and shimmer, drawing
you onwards to dream-mountains 'between the sunset and
the sea'. One of these dream-mountains, arguably the finest, is
Ladhar Bheinn, the most westerly Munro in mainland Scotland,
situated in prime position on the remote and romantic Knoydart
peninsula. Knoydart has long been a revered destination for
lovers of solitude and sanctity, for those who revel in the peace
and tranquillity of far-flung places. Bounded south and north
by two long, indented sea lochs, Nevis and Hourn, Knoydart's

grand, glaciated mountains soar from sea level to airy summits, displaying its true nature as the quintessence of Western Highland maritime landscape. Yet another meaning of Nevis is 'heaven' and since Hourn translates as 'hell', Knoydart literally lies between heaven and hell, though most would place it closer to the former. The weather may give some substance to this notion: dominated by Atlantic airstreams, the notoriously fickle west coast conditions can and do shift from heavenly to absolutely hellish, often by the hour.

Ladhar Bheinn's high esteem and allure are due not only to its relative inaccessibility, but also because it embraces that heady and addictive blend of mountain and sea, a marriage consummated in the briny freshness and sparkle of maritime, mountain air... a marriage made in heaven. Also, high on the list of favourable attributes is its astonishing complexity of dramatic corries, narrow ridges and subsidiary summits – a magnet for all adventurous walkers. Ladhar Bheinn is more a mountain range than a single mountain. Its finest feature is the huge, cavernous cauldron of Coire Dhorrcail, backed by a magnificent headwall of soaring buttresses and deep gullies, a rare domain of winter climbing potential whose remoteness ensures few visitors. Some have translated Coire Dhorrcail as 'the corrie of the devil', and with the 'Loch of Hell' directly below, it would appear to hold ominous omens... but its hillwalking circuit on a clear day is probably the finest 'horseshoe' route in the entire country. I say 'probably' because my first ascent of Ladhar Bheinn by this very route was completed in thick mist.

Just reaching Ladhar Bheinn is an expedition in itself. The main walking approach is from the road end at Kinloch Hourn, from which it is a seven-mile trudge on a switchback path, following the south side of Loch Hourn, to Barrisdale and a small estate bothy. This route gives direct access to Coire Dhorrcail. The easiest approach is from Arnisdale on the opposite side of Loch Hourn, where it is possible to book a small ferry in advance. Most people access Knoydart by the scheduled ferry from Mallaig to Knoydart's sole settlement at Inverie, the only village in mainland Britain not accessible by road. Inverie has accommodation, a shop and a legendary pub, The Old Forge, where, according to its website, Munro-baggers, deer stalkers, anarchists, hippies and musicians are all welcome. I have enjoyed many a memorable night in this remote, homely haven.

Inverie was the base for a special ascent of Ladhar Bheinn in 2014 – the last Munro of my second round, and a common 'last' for many baggers. Thankfully, the weather was improved from my first ascent, though strong winds and some low cloud showed their hand. A fine round was made of the vast, western corrie, ending unceremoniously in a dire descent through deep bracken, briars, nettles, rocks and hidden holes providing a real sting in the tail... literally!

An improvement in the weather later in the day saw my summit companion, Andy Oldfield, and myself cycling down from our rented cottage to Inverie village, where we ensconced ourselves outside The Old Forge, savouring the cool smoothness of a pint of Guinness. Basking in the balmy ambience of a golden west coast evening, watching wisps of cigar smoke melt into soft Highland air and hearing the rhythmic lapping of wavelets on the shore, was one of those 'rare malt' moments now bottled and stored in my cellar of memories. In the warm glow of true companionship and that familiar post-Munro, pre-meal contentment, we laughed, joked, picked on the bones of the day, sunk more of the black stuff and reflected on life; the precious pearl between dreams and memories. That wonderful hour outside The Old Forge was what I call a 'snowflake moment', as in Robert Burns' 'Tam o' Shanter':

> But pleasures are like poppies spread
> You seize the flower, its bloom is shed;
> Or like the snow falls in the river,
> A moment white... then melts forever.[5]

This exemplifies the tragic transience and fragility of beauty. The magic of the far west had claimed us both.

Far, far in the west
Is peace profound.
Clouds pillow the hill's Crest,
Seas suck at the shore's breast
With rhythmic sound.
          – Douglas Fraser[6]

THE SADDLE

The 40-mile road trip from Invermoriston, in the Great Glen, to Shiel Bridge, on the west coast, is the last motorable stretch crossing the West Highland Heartland before Strath Bran, 30 miles to the north. The muted beauty of Glen Moriston, with its subdued hills and sylvan slopes, runs seamlessly into the grand, lofty offerings of Glen Shiel. Here, the mountains are no retiring wallflowers, but flaunt their finery of graceful corrie and ridge-line in almost unending succession on both sides of the road. No less than 21 Munros queue up in line, ripe for the picking, with the low-hanging fruit of the South Cluanie ridge providing the staple fare of my formative hillwalking years in the late '70s and early '80s. As the road begins its long descent to Loch Duich and the sea, the view is dominated by the fine, pointed form of Faochag (the Whelk), but it is the mountain to the right that draws the eye, its serrated skyline and tangle of corries and spurs quickening the heartbeat of the aspiring Munro-bagger. This is The Saddle, one of the finest mountains in the West Highlands.

The Saddle is sometimes wrongly claimed as the only Munro with an English name, but Broad Cairn is another. The great, curving summit ridge of The Saddle, sporting three other Tops, encloses a massive north-facing corrie, the round of which is a classic outing from Shiel Bridge. The most famous feature of the mountain is the celebrated Forcan Ridge, a superb scramble and the common ascent route. The Saddle is unique as the only Munro outwith the Skye Cuillin that has a scrambling ascent to its summit as the 'via normale'. Other mountains, such as Ben Nevis and Buachaille Etive Mòr, have excellent scrambling lines, but are not the 'normal' tourist routes to the top. Similarly, classic scrambles, such as Aonach Eagach and Corrag Bhuidhe on An Teallach, are ridge traverses and not ascent routes.

In many respects, The Saddle is the perfect mountain. It possesses all the rugged and wild characteristics associated with West Highland scenery and yet is easily accessible from the A87. Some would view this last observation as a disadvantage – on a summer's day, parked cars can be bumper to bumper, and it is then that the longer Shiel Bridge approach has its advantages. This is a mountain I must re-explore; all my four ascents were made last century. The Saddle is ripe for re-ascent; it is one of those mountains which demands return visits to learn more of her secrets and intimacies.

SGÙRR FHUARAN

From the crest of Mam Ratagain, on the Glenelg road south of Loch Duich, there is a classic view of the northern five peaks of the north Glen Shiel ridge – the famous 'Five Sisters of Kintail'. The highest of these, in the centre, is the Munro of Sgùrr Fhuaran, a graceful pyramid standing proudly above all else, the highest summit in Glen Shiel west of the Cluanie Inn. To its right are Sgùrr na Càrnach and Sgùrr na Ciste Duibhe, both Munros over 1,000 metres high, while to its left are the double summited Sgùrr nan Saighead (a Top) and the more rounded Sgùrr na Moraich.

The first time that I gazed upon this mesmerising scene, from the road viewpoint at Mam Ratagain, I was captured 'hook, line and sinker'. The very name, 'Five Sisters of Kintail', combined with the truly sublime image, engraved an indelible imprint on heart and mind. Some mountains enter your psyche and soul and stay there; Sgùrr Fhuaran and her four sisters were such mountains. The switchback ridge connecting them ranks as one of the iconic ridge walks in Scotland. Not surprisingly, I accepted the challenge offered by this exalted ridge in late October 1979, along with my sadly missed colleague and friend, Bill Houlsby. We witnessed dawn breaking over the mountains as we began what was to be a truly magnificent day striding the high tops, with Sgùrr Fhuaran itself offering one of the finest viewpoints from any Scottish mountain.

The most memorable traverse, however, occurred in the summer of the following year, when I took a party of four Fort Augustus Abbey school pupils with the ambitious intention of camping high on the ridge. These were the days before the creeping tentacles of Health and Safety, Mountain Leader Certificates and other assorted 'paper qualifications' smothered and choked the impulsive passions of free-thinking individualists! For some reason, I had decided on a west to east traverse, maybe as a change from the previous year, so in late May of 1980, we found a grand perch just below Sgùrr na Moraich's summit, making camp and enjoying a supper of gammon steaks – we ate like kings. Later, we sat in awe as the soft, Highland evening light faded gradually into pale yellow, orange and finally into glorious, emblazoned red, behind the serrated skyline of the Skye Cuillin, where more dreams were yet to be realised. We even had our own natural fridge of a pocket of old snow to keep the milk fresh until morning. We were indeed kings of all we surveyed.

At 4.30 the next morning, I again watched the sun rise. Upon our departure at 7 o' clock, the sun was already warm, pointing to a scorching day ahead. Somewhere around the second summit of Sgùrr nan Saighead, we stopped to remove unnecessary items of clothing, and inadvertently, one boy allowed his rucksack to fall from the edge of the narrow ridge. We all watched, mouths wide open, as it tipped and tumbled its way down the steep, grassy slope, only for the rolled up sleeping bag to detach itself and continue to bounce downwards after the rucksack finally came to a halt. The unfortunate lad in question, Mark, upon asking what we should do, was told in no uncertain terms, by myself, that he would have to go down and fetch it. Sympathetic to his predicament, we both descended, with yours truly 'going the extra mile' to retrieve the sleeping bag. On finally reuniting with the other three, who had enjoyed a prolonged ridge fester, the now hot and sweaty Mark, desperate with thirst, pulled out a now bulging can of lager from the wayward rucksack. Before I could even utter the words 'don't open it!', we all were anointed with a lukewarm lager shower, accompanied by some choice phrases. We all reeked of a brewery for the rest of the day. Thankfully, this was the only major incident of the trip, but it and the oppressive heat would contribute to an astoundingly slow ridge traverse... it was 7.00pm when we finally reached the road in Glen Shiel for a pre-arranged pick-up. My memories of that wonderful trip are still vivid and hopefully remain so for the four boys also – especially Mark!

As I write these words, it is now over 40 years since that unique expedition, and unbelievably, the last time I ascended Sgùrr Fhuaran, making it potentially my longest period between two successive ascents of the same Munro. I do aim to climb it again, hopefully on the special occasion of the last Munro of my third round... a few years from now.

LIATHACH

The name, Torridon, evokes images of wild, rocky terrain and hulking mountain giants stirring passion in the hearts of most hill lovers. Torridon is widely accepted as the epitome of true Highland beauty. Mountaineering legend WH Murray remarked:

> Glen Torridon, its lochs and the mountains to either
> side exhibit more mountain beauty than any other
> district in Scotland including Skye.[7]

Coming from a typical hill-goer, this is praise indeed, and from WH Murray, it is an accolade of the highest order.

Yet there is a paradoxical nature to this beauty. The Torridon trio of Beinn Alligin, Liathach and Beinn Eighe possess an ancient, brooding serenity, but also have a savage, stark and almost hostile side to their character, especially Liathach. This is in no small part due to the fact that their quartzite-topped sandstone forms, tens of millions of years old, stand on an archaic bed of gneiss, some 2,600 million years old. They are among the oldest hills in the world. Hamish Brown has remarked that 'Torridon is a glen of brutal beauty'.

For sheer elegance and beauty, Beinn Alligin, the 'jewelled mountain', wins hands-down, but for presence, attitude and drama, Liathach is the ultimate personification of all three... and more. On the drive down Glen Torridon, the mountain's south-eastern ramparts hem in the north side of the glen for five miles. Its tiered, castellated, sandstone flanks, rising steeply to an angular, ice-sculpted summit ridge, produce an air of utter impregnability. Liathach not only deserves awe and admiration, but also respect.

Like its other Torridonian neighbours and massifs such as An Teallach and Buachaille Etive Mòr, Liathach has progressed from its single Munro status to a more deserving double-Munro position. The two Munros are separated by a magnificent, high-level traversing scramble along a series of shattered sandstone pinnacles, known as Am Fasarinen, the exhilarating highlight of the whole ridge. I have made several ascents of the mountain by a variety of routes, including the notorious Northern Pinnacles ridge on the remote north side. Liathach is another of my 'early years' mountains, receiving many ascents in the 1980s and early 1990s, but none since. There seems to be a pattern here, with the classic Munros of the Northwest not receiving their fair share of ascents in later years. I intend to remedy this sad state of affairs sooner rather than later!

SLIOCH

If I was asked to choose only one view which captures the true essence of the Northwest Highlands, it would be the vista along Loch Maree from the north looking to Slioch. Slioch rises in splendid isolation north of Loch Maree, forming an effective barrier between Torridon to the south and the 'Great Wilderness' of Fisherfield to the north. In stature and nature, it possesses that distinctive Torridonian 'feel', with its grand, soaring, sandstone buttresses rising to a squat, castellated summit. Defended on almost all sides by these steep bastions of rock and riven by gloomy gullies, the mountain is the natural embodiment of an impregnable fortress.

Viewed from the north-west on a late summer evening, its buttresses and gullies emboldened into sharp relief, and the tree-fringed shores of Loch Maree provide an exquisitely contrasting foreground. I defy any devotee of mountain scenery, not to reach for a camera in the skip of a heartbeat. There is a saying that 'great artists are the gatekeepers of truth'. As all good landscape photographers are also, in a sense, artists, a single, well-composed photograph has the ability to convey the observer from what is essentially 'just' a landscape to a mindscape of beauty – from reality to ethereality. A vivid example of such a photograph is Colin Prior's image on pages 54–5 of his book *Scotland, the Wild Places*. Oddly, the finest image of Slioch that I have seen is not from Loch Maree but from the flat, rocky summit of Beinn a' Chearcaill, a Graham on the south side of the loch. The photographer is Joe Cornish, and the photograph appears on page 117 of his stunning book, *Scotland's Mountains, a Landscape Photographer's View*.

In many images of Slioch, the foreground dominates the picture. In Joe Cornish's photo, Slioch appears in only the upper quarter. Similarly, in Prior's shot, Slioch forms only a small part of the overall image. This tends to accentuate the mountain's air of inaccessibility and inviolate nature. On an autumn holiday some years ago, I spent a day of particularly fine weather driving around and photographing classic mountain scenes. On arrival at Loch Maree in late afternoon, the golden light, autumn colours and contrasting dynamic interplay of cloud shadows and bright, spotlit, russet hill slopes, was a revelation. Add to that the deepest blue of the loch highlighted with wind-flecked white crests and the ancient, gnarled remnants of Scots pine trees and the picture was almost complete. Almost, apart from majestic and mysterious Slioch rising above everything. I spent over an hour hunting down every compositional opportunity, hoping for that sublime image which probably lay more within myself than beyond the lens. Whether I was a 'gatekeeper of truth', only the viewer can decide.

Of Slioch's grand buttresses, one in particular holds a great fascination for myself. The SMC's book, *Highland Scrambles North*, describes the North-West Buttress as in a 'splendid situation' and 'not particularly exposed'. Having climbed Slioch twice by the standard hillwalkers' approach, this more remote and challenging route is a beguiling attraction that appeals to my scrambling sensibilities. There is a saying, 'never let dreams become regrets', and the dream of wandering up the rough bands of sandstone outcrops of this buttress while the sun sinks slowly beyond island-studded Loch Maree is one I will endeavour to turn into reality. We are all prisoners of time, but not from opportunity.

A' MHAIGHDEAN

My ancient, dog-eared OS Landranger map number 19 – old, creased, folded and characterful – is a bit like the land it represents. Yellowed, crumpled and with strategically placed strips of Sellotape covering the worst tears, bearing the words 'Crown Copyright 1976', its value over the last half-century has far exceeded the meagre £1.50 price marked on its cover. Many of my other 80-odd maps covering Scotland have been replaced by newer versions with updated changes. However, the vast tract of wild terrain between Loch Maree and Loch Broom, known romantically as the 'Great Wilderness', has seen little or no change over this period, so why buy another?

Unfolding Sheet 19 always sends through me a frisson of anticipation and a deep longing to experience this elemental domain. Spread out in full, the general impression of a north-west to south-east grain is immediately apparent. Loch Maree, Lochan Fada, Fionn Loch, Loch na Sealga, Little Loch Broom and Loch Broom itself are all aligned in this same direction, an indicator of the monumental geological upheavals, over aeons of time, that created this extraordinary area. Looking closer, the densely packed, contorted contours resemble the whorled tree-rings of the ancient pinewoods that once covered this crinkled landscape, known poignantly as the Fisherfield Forest. Their dominating presence is enhanced by a host of smaller lochans, rivers, streams and marked crags and cliffs, not only reflecting the underlying topography and geology, but also the antiquity of the region. Here, the landscape is stripped back to reveal the skeleton; the bare bones of its creation.

Almost in the exact centre of the map, surrounded by a cluster of high, hill lochans, is the mountain known as A' Mhaighdean (The Maiden), described by the third Munroist, JA Parker, as 'that most un-get-at-able of all hills', and generally considered to be the remotest Munro of all. For most Munroists, the very name, 'A' Mhaighdean', is enough to send shivers of delight, as it conjures up images of remote, high camps, craggy skylines, glorious sunsets, utter solitude... and midges! The mountain's magical position in the heart of the region is reliably confirmed when one realises that a full 14 miles of rough walking is required to reach its summit from the three main access points of Kinlochewe, Poolewe and Dundonnell.

For this reason, and the fact that approach paths are generally not ideal for cycling, most hill-goers opt for a backpacking and camping plan over several days, giving time to include the other four Munros in the region, together forming the illustrious 'Fisherfield Five' – down from six, following the demotion of Beinn a' Chlaidheimh. Camping has always been my preferred option for tackling this revered mountain. My first ascent, from a Lochan Fada camp, occurred less than a month before the final Munro of my first round back in July 1988. The finest approach, however, begins at Poolewe, in the west, from where a path gradually encroaches into the lonely majesty of mountain and loch, crossing a causeway between Fionn Loch and Dubh Loch, to reach the remote outpost of Carnmore below the imposing crags of Beinn a' Chaisgein Mor, a Corbett. I have enjoyed several camps in this wonderful area, climbing Munros, Corbetts and Grahams, and all hold precious and abiding memories.

I fondly recall one early summer evening, having arrived at the brooding Dubh Loch, near Carnmore, tent up, meal finished and a low, red sun bathing the surrounding crags in a fiery, late evening glow. The drop in temperature soon saw me cocooned in eiderdown, listening to the chattering gurgle of the stream and the melancholic, rhythmic wailing of a black-throated diver on the aptly named Dubh (black) Loch, home to the very sound and soul of wildness. The following morning, I was woken by the plaintive call of a cuckoo heralding the promise of longer days – for myself, a magnificent day wandering the high tops.

I have been asked if I ever experience loneliness or fear on these solo ventures, and my reply is that I feel the exact opposite. Being alone is not necessarily being lonely, and with divers, plovers, cuckoos and eagles as company, who needs the distraction of other companions? Fear, too, is something I never experience. The head may conjure up vulnerability and fragility rather than fear, but the heart soars above these 'concerns' and feels nothing but elation, peace, connectedness and privilege. We spend much of life reflecting pensively on the past or musing wistfully of a brighter future, ignoring the present. Being alone in wildness reconnects us with the reality and beauty of the moment and allows us to touch base with the landscape and, ultimately, ourselves.

The classic route up A' Mhaighdean is the north-west ridge, providing optional, easy scrambling on a succession of steeper rock terraces and an increasingly sublime views of secret lochans and mountain sanctuaries. A gap in the ridge and the bypassing of some sandstone pinnacles leads to broad, grassy slopes sweeping up to the small summit cairn.

The general rule that views *of* mountains are better than views *from* mountains is decisively broken on A' Mhaighdean.

I believe the view north-west from this mountain to be the finest vista of any Munro. Magnificent desolation might be one way to describe it, or perhaps subtle and sublime splendour. The eye is led across Dubh Loch to the blue expanse of Fionn Loch and finally to the hazy harmony of sea and sky. But bewitchingly juxtaposed with these horizontal elements are the craggy verticalities on either side, with the tiny, white dot of Carnmore adding a human touch to the wild scene. Sitting alone on A' Mhaighdean's summit on a good day is a privilege beyond measure. On most summits, I rarely feel that I spend long enough to fully appreciate the view, but on my last visit to this mountain, a full hour passed before I moved on. Beyond the practicalities and trivialities of photography, snacking and identifying other peaks and points of interest, there comes a period of quiet reflection when the eyes and mind wander, unconstrained by the frivolous. In Frank S. Smythe's words,

> Absorb and be absorbed by the beauty of the surroundings. Escape from the shell of your small affairs and tread for a while those mysterious paths of the spirit that lead nowhere and everywhere. Then you will know beauty.[8]

Such quiet reflection may only last a few minutes, but during that time, we become part of something greater. The mind becomes a prism transforming the bland and trivial into the grand and spiritual… we are one with the landscape.

AN TEALLACH

A chain of rocky mountains with sides dark, deep and precipitous; with summits broken, sharp and serrated, and springing into all terrific forms; with snowy glaciers lodged in the deep shaded apertures.
– Thomas Pennant, 1772[9]

This description of An Teallach from an early Scottish traveller and admirer is surprisingly accurate, given the propensity for early tourists to over-exaggerate and embellish the mountain scene. Okay, there are no glaciers, but we know what he means!

An Teallach, standing on the northern edge of the 'Great Wilderness' of Fisherfield, is regarded by many as Scotland's finest mountain. Some would even say that Pennant's description is understated, but he is certainly correct in regarding An Teallach as a chain of mountains rather than as a single peak. The mountain's impressive topography boasts no less than two Munros and seven Tops, a full traverse of which is a major undertaking.

I have made several visits to this grand massif latterly in order to claim some outstanding Tops, scattered on subsidiary ridges, but the real draw and drama is the southern section of ridge, known as Corrag Bhuidhe (Pennant's 'terrific forms'), a succession of weathered sandstone towers; a classic scramble and the highlight of any traverse. Anyone who summits the two Munros without exploring Corrag Bhuidhe cannot really claim to have 'done' An Teallach. My second trip to the mountain, with two companions in July 1990, had the intention of securing suitable photographs for inclusion in my first literary offering, *Classic Mountain Scrambles in Scotland*, published by Mainstream in 1992, and subsequently reprinted and updated and appearing in paperback form in 2016 from Luath Press. Little did I know that this one particular image would end up adorning the front cover and to a large extent encapsulate the pure enjoyment and freedom of scrambling.

Perhaps the finest and certainly the most dramatic feature of Corrag Bhuidhe is the northernmost pinnacle, known as Lord Berkeley's Seat, whose north face drops sheer for several hundred feet into the gloomy depths of Toll an Lochain, the dramatic eastern corrie. Reaching the top is an easy scramble on a staircase of huge sandstone blocks, and it is probably the most exposed situation accessible to the ordinary pedestrian in the entire country. Such is its notoriety, that a daredevil soul paraglided from here and almost killed himself, whilst another launched himself off in a wingsuit.

An Teallach is one of those mountains that always amply rewards return visits, and its relative accessibility and classic status ensures a steady stream of acolytes all too willing to worship at the shrine of the 'Mighty Forge'.

BEN MORE (MULL)

Months could be spent exploring Mull's countless natural attractions... the fascinating coastline, its 27 listed hills, its offshore island havens of Iona, Ulva, Gometra, Staffa and Treshnish, not to mention its many historical and cultural centres – yet many Munro-baggers come, see and 'conquer' the only island Munro outside Skye before turning tail and scurrying back to the mainland.

Ben More's unique status has made it by far the most common mountain to be one's 'last Munro', and indeed, it was my own final summit in 1988. Reaching Mull in the first place obviously requires a ferry and, more than likely, a night on the island. This naturally leads to many baggers 'making a weekend of it', and so results many a celebratory weekend with friends and family under the focal point of the last Munro, Ben More.

In my own case, I booked a cottage in Salem several months in advance and invited various friends, wives and assorted kids to join me for a week in August 1988. Being on the island for a whole week would give the added flexibility of choosing the best day, weather-wise, to tackle the hill... at least, that was the theory. I wound up choosing the least terrible day out of a pretty bad week of mainly rain for myself and four companions to make the classic ascent via the subsidiary peak of A' Chioch, giving us a fine, easy scramble for the final climb to Ben More. The statutory champagne was pulled from a rucksack and hastily demolished in a glug of fizz and bubbles, marking the end of my ten-year campaign.

For those 'continuous rounders' (see chapter 6), Ben More is usually the first Munro, as the self- propulsion ethic obviously benefits from starting on the 'out on a limb' Munro, thus saving a long outward walk or cycle and an extra sea crossing. Being close to the sea and the most westerly Munro south of Skye, Ben More receives more than its fair share of foul weather, but on those magical, sparkling days of spring and early summer, when the sun picks out everything, from nearby crags to breaking waves and distant islands, the summit of Ben More is more than a hint of heaven.

SGÙRR NAN GILLEAN (SKYE)

I make no apologies for the last three Munros in this chapter being situated in the celebrated Cuillin mountains of Skye. The Cuillin are well-known as being unique in the British Isles, not only for their extremely challenging terrain, but also for their savage beauty, rugged grandeur and unrivalled maritime position. For the walker and Munro-bagger, they are a radical departure from the mainland hills, as different as rugby from football, requiring full, hands-on scrambling to reach their dizzying heights. Some refer to the range as the 'Cuillin Hills', which is a bit like placing them in the same category as the Cotswold Hills. In the Cuillin, there is no such thing as hillwalking, only mountaineering. Here, the progression from rambling to scrambling is not a choice, but a necessity.

The Cuillin are undoubtedly a scrambler's and rock climber's heaven, and a host of mountaineering legends have extolled their virtues in no uncertain terms. Himalayan climber Frank Smythe claimed that they were 'the only real mountain range in Britain', while Ben Humble went one further and reckoned that 'they have no equal in all the world'. Hamish Brown, meanwhile, describes the Cuillin as 'Valhalla, Mecca, the Ultimate'. All this praise may seem 'over the top' to those who have not experienced the touch of gloriously rough gabbro and the dancing fluidity of free movement, high on airy ridges above glassy seas. Nothing prepares you for such wonders. The praise is thoroughly validated.

Despite all these superlatives, the Cuillin tend to conceal their grandeur, and once on Skye, there are few places where it is possible to gain a true appreciation of the whole ridge; even then, one can capture only a distant view. For the car-bound tourist, one of the few peaks to reveal itself in glorious splendour is Sgùrr nan Gillean, seen to advantage from the Sligachan Hotel and campsite, from where its elegant pyramid rises gracefully to the left of Am Basteir and the improbable-looking Basteir Tooth. The tempting profile and relative proximity to the Sligachan 'fleshpot' have made it a popular objective for tourists with little or no experience of Scottish mountains. Its south-east ridge, hosting the so-called 'Tourist Route', is something of a misnomer, as its last section involves quite serious scrambling. It was the first Cuillin peak to be climbed, back in 1836, by Professor William Forbes, guided by local forester Duncan MacIntyre.

Sgùrr nan Gillean is often described as the Monarch of the Cuillin, and although not the highest peak in the range, it is certainly the shapeliest, with three superb ridges converging to a magnificent, pointed summit. The view from Sligachan only reveals the profiles of the west ridge on the right and the south-east ridge on the left. The mountain's finest feature is Pinnacle Ridge, which directly faces the viewer and is consequently seen 'end on'.

The peak was my introduction to the Cuillin back in April

1980, and was something of a baptism of fire. In those hazy, crazy days of relative youth (I was 25 at the time), I was a Cuillin 'Green horn'; the name Sgùrr nan Gillean, or 'Peak of the young men', was apt. Fired by Poucher's dramatic prose in *The Scottish Peaks* and self-assured by the bullishness of youth, I found myself on the bealach between my intended peak and Am Basteir, which was the foot of the west ridge and not my planned south-east ridge. This was seven years before the notorious pinnacle known as 'the Gendarme' collapsed, subsequently making the route significantly easier, though I was totally ignorant of its existence then. I somehow shuffled my way up to this awkward obstacle and my diary of the ascent records,

> a pillar of rock which seemingly blocks all passage and with dizzy drops on both sides! I somehow manage to bypass it on the left with some acrobatic moves and much adrenaline and then it was a good romp to the top.[10]

Reading this today makes me grimace and chuckle at the same time. Such was the desire to 'bag' Am Basteir – another Munro – that the sheer brashness of immaturity saw me descend the same ridge in order to do so. Crazy days indeed.

The following summer, I climbed the south-east ridge accompanied by three enthusiastic Abbey school boys who revelled in the rough gabbro scrambling and were genuinely disappointed when the ridge ended too soon at the summit. We even descended the west ridge, avoiding the Gendarme 'by a rope-aided descent down a gully which everyone found slightly alarming', according to my diary. Health and Safety? Mountain Leader Certificate? Nothing... just boyish enthusiasm and good luck. One of the three boys, a German, was so enthralled by his Skye experiences that on Prize Day that year, his parents presented me with a bottle of best German wine as thanks for his memorable trip. They did not mention his maths results!

Two years later, I took some boys up Pinnacle Ridge. Altogether, I have ascended Sgùrr nan Gillean a dozen times, including once on my Skye honeymoon in 1997. I am often asked as to my favourite Munro, and Sgùrr nan Gillean is my inevitable reply, although these days I gravitate more towards less vertiginous hills, such as Blaven or Ladhar Bheinn. Still, the 'peak of the young men' was certainly the favourite peak of my younger days, and it holds a host of intense, enduring and fond memories.

THE INACCESSIBLE PINNACLE

The notoriety and hyperbole surrounding the 'hardest Munro' is, I believe, somewhat misplaced and misleading. The name 'Inaccessible Pinnacle' was conjured up in the mid-19th century, perhaps to overemphasise and embellish this innocent rock wedge with traits to strike fear and terror into the hearts of ordinary pedestrians. Indeed, the wonderfully inflated Victorian description of it as possessing

> an overhanging and infinite drop on one side and a
> drop longer and steeper on the other[11]

is even more nonsensical than portraying it as 'inaccessible'. In truth, the 'In Pin', as it is often shortened, is neither inaccessible nor a pinnacle. Seen in profile, it assumes the shape of an enormous door wedge, with a long, relatively easy-angled east ridge and a short, steep, western drop, standing only eight metres above its parent top of Sgùrr Dearg. From this side, it certainly gives the impression of a pinnacle, but its eastern aspect is a long, stepped ridge, averaging only about 30 degrees in steepness.

This east ridge, the usual ascent route, is graded as a Moderate rock climb, but an easy one at that. Unlike many rock climbs, it does not have a dreaded 'crux' where an awkward, acrobatic move is required to surmount a particularly troublesome obstacle. The whole route is a steady succession of big ledges, excellent 'jug' handholds and reliable rock, albeit somewhat polished in places. Yes, it narrows significantly nearer the top, where the exposure is all too obvious and the consequences of a fall unthinkable, but the Cuillin ridge possesses a host of similar moments and significantly harder ascents. The Thearlaich-Dubh Gap, Bidein Druim nan Ramh and the Basteir Tooth, to name a few, all surpass the In Pin in terms of technical difficulty. Simply because the In Pin is a Munro, it has entered the public imagination with its difficulties exaggerated to the point of blind terror.

My first ascent of the In Pin was in July 1981, the final 'piece de resistance' of the classic 'Round of Coire Lagan', arguably the finest circular scrambling route in Scotland. It includes the Cuillin's highest summit, Sgùrr Alasdair, Collie's infamous ledge and the grand An Stac Buttress, a feast of delights for the competent scrambler. Luckily, I met some folk on Sgùrr Alasdair who agreed to let me use their rope in order to abseil off the steep side of the In Pin. The whole experience was so enjoyable that I promptly descended to the base of the east ridge and claimed a second ascent, followed by a further abseil!

My growing love affair with the Cuillin came to a head on the last day of May 1982, when I finally laid a long-held obsession to rest. Following a bivouac near the summit of Sgùrr nan Eag, the most southerly Munro on the ridge, I set off at 3.30am, with the first rays of the sun glinting on the tops, to traverse the full 11 Munros of the Cuillin ridge, arriving 11 hours later on Sgùrr nan Gillean in perfect weather. As I was not carrying a rope, I knew I would have to descend the In Pin by the route of ascent. Climbing down is much harder than climbing up, and I can remember being somewhat unnerved by a curious onlooker watching me as I delicately descended the east ridge at 6.00am.

Less than a fortnight after this memorable day, I was back on Skye for a weekend with another group of four eager and enthusiastic youngsters, desperate to sample the scrambling delights of the Cuillin. Armed with a rope and an abseiling device, known as a 'figure-of-eight-descender', myself and two brave souls made a free ascent of the In Pin by the usual east ridge. It was not until we had all reached the top that one of the two boys admitted he suffered from vertigo. Now, of all places to make this admission, the top of the In Pin is probably the most unlikely and unwanted. As I uncoiled the rope in preparation for the abseil descent, I admit to feeling a lump in my stomach, but I knew that any sense of dread could not be imparted to my two charges. I was also well aware of the fact that on the previous evening, I had practised 'classic abseils' in my living room from the back of the sofa! As I nervously fed the double rope through the metal descender and flicked the rope over my left shoulder, grabbing it with my right hand, I chatted with mock reassurance to the two lads...

Just gradually let the rope slide through the descender, and don't let go of the rope with your right hand – it's easy – you can't fall.[12]

I am not sure they believed me, but anyway, as I leaned back over the edge, letting the rope take the strain, they both seemed slightly relieved. I pulled back from the abyss, unclipped the rope and prepared the vertigo-sufferer for the longest five minutes of his life. Within minutes, he was over the edge, staring at me intently, the sheer terror in his eyes only partly appeased by my flimsy, unconvincing words of encouragement. Staring up in awe, the remaining two boys who, probably wisely, had declined to make the ascent, shouted supporting noises. Slowly but surely, the roped crusader made it safely to the bottom. The second lad followed, in somewhat quicker time, and finally I joined them, to the huge relief of all.

Looking back at this edgy saga today, with all the benefit of hindsight, experience, and health and safety awareness, I sometimes shudder at the possible consequences of those risky abseils. Not only was there no safety rope and no helmets worn, but I had no abseiling qualifications and only limited experience with this potentially dangerous technique. In today's risk-averse climate, an individual would not even think of taking kids abseiling unless he or she was certified to the hilt and highly experienced. The truly wise would outsource it to a reputable, qualified climbing guide.

A large proportion of Munro-baggers follow this last course of action, while others rely on a suitably qualified friend or relative to guide them up and down what for many, will be their last Munro. Forty years ago, the In Pin could be climbed with few people around. Today, there is likely to be a queue of folk waiting patiently and nervously at the foot of the east ridge to enact their likely sole ascent of this famous blade of rock. I doubt if I will ever top my six ascents – unless I ever actively pursue a seventh Munro round... highly unlikely, at my age, given that I have not yet compleated three.

BLA BHEINN (BLAVEN)

Alexander Nicolson, a Skye local and early pioneer of the Cuillin, considered Blaven to be the finest hill on Skye. Naturalist Jim Crumley describes it as 'the most hypnotic mountain profile in all Scotland'.

All this praise is fully justified. Blaven's majestic grandeur and isolation make it one of the most photographed mountains on Skye, on a par with Sgùrr nan Gillean. Blaven is the only Skye Munro not on the main Cuillin ridge, and along with the other Cuillin outlier satellite peaks of Clach Glas, Garbh-bheinn, Sgùrr nan Each and Belig, forms a magnificent, high level ridge. Blaven's awesome skyline is first glimpsed on the drive from Broadford to Elgol, where Loch Cill Chriosd, on the right of the road, provides a picturesque foreground to its rocky facade. But the classic view is three miles further on, past Torrin, where the 'hypnotic mountain profile' is seen in all its splendour towering above the head of Loch Slapin. This view vies with that of Slioch and Loch Maree as the quintessential West Highland image, the foreground presence of the sea loch endowing the scene with that extra magical, coastal element.

The great massif is a wonderfully complex wall of rock, split by deep corries and weaknesses, riven by crisscrossing gullies that separate soaring buttresses, all rising to a contorted and castellated skyline. The highest point is Blaven itself, on the left, with Clach Glas in the middle and Sgùrr nan Each to the far right. The normal route to Blaven's summit is, ironically, one of the easiest in the Cuillin and follows the obvious left-to-right line of weakness above the cliffs, directly under the summit. This was my first ascent route, back in April 1981, but was soon superseded by what I regard as one of the finest ridge scrambles in the whole of Scotland and an absolute classic in its own right: the Clach Glas-Blaven traverse.

The full traverse of this magnificent ridge has a truly Alpine feel, full of interest, sensational situations and a panoramic view of the Cuillin ridge. Clach Glas is sometimes called the 'Matterhorn of Skye' and involves Moderate rock climbing to reach its airy summit, though nowhere near as exposed as the Inaccessible Pinnacle. The sting in the tail, or crux, is the route onto Blaven, with oddly the least scary of three options being the highest grade in terms of difficulty – the 'Difficult' ascent is an 18-metre chimney that is not exposed and, in my opinion, only rates as Moderate. The fact that I have now traversed this ridge, countless times, with kids as young as ten, gives an indication of its appeal and amenable nature.

The majority of these traverses have been accomplished from the south, at a beautiful bay known as Camas Fhionnairigh, 'Bay of the White Shieling', usually shortened to Camasunary or Camasunarie. This bay sits at the foot of the long, south ridge of Blaven and directly underneath the dramatic little Cuillin viewpoint of Sgùrr na Stri. With its glorious sea views to Eigg, Rum and Soay, it is a truly magical and romantic spot. The name derives from both the large white lodge standing on the east side of the bay and a smaller white cottage on the west side. The latter was a former MBA bothy and the base for a highly memorable and ultimately game-changing experience in New Year 1985–6, when five of us enjoyed the novelty and camaraderie of a bothy Hogmanay in superb weather and idyllic surroundings; so good, in fact, that we repeated the venue every second year until 1989–90, with other bothies used in the intervening years. This bothy has now been reclaimed as a private residence by the owner of Camasunary Lodge, but a fine, new, natural stone replacement has been erected on the far eastern end of the bay.

The Lodge had always been rather a question mark in these early years, but a fortuitous set of events was to ultimately lead in a productive and life-changing direction. A photograph of the bay, taken on our first bothy visit, wound up as a large print adorning the wall of the staff room of my school. This was noticed by a pupil who had been injured during a hockey match and taken to the staff room. Upon seeing the photo, she immediately said, 'that's my uncle's holiday house!' Not only that, but he rented it out, during the summer months, to interested parties. Of course, I got wind of all this and the rest is history, as they say.

Since the early 1990s, I have enjoyed regular holidays at this marvellous location, usually on an annual basis and mainly in the summer. As the Lodge sits directly beneath the south ridge of Blaven, this long, varied and scenic route has almost become a rite of passage when staying at the Lodge. Compared to the standard route of ascent, this approach wins, hands down. The ridge soars from sea to summit in one long, continuous sweep of about two miles. Several steeper rock steps and terraces provide optional scrambling possibilities, but the route's real charm is the stunning view it provides, not only of the entire Cuillin ridge, but south to Camasunary bay and sublime, seaward vistas of Soay, Rum and Eigg. A 'stairway to heaven' would be a good description. The only drawback of this approach is its termination on the south summit of Blaven, from which a slightly awkward scrambling descent precedes the final ascent to the true summit.

Gazing across Glen Sligachan, from Blaven's summit, to Sgùrr nan Gillean and its Pinnacle ridge, is for me like looking back in time, back to the 'peak of the young men' and to my own 'dancing days of spring'. Over the course of four decades, my allegiance has steadily shifted from Gillean to Blaven, the latter's 14 ascents now surpassing Gillean's 12. Bald statistics, however, are an uncouth and superficial measure of Blaven's real pull and prestige. Blaven has gradually burned its way into my psyche and soul; no love at first sight, but a slow awakening and appreciation of its many moods and facets. It has now become the quintessential 'dream mountain' of the west... Sgùrr nan Bodach, or 'peak of the old man', in my misty, mellow days of autumn.

An unhurried descent of Blaven's south ridge on a late summer's day is always a pleasure to slowly savour. I never hurry a descent anyway, but especially not this one. Far to the west, beyond the 'antlered Cuillin', the bulbous, orange orb of the sun throws the landscape into burning, sharp relief, and the clouds are lined with golden thread. I often stop and sit on a convenient rock, absorbing the scene; the changing light, the lengthening shadows, the bronzed sea, Soay's lobster claw shape... Then, after ten minutes, just a blink in Blaven's eternity, I continue down through boulders and scree, trying to refocus my mind on the banalities of balance and foot placements, but simultaneously revelling in the rhythmic movement and the physical contact with the mountain.

At a crest in the ridge, the bay appears without warning, still 2,000 feet below; a half-mile wide tongue of green and ochre machair, fringed by a curving filament of sand and a burnished shield of ocean beyond. The two sugar grain shielings of Lodge and old bothy add human flavour and focus to the timeless scene. There is a 'spirit of place' here which seems to transcend space and time, a time-worn yet timeless ancestral simplicity that will outlive and outlast the petty beyond. Descending further in mesmeric thrall into the protective palm of the bay itself, the Lodge graduates from sugar grain to substance, its four whitewashed walls offering protection from the frequent battering from squalls and westerlies. Another stop to absorb the briny scent of the sea and the smell of bog myrtle wafting upwards in the still, summer evening air, then downwards again, attended by the mournful peep of a Golden Plover. I notice a faint wisp of woodsmoke emerging from the Lodge chimney, hinting at the warmth within. Central heating? Absolutely not, and no electricity either. At Camasunary, all electronic devices lose their charge – and their meaning. Meanwhile, we recharge and find meaning by relaxing, unwinding and ultimately regressing back to childhood. It is a place where worldly worries are washed away by the tide, and a diet of fresh mackerel and malt whisky does wonders for both heart and soul.

Crucially, the Lodge has witnessed a rich seam of rock-solid friendships, revitalised and reinforced within its cosy confines. Here, cosseted in companionship and cocooned in camaraderie, the outside world is airbrushed from existence – if only for a flicker in Blaven's infinitude. But the timelessness of Camasunary is assured. It is a place where the material and imagination merge, where the real and ethereal blend seamlessly, like water and whisky. For me, in a strong sense, Camasunary has become a spiritual home, and Blaven its guardian.

CHAPTER 10

Wildness And Well-being

IN MAY 1961, distinguished mountaineer, author and conservationist WH Murray was commissioned by the National Trust for Scotland to survey the Scottish Highlands, with the intention to identify specific areas of exceptional landscape value and outstanding beauty. In the eyes of the Trust, there was a pressing need to engender good land management and to create and maintain a natural balance between mankind's material and spiritual needs; in more prosaic terms, between money and natural beauty.

That WH Murray had been requested for this task was a reflection of his extraordinary and profound recognition of natural beauty and his ability to convey this to his readers, with exceptional passion, in finely crafted prose. Anyone who has read his two classics, *Mountaineering in Scotland* and *Undiscovered Scotland*, will fully appreciate his impact. But it was Murray's connection with the landscape through the act of mountaineering which enabled him to experience beauty in a deeper and more meaningful way. As far back as 1902, the great Impressionist painter, Paul Cezanne, commented, 'we no longer see nature; we see pictures over and over again'. In other words, most of us never experience nature first-hand, but only through images, like calendar pictures – or, in the present day, television and digitised footage. Yet it is only through physical connection with the natural world that we can gain an understanding and appreciation of its true worth and, crucially, the need for its protection.

The National Trust's impetus for action had emerged on

account of the stubborn North of Scotland Hydro-Electric Board, which was hellbent on damming the narrow gorge of upper Glen Nevis. Those who are familiar with this famous, rocky, wooded defile, will be well aware of its uniqueness and beauty, and indeed, Murray himself compared it to a Himalayan gorge. The Hydro Board had already blighted three of Scotland's grandest glens – Affric, Cannich and Strathfarrar (see chapter 1) – with dams, bloated reservoirs and new roads severely detracting from and eroding their natural atmosphere and wild essence. The proposed inclusion of Glen Nevis was the final straw, and in a sense, the fight to secure Glen Nevis's natural state marked the beginning of a long and embittered battle to protect Scotland's wild areas that still continues today. Thankfully, the fight for the sanctity of Glen Nevis was won, and the glen has retained its natural beauty.

Following Murray's identification of 21 areas of outstanding beauty, the final paragraph in his report pointed out that Scotland's finest asset was slowly being wasted, and this wastage would accelerate unless a statutory body was created and granted powers to act accordingly. What made the formation of such a body even more imperative was the great outdoor revolution following World War Two, which sent scores of people into the Highlands – and of course, up Munros. Upon meeting the secretary of the National Parks Commission to discuss a possible Countryside Commission for Scotland, Murray probed him as to the most important factors to consider. The secretary's reply was first and foremost, conservation, but he also added,

If you want to keep the best of your landscape, you'll have to fight for it – if you don't, no one else will.[1]

The upshot of all this was the creation of the Countryside Commission for Scotland (CCS), established by Act of Parliament in 1967. Although a positive step forward, the CCS had several crucial weaknesses. Firstly, it only possessed an advisory capacity, with no real powers or 'teeth'. Furthermore, its stated aims,

to develop facilities for the enjoyment of the Scottish
countryside and to conserve its natural beauty[2]

were expressed in the wrong order. Also, few of the commissioners
had any close association with the countryside, and they were
essentially blinkered towards development as opposed to
conservation. Despite these concerns, the Commission was a
force for good during its 25 years in office, and its successor
of 1992, Scottish Natural Heritage (now NatureScot), had
excellent foundations on which to build its ultimate success in
legislating for National Parks.

Since publication of *The Munro Phenomenon* in 1995,
there have been several significant developments relating to
outdoor access, conservation and land use, some of which
are positive, some inappropriate and some which have been
met with mixed opinions. These include the formation of the
Scottish Government, the creation of two National Parks, the
Land Reform Act of 2003 and the huge rise of industrial-scale
wind farms. Before looking at these developments in further
detail, it would be salutary to examine the basis of the notion
of beauty in natural landscapes and how our perceptions of it
have changed over time.

Murray's 21 chosen areas were based on his own criteria
for natural beauty and included such regions as Loch Lomond
and the Trossachs, the Cairngorms, Glen Lyon, Torridon and
Loch Maree, Fisherfield and the Cuillin. The vast majority of
hillwalkers and outdoor enthusiasts would nod in agreement
along with his selection. Yet, we only need to look back a few
hundred years to discover an era when the scenery conjured by the
above list was regarded as anything but beautiful. As we saw in
chapter 1, Samuel Johnson and James Boswell saw mountains as
'considerable protuberances' and wild landscape as a 'wide extent
of hopeless sterility'. Most folk of the time viewed wild country
as wasteland, full of danger and entirely alien. One tourist, upon
reaching Loch Coruisk on Skye, described the scene as 'nothing
but dead and stony, seemingly a God-forsaken world'.

How we see and perceive the natural world is influenced by the values and cultural pressures of the society within which we find ourselves. In other words, our perception of beauty, or ugliness, is prejudiced by a dense filter of fashion and preconceptions relating to the zeitgeist of the time. This idea is strongly related to what David Attenborough has called the 'shifting baseline syndrome', the notion that each generation defines the normal by what it experiences.

Prior to the 18th century, beauty in landscape was generally appreciated more in rural settings, particularly forest and woodland scenes. At that time, more wild land was covered with natural forest, with fewer of the typically denuded mountain landscapes we see today. Most of Scotland's 'wild' landscape is not in any sense 'natural' compared to how it was many centuries ago. In fact, the great Caledonian Forest of Scots pine, oak, birch and alder, which grew to an altitude of 2,000 feet in the east and 1,000 feet in the west, had largely disappeared by the 18th century, and any chance of its natural regeneration was obliterated by the introduction of cloven-hoofed destroyers – the ubiquitous sheep. Much of the perceived beauty we see today, such as a purple, heather-clad hillside dotted with sheep, or the extensive Flow country of Caithness, has come about largely by the hand of man. The true enormity of this destruction was compellingly captured by Hugh MacLennan, a Canadian visitor to Scotland in the 1950s, who was directly descended from a Highland emigrant:

> Such sweeps of emptiness I never saw in Canada
> before I went to the Mackenzie River later in the
> same summer. But this Highland emptiness, only a
> few hundred miles above the massed population of
> England, is a far different thing from the emptiness of
> our Northwest Territories. Above the 60th parallel in
> Canada you feel nobody but God has ever been there
> before you, but in the deserted Highland glen you feel
> that everyone who ever mattered is dead and gone.[3]

He was, of course, referring more to the eviction of the native population during the Highland Clearances than the removal of forest cover.

Nor has this change in land use relented. The monotonous monoculture of densely packed, uniform Sitka Spruce now covers vast swathes of Highland landscape and is another destroyer of biodiversity. Massive, concrete dams have grotesquely enlarged former, natural, freshwater lochs, such as Quoich, Loyne, Cluanie, Mullardoch and Monar. Associated gaunt pylons and wires march relentlessly through the glens, and forests of towering steel turbines are the latest sorry additions to this wanton destruction of a less industrialised, natural-looking landscape. Common to all these changes is mankind... and money. Regardless of arguments concerning energy needs and 'saving the planet', the core driving force behind many of these developments is economic in nature. Capitalism and greed have replaced caring and need. For too long, man has viewed wilderness as prime territory to use, abuse, tame and profit from, oblivious to the loss of the biodiversity upon which the planet ultimately depends. Colin Prior puts it well when he says, 'Rather than defend ourselves against nature, we need to defend nature against ourselves'. In a similar vein, David Attenborough remarks: 'We moved from being a part of nature to being apart from nature'.

As briefly mentioned above, by far the most repulsive episode in Highland history was the large-scale eviction of tens of thousands of working people from the Highlands by greedy lairds in order to make way for sheep – another profit-driven horror. The Clearances tore out the heart of once-thriving glens, leading ultimately to the creation of vast sporting and farming estates owned by powerful landlords, where 'deer forests' became the fashionable recreation grounds of Victorian gentlemen.

The hand of man has been so influential in moulding the Highland landscape we see today that it is increasingly difficult to assess and understand the true character of the wild places in need of protection. Are we trying to protect wild places and leave them as they are now, or recreating them as they were in the past? Does an ideal state exist? These complex questions continue to be bones of contention between various opposing parties with sometimes vociferous points of view. Bodies such as NatureScot, the National Trust for Scotland, the John Muir Trust and the Scottish Wild Land Group all have done a power of good in addressing these questions and acting with best intentions.

Two of the most significant developments since the mid-1990s have been the creation of two National Parks and the Land Reform Act, the latter resulting in the Scottish Outdoor Access Code, enshrining land access in law rather than as a longstanding tradition. Both these developments are linked in many respects, so they will be discussed in parallel. In a nutshell, the twin aims of a National Park are conservation and recreation. In theory, this sounds positive, but in practice, a fine balancing act exists between the two that requires constant analysis and fine-tuning. Encouraging folk to enjoy the great outdoors is a laudable aim, and the health and well-being benefits of immersion in the natural world are well-documented. Also, as already mentioned, direct experience of wild country through the act of walking gives the individual a more sympathetic and empathetic relation to 'wildness', which can only be a good thing.

However, the hard truth is that when visitor numbers pass beyond a crucial point, path erosion is inevitable, scars will appear and wildlife are threatened. Unrestricted access is a double-edged sword, as too is the entire National Park ethos. What is the solution? Part of the answer revolves around an influential conservationist, Percy Unna, a former president of the SMC, who spearheaded the successful buyout of Glencoe for the NTS. Unna died in 1950 but is remembered for his 'principles for the management of mountainous country for the use of the public', which eventually became known as the 'Unna Rules'. Unna was a visionary who had foreseen the increased pressure on the land back in 1937 when he forwarded his 'Ten Commandments' to the Trust.

The gist of these rules is given here. Wild land was to remain in its primitive condition, but with unrestricted access for the public. Hills were not to be made easier and safer to climb by the construction of new paths, bridges, signposts or shelters, and there was to be no access for mechanical transport or refreshment facilities. Any hotels or hostels had to be situated by the roadside and suitably screened by trees. From a conservation angle, these 'rules', though not legally binding, made much sense, and Unna's financial generosity to the NTS suggested a moral duty to adopt them. However, those who remember the hideous Ben Lawers Visitor Centre and the original Glencoe Visitor Centre, to name a few, will realise that Unna's rules were not exactly high on the Trust's priority list. The rules demanded that preservation of wild quality have absolute priority over visitor attraction and the creation of tourist honeypots.

There are some instances, however, where strict adherence to Unna's rules would lead to further erosion or damage, and a policy of common sense rather than blind tenacity should be adopted. A good example is the original 'path' up Schiehallion, which had become a hideous quagmire due to the passage of thousands of feet. On the acquisition of the north-east side of the mountain by the John Muir Trust in 1999, a new, properly engineered and drained path was constructed, which is coping well with the increased level of foot traffic.

WH Murray was a founding member of the John Muir Trust. His principles went further than Unna's in his wish to withhold positive promotion of access. In other words, he was against the encouragement given by books and magazines for the attraction of hills, and in particular, of Munros. His concern was based on the hordes of hillwalkers who followed guidebook routes and rarely sought out their own way. In my opinion, this is not an argument for withholding promotion of access, but for educating the Munro-bagger to be more imaginative in their route choices. Murray also talks about collecting Munros for collection's own sake, indicating a disparaging attitude towards mere hillwalkers (see related discussions in chapter 7).

'The Right to Roam' has always been a rallying cry for hill lovers, harking back to the 1930s and before. Open access to moor and mountain has always been an ideal worth fighting for, and finally, in 2003, this worthy principle was enshrined in law with the introduction of the Land Reform Act. However, with rights must come responsibilities, and it is essential that the right to roam is seen as a privilege and not an open invitation to abuse that privilege by littering paths, cairns and bothies. Ultimately, the Land Reform Act is based on a mutual respect between land users and landowners, whether these landowners are private, the National Trust or others. The old adage of 'take only photographs and leave only footprints' has never been more salient than in our world besieged by litter and especially plastic waste.

Land ownership in Scotland has always been a contentious issue, and the image of 'tweedy' lairds and their 'toff' companions hunting, shooting and fishing on huge, heather-covered estates, is one that continues to reinforce the notion that Scotland has the most unequal land ownership system in the free world. There are those who concur with Marx, holding that private land ownership is as ludicrous and immoral as the private ownership of human beings, and in the fullness of time, this belief may well reveal itself to hold much truth. It is reckoned that around 60 per cent of rural Scotland is owned by private landowners, some good, some bad and some indifferent. Although easy to tar all with the same brush – usually negatively – there do exist a significant proportion, who are genuinely committed to the conservation and rewilding of Scotland's rural landscape. One of these, who is now the largest private landowner in Scotland, is a true visionary who should hopefully dispel the notion that landowners are inherently bad for Scotland. This individual is Anders Povlsen, who will be discussed later in this chapter.

Meanwhile, we turn to one of the most controversial issues affecting the Scottish landscape in the last quarter century – the rise of large-scale wind farms. An older adage, conjured up by anti-wind farm adherents, which proclaimed:

There are only two types of people who like wind farms... those who don't know enough about them and those who have a vested interest in them.[4]

It is the first group to whom the following discussion is aimed.

Wind energy, when used sensibly and sensitively in locations where the wind does not have a fickle and unpredictable nature, can be a valuable local resource. Small communities like the island of Eigg and Scoraig, on the west coast, utilise wind power in an efficient and sustainable way. However, the industrial scale use of wind as a supplement to base load electricity will almost certainly be recognised in years to come as one of the greatest follies of the 21st century.

To the many proponents of wind farms, this bold assertion will require a great deal of backing up, so I will attempt to persuade you. Firstly, wind power on the industrial scale is both inefficient and uneconomical. Wind turbines cannot produce electricity if the wind speed is too low or too high, and the fickle nature of wind ensures that they only produce around 27 per cent of their rated capacity. Vast subsidies are paid to wind farm companies under the Renewable Obligation scheme, which amounted to £1.3 billion in 2019 alone. But the real economic folly is the renumeration of so-called restraint payments. As more turbines come on-line, the National Grid is under increasing pressure to maintain a steady flow of power and minimise congestion through wind farms, much like traffic lights controlling traffic flow. This is done by temporarily constraining power from specific producers, but compensating them accordingly for the value of the power they would have generated and for the loss of subsidy. This results in over-compensation, meaning that wind farms earn more for sitting idle than for generating power, and you and me are paying for this idleness in our energy bills. In 2020, a quarter of a billion pounds was paid out in constraint reimbursements. Indeed, so profitable is the bonanza or these payments that developers are financially encouraged to construct more turbines in areas already over-provided with wind power. In other words, they are hiding behind bottlenecks in the grid and receiving enormous cash sums for sitting idle. The profusion of wind farms is being driven by greed, not need.

Were wind farms truly efficient and economic, their ugly intrusion into the countryside might be tolerated, but their existence is the biggest white elephant of modern times and one which future generations will regard as a monumental folly. The second drawback of large-scale wind power is the vast amount of space required in order to produce a relatively small amount of electricity. One thousand square miles of land is needed for a one-gigawatt wind energy source, but as the correct wind speed blows only a quarter of the time, a near full-sized, one-gigawatt power station, occupying a mere 30 acres, would be required as back-up when wind speeds are insufficient.

None of these serious concerns have even hinted at the chief dislike of wind farms among many hill-goers – their visual impact. Again, if wind power were truly the saviour and giver of our energy needs, we may just grit our teeth and endure it; but it is not. Industrialising vast swathes of wild land with monstrous turbines is as philistine as placing a sewage plant in the middle of the Cairngorms. Hydro power is at least efficient and reliable, so to some extent, endurable.

All wind farm applications are supposedly subject to consultation with the public and interested parties, but more often than not, this turns out to be a massive sham. Local opinion is often completely disregarded, and communities lack the funding to take on the usually foreign, rich, faceless players in the wind energy industry. Even where wind farm applications have been rejected by local councils, government ministers frequently overrule their decisions – in the past five years, 19 out of 24 rejected applications were nodded through at a government level.

One of the main 'attractions' of wind turbines, to politicians, is their supposed zero carbon emissions. This may be true when they are 'up and running', but the carbon emissions involved in their construction and associated infrastructure are often conveniently overlooked. Mining and smelting of various metals for the turbines, along with carbo-intensive concrete for the massive 5,000-ton foundation of each turbine and the building of access roads, all contribute to an enormous release of CO_2. It is reckoned that a typical wind farm would have to operate for at least half its nominal lifetime to offset the carbon released in its construction. And it is now generally recognised that a wind farm's typically suggested lifetime of 25 years is grossly exaggerated.

It is now almost impossible to stand on a Munro summit without seeing the tell-tale turning of massive blades in the distance. What we are really seeing, however, is the price we have been paying over the last quarter-century for an energy policy which has become hopelessly skewed and distorted by the heated calls of 'environmentalists' who have fallen for the chimerical dream of gambling our future on the 'free' and 'clean' power of wind.

If there are still any pro-wind farm individuals reading this, they will no doubt be asking the question: 'What is the alternative to wind power?' Surely, fossil fuels and nuclear energy are un-'green' and dirty, so we can count them out. But this last statement is only half true: nuclear energy produces no carbon emissions at all, and it is the only long-term hope we have for securing an energy-rich future. The propaganda spouted concerning the favourable qualities of wind energy is equalled by the negative propaganda and untruths propagated about nuclear energy.

Planetary scientist and originator of Gaia theory, James Lovelock, who was described by the *Guardian* as 'a prophet who deserves every honour the human race can bestow' and by *The Sunday Times* as 'the greatest scientific thinker of our time', another rejector of wind power, is a positive advocate of nuclear energy. He writes:

> I think we fail to welcome nuclear energy as the one good and reliable power source because we have been grievously misled by a concatenation of lies. Falsehood has built on falsehood and is mindlessly repeated by the media until belief in the essential evil of all things nuclear, is part of an instinctive response.[5]

It is beyond the scope of a book on Munros to argue the pros and cons of nuclear energy, but there is one other form of energy generation already mentioned which has significantly altered many remote glens of the Highlands – hydro power.

As indicated previously, hydro power is both efficient and reliable, but its visual cost is the construction of massive concrete dams and the 'drowning' of once peaceful, wooded glens with often un-naturally large reservoirs which produce unsightly high and low water erosion along their banks. This is very evident with, for example, Loch Lyon, Loch Mullardoch, Loch Quoich, Loch Cluanie and Loch Monar – all artificially enlarged lochs in once attractive and often occupied glens.

Many hill-goers are willing to accept these intrusions for two main reasons. Firstly, the visual impact of dams and reservoirs is not perceived to be as bad as, say, that of wind farms. Secondly, hydro power is 'green', efficient and reliable – it is in fact one of the most efficient means of generating electricity and therefore more readily accepted, despite the damaging impact on glens.

The general trend today is a shift from large hydro schemes to smaller, local projects, which obviously have less impact on the natural environment. I strongly believe that this is the direction in which wind farms should be heading.

There is a general recognition that hedging all hopes on too small a range of types of power generation is unwise. Having 'all our eggs in one basket' is a recipe for future blackouts and a reliance on importing energy from overseas. In the UK, there is also huge potential for tidal and wave power, two forms of energy generation which hold promise to be as efficient and reliable as hydro power. The developing technologies of tidal power in particular, harnessing electricity from the regular and reliable tidal shifts, have a huge part to play in an energy-rich future.

We now return to yet another thorny issue – land ownership in Scotland. As mentioned previously, there is a generally negative view regarding ultra-wealthy individuals or groups owning large tracts of rural country. A study by the Scottish Land Commission, a government quango, asserts that in extreme cases where landowners abuse their power, they could face compulsory purchase orders or community buyouts. In the worst cases, where landowners actively exploit the land for monetary profit and are uninterested in conservation or local communities, concerns are obviously justified, but at the same time, we must tread this ground with care.

Regardless of the rights and wrongs of owning land, at the end of the day, how land is managed is more important than its ownership. For an example of excellent land management, look no further than Danish billionaire Anders Povlsen, who is currently the largest private land owner in Scotland and the nation's wealthiest man. These facts alone, are enough to raise the hackles of those with more socialist leanings, but the former fashion retail tycoon who owns 13 Highland Estates is totally committed to a 200-year rewilding vision to completely transform the Scottish Highlands. Mindful of David Attenborough's 'shifting baseline syndrome', Povlsen remarks:

> I generally think, over generations, we have lost the baseline. The Highlands is not a natural environment any more, when you're out there and there's only heather, heather, heather. In some places you will not be able to see a single tree for miles. Then we dig into the peat and you will find it used to be a forest, and not only that, we can change it back to its splendour and natural state.[6]

Anders Povlsen is often remembered for the tragic loss of three of his four children in a terrorist atrocity in Sri Lanka. He pays tribute to them by describing his children as 'always looking at the environment'. Personally, I echo these sentiments when looking generally at the young people of today. Environmental awareness seems to be almost hard-wired into many children – not just Greta Thunberg – and again, the notion of a shifting baseline is evident. However, we are also in danger of 'greenwashing' young minds in ideas such as the mad rush for wind power or the rejection of nuclear power. Povlsen's long-term aim of restoring

Scotland's ancient woodland is one proven to lower carbon dioxide levels and restore biodiversity to large areas that have been ravaged by the hand of man for hundreds of years. As David Attenborough points out, the planet's climatic stability has wavered in conjunction with a decline in biodiversity, and the two are intimately bound together. Restoring biodiversity is a 'call to arms' with which we all must actively engage, for our own sake and for the planet's. As far back as 1983, Cairngorms expert Adam Watson commented that

> many of the grandest relics of the old Caledonian
> Forest are steadily disappearing and heading for
> extinction. Time is short, and fast running out.[7]

I wish I could relate that the situation has vastly improved since this observation, but sadly, this is not the case. While isolated pockets of denuded land have seen serious replanting of native species, such as the Creag Meagaidh National Nature Reserve, these essentially piecemeal approaches have only recently begun to be replaced by more extensive, government-backed schemes.

Although mass tree cover is seen as desirable by conservationists, there also exist other valuable habitats, such as peatland and blanket bog, exemplified by the Flow Country in Caithness. This vast blanket bog acts as a 'carbon sink' capable of absorbing and storing huge amounts of carbon dioxide. These areas store at least twice as much carbon as standing forests, but this has not stopped wind farm developers ploughing up bog areas and releasing vast amounts of carbon and methane into the atmosphere, then replacing them with thousands of tonnes of concrete... in the name of 'green energy'. In addition to carbon storage, blanket bogs are a unique ecosystem that provides home for a variety of wildlife. They also help with flood mitigation.

Of course, restoring biodiversity is not just restricted to flora, but also fauna. By far, the biggest problem in the restoration of natural forests is the presence of deer and sheep, whose overgrazing of wild areas prevents the growth of new trees and a wealth of wild flowers. Quite simply, Scotland's deer population is far too high, which is why large estates have adopted a policy for culling in the autumn – with the added bonus of extra revenue! The problem is that deer in Scotland have no natural predators (apart from man), and so their numbers will naturally increase unless artificial controls, like culling, take place.

Even with culling, however, deer are still a destructive force. The absence of a top predator has stifled their normally migratory nature, resulting in deer spending too long in single locations and eating too much of the foliage. Deer also are partial to tree bark, which in turn threatens woodland bird populations. We are all aware that birds are fond of insects, and midges in particular, so fewer deer should result in a rise in bird populations, resulting in a decline of the much-berated midge! All this should help clarify the intimate interconnectedness of life, from the humble midge all the way up to apex predators such as the magnificent Golden Eagle and... wolves.

There are some who maintain that if we are serious about restoring biodiversity in the Highlands, then at some stage, the reintroduction of wolves is a necessity. Anders Povlsen and 'celebrity' gardener, Monty Don, are both advocates of the idea, but another private landowner, Paul Lister, who owns the 23,000-acre Alladale Wilderness Reserve near Ardgay, is the chief instigator of the 're-wolfing' notion. On the subject of deer, he says,

> we have to keep [deer] numbers down to allow the land
> to regenerate and the most natural way to do this is by
> introducing once indigenous carnivores like wolves and
> bears for whom they are natural prey.[8]

The problem with Lister's plan of introducing two packs of ten wolves to his estate is that the wolves would not be roaming free, but contained within a large enclosure, surrounded by a nine-foot fence. With this plan, the result will be little more than a glorified zoo, and it does not serve the intended motive for wolf reintroduction. Professor Alastair Driver, director of the charity Rewilding Britain, has commented that within the next 20 years, we might see wolves in large enclosures, but due to people's obvious caution and distrust, wolf reintroduction would have to be done by a slow 'toe in the water' approach. Povlsen believes that the whole rewilding process – including wolf reintroduction – must be carried out over several generations and be done on a grand scale.

Despite evidence to the contrary, wolves are not a great threat to man, and the bad press they receive is largely unjustified. However, there is no question of their danger to sheep and lambs, and the National Farmers Union is quite rightly concerned about any reintroduction. Andrew Midgley, environment and land use policy manager at NFU Scotland, has commented that such proposals

> have the unfortunate effect of driving a wedge between farmers and environmentalists, at a time when we all need to be working together to focus our collective efforts on safeguarding existing wildlife.[9]

There may come a time in the future when the notion of domesticated animals like sheep and cattle is a quaint memory, as our food sources shift away from a focus on meat, while wolves roam completely free. But that vision is still, if ever, a long way off.

In the USA, wolves were successfully reintroduced in large National Parks, such as Yellowstone, with a resulting massive renewal of an entire ecosystem, but Scotland is a tiny country compared to the USA. However, Yellowstone National Park is only double the area of the Cairngorms National Park, so perhaps the Cairngorms would be able to cope with half of Yellowstone's wolf population?

Regardless of the scope and timeline, Scottish Gamekeepers Association chairman Alex Hogg's comment that bringing back wolves to Scotland is akin to 'reintroducing killer whales to a swimming pool' is sensationalist nonsense – if wolves were here before, then they can be here again.

Wolf reintroduction is a bit like the canine equivalent of a full focus on nuclear power generation, but I believe both will transpire eventually. Any decision concerning wolves ultimately resides with NatureScot, whose current position remains that they have no plans for wolf reintroduction. However, circumstances must change for biodiversity to flourish. A scheme of large-scale reforestation in the Highlands is long overdue, and once this is reasonably established, the reintroduction of wolves is the next logical step.

Another apex predator that carries much less negative emotional baggage is the European lynx. The lynx last prowled through Scottish forests over 1,000 years ago, and there has never been any recorded attack by a lynx on a human. Believe it or not, a year-long study has already begun to assess the feasibility of their reintroduction. 'Scotland: The Big Picture', one of three groups leading the research, is partly funded by Anders Povlsen. Peter Cairns, of this group, remarks that lynx could be back in Scotland within five to ten years if feedback is favourable. The lynx discretely advertises its presence through faeces, urine and scrapings, keeping deer on the move and thus reducing overgrazing. But crucially, as with wolves, lynx will naturally kill and eat deer, the first step toward restoring biodiversity.

The main focus in this chapter so far has been on wildness and the wilderness, but little has been mentioned of 'well-being'. Restoration of wilderness is key to the well-being of the entire world, but recreation *in* wilderness is key to the well-being of the individual. Re-creation and recreation are dual aspects of revival and renewal. We can both save and savour the natural landscape with minimal conflict.

In a purely physical sense, the very act of putting one foot in front of the other is a wonder-drug, one that does not appear on any prescription, though perhaps should. Walking, and particularly wild walking, lowers blood pressure, reduces the risk of heart problems, improves memory and thinking skills, staves off depression and Alzheimer's, and improves sleep patterns. If anything positive has stemmed from the recent COVID-19 restrictions, it is the upsurge in people going out for a leisure walk – and hopefully reaping the benefits.

Not surprisingly, physical health benefits translate naturally into mental health benefits, and this connection can go much deeper. For Munro-baggers, the initial lure and allure of the Munros soon gives way to a more profound craving for space, freedom, discovery and the ability to 'connect' with the landscape more intimately. The act of climbing upwards, rather than mere horizontal walking, raises the heart rate and gets the lungs pumping, but these physical benefits, though important, parallel deeper insights into our nature.

The higher we climb, the smaller and more insignificant we feel against the majestic backdrop of mountain scenery. Concurrently, any worries and petty problems seem to slide away and recede into the distance; we gain a better sense of perspective. Massaging of the ego, which often assumes great importance back in 'civilisation', also loses substance; our vanity is replaced by sanity. This reconnection to the natural world returns us to our ancestral roots and reminds us that we are a part of nature. Wilderness is a necessity, not just for our own recreation, sanctity and sanity, but for the future of ourselves and our planet. It is apt to conclude this book as I concluded *The Munro Phenomenon*, with the wise words of Scotland's greatest champion of wild places, John Muir:

> Thousands of tired, nerve-shaken, over-civilised people are beginning to find out that going to the mountains is going home.[10]

Bibliography

Allan, Elizabeth, *Burn on the Hill*. Bidean Books, 1995.

Bennet, D, *The Munros*. SMT, 1985.

Borthwick, A, *Always a Little Further*. Diadem, 1983, republished.

Brown, HM, *Hamish's Mountain Walk*. Gollancz, 1978. Republished by Sandstone Press.

— (editor), *Poems of the Scottish Hills*. Aberdeen University Press, 1982.

Brown, HM, *Chasing the Dreams*. Sandstone Press, 2019.

Butterfield, I, *The High Mountains of Britain and Ireland*. Diadem, 1986.

— *The Magic of the Munros*. David and Charles, 1999.

Caldwell, C, *Climb Every Mountain*. Macdonald, 1990.

Campbell, C, *Millennial Munros: A Postman's Round*. Ringwood Publishing, 2017.

Campbell, RN, *The Munroist's Companion*. SMT, 1999.

Dawson, A, *The Relative Hills of Britain*. Cicerone, 1992.

Dempster, A, *The Munro Phenomenon*. Mainstream, 1995.

— *The Grahams*. Mainstream, 1997.

— *The Hughs, Volume 1*. Luath Press, 2015.

Docharty, W, *A Selection of Some 900 British and Irish Tops*. Private publication, 1954.

Drummond, P and Mitchell, I, *The First Munroist*. Ernest Press, 1993.

Gray, M, *The First Fifty*. Mainstream, 1991.

Haswell-Smith, H, *The Scottish Islands*. Canongate, 1996.

Johnston, H, *Matthew Forster Heddle, Mineralogist and Mountaineer*. NMS Enterprises Ltd, 2015.

McNeish, C, *There's Always the Hills*. Sandstone Press, 2018.

Mitchell, I, *Scotland's Mountain's Before the Mountaineers*. Luath Press, 1988.

Moran, M, *The Munros in Winter*. David and Charles, 1988. Republished by Sandstone Press.

Murray, WH, *Scotland's Mountains*. SMT, 1987.

Murray, WH, *The Evidence of Things Not Seen*. Baton Wicks, 2002.

Poucher, WA, *The Scottish Peaks*. Constable, 1965.

Price, RJ, *Highland Landforms*. HIDB, 1976.

Prior, C, *Highland Wilderness*. Constable, 1993.

Rowan, A, *Moonwalker*. BackPage Press, 2014.

Steven, C, *The Story of Scotland's Hills*. Hale, 1975.

Storer, R, *The Ultimate Guide to the Munros*. Luath Press, 2008.

Symonds, H, *Running High*. Lochar, 1991.

Thomson, IDS, *May the Fire Be Always Lit*. Ernest Press, 1995.

Various authors, *Scaling the Heights*. The Munro Society, 2018.

Various numbers of *SMC Journal*, *TGO* magazine and *The Scots Magazine*.

Acknowledgements

A HEARTFELT THANK-YOU must be extended to all those individuals and sources who have directly, or indirectly, supplied photographs, quotes, advice and valuable information. In particular, I would like to thank Elizabeth Allan, Hamish Brown, Donnie Campbell, Robin Campbell, Joy Hodgkiss, Hamish H Johnston, Kathy Murgatroyd, Ian Mitchell, Tom Prentice, David Stone, the Scottish Mountaineering Club, Aberdeen University Archive Department and The Munro Society. I also wish to thank my editor, Gwyneth Findlay, Jennie Renton and the team at Luath Press.

Endnotes

Introduction

1 From Foreword by Hamish Brown, in Dempster, A, *The Munro Phenomenon*, Mainstream, 1995.

Chapter 1

1 Munro, H, 'Notes on Carn Liath and Beinn Vuroch' in *Scottish Mountaineering Club Journal* volume 1, 1891, p. 243.
2 Ibid.
3 Ibid.
4 Munro, H, 'Winter Ascents' in *Scottish Mountaineering Club Journal* volume 1, 1890, pp. 20–24.
5 McNeish, C, *There's Always the Hills*, Sandstone Press, 2018, p. 28.
6 Ibid.
7 Dunbar, J (editor), *Sir William Burrell's Northern Tour, 1758*, pp. 80–82.
8 MacCulloch, J, *Highlands and Western Islands of Scotland* volumes 3 and 4, Longman, Hurst, Rees, Orme, Browne, and Green, London, 1824.
9 Ibid.
10 In Goodchild, J, 1899, p. 319.
11 Heddle to Geikie, April 1879, University of Edinburgh Library Special Collections, Coll 74/12/2.
12 Heddle, M, in *Mineralogical Magazine* volume 4, January 1881, p. 144.
13 Ibid., p. 136.
14 For a first-hand appreciation of one man's experience of shepherding in the Loch Monar area and the subsequent destruction and flooding of his Highland home, the best-selling book *Isolation Shepherd*, by Iain R Thomson, is a must-read.
15 Heddle to Geikie, April 1890, University of Edinburgh Library Special Collections, Coll 74/12/2.
16 Munro, H, in *Scottish Mountaineering Club Journal* volume

   5, 1898,
   p. 115.
17 Ibid.
18 Heddle, M, 'Minute', St Andrews Literary and Philosophical Society, February 1891.
19 Heddle to Harvie-Brown, July 1891, National Museum of Scotland Library, File 422.
20 Munro, H, in *Scottish Mountaineering Club Journal* volume 5, 1898, pp. 114–115.
21 Douglas, W, in *Scottish Mountaineering Club Journal* volume 15, 1919, pp. 214–219
22 Munro, H, Scottish Mountaineering Club Minutes, 1904.
23 Munro, H, 'Winter Ascents in the Cairngorms' in *Scottish Mountaineering Club Journal* volume 1, 1890, pp. 20–24.
24 Ibid.
25 Ibid.
26 Ibid.
27 Ibid.
28 Munro, H, 'A' Mhaighdean' in *Scottish Mountaineering Club Journal* volume 6, 1900, pp. 99–101.
29 Ibid.
30 Ibid.
31 Ibid.
32 Munro, H, 'Tomdoun' in *Scottish Mountaineering Club Journal* volume 12, 1912, pp.177–181.
33 Ibid.
34 Ibid.
35 Munro, H, in *Cairngorm Club Journal*, 1917.
36 Garden, W, in *Scottish Mountaineering Club Journal* volume 10, 1909, p. 230.
37 Ibid.
38 Ibid.
39 Reported in Tarascon, 22 March 1919.
40 Scott, J, 'Munro's Tables' from the Scottish Mountaineering Club, 1891.

Chapter 2

1   Robertson, A, *A Mountaineering Notebook*, National Library of Scotland, 1901.

2   Robertson, A, in *Scottish Mountaineering Club Journal* volume 7, 1902, pp. 10–14.

3   Robertson, A, *A Mountaineering Notebook*, National Library of Scotland, 1901.

4   Ibid.

5   Ibid.

6   Robertson, A, in *Scottish Mountaineering Club Journal* volume 7, 1902, pp. 10–14.

7   Ibid.

8   Aikman, JL, Diaries 1924–1930, National Library of Scotland, or see Campbell, R, *The Munroist's Companion*, Scottish Mountaineering Club, 1999, pp. 71–76.

9   Ibid.

10 Allan, E, *Burn on the Hill*, Bidean, 1995, Chapter 1.

11 Burn, A, Diary 1, Aberdeen University Archives Department, or see Allan, E, *Burn on the Hill*, Bidean, 1995.

12 Ibid.

13 Ibid.

14 Burn, A, Diary 4, Aberdeen University Archives Department, or see Allan, E, *Burn on the Hill*, Bidean, 1995.

15 Ibid.

16 Ibid.

17 Burn, A, Diary 5, Aberdeen University Archives Department, or see Allan, E, *Burn on the Hill*, Bidean, 1995.

18 Burn, A, Diary 7, Aberdeen University Archives Department, or see Allan, E, *Burn on the Hill*, Bidean, 1995.

19 Burn, A, in *Scottish Mountaineering Club Journal* volume 16, 1923, p. 329.

20 Robertson, A, in *Scottish Mountaineering Club Journal* volume 7, 1902, pp. 10–14.

21 Burn, A, in *Scottish Mountaineering Club Journal* volume 14, 1917, p. 22.

Chapter 3

1 Nimlin, J, 'A Hundred Times Up Ben Lomond' on BBC *Talk*, 19 April 1940. See also Thomson, IDS, *May the Fire Be Always Lit*, Ernest Press, 1995, pp. 23–24.

2 Ibid.

3 Ibid.

4 Borthwick, A, *Always a Little Further*, Diadem, 1983, p. 75. First published by Faber, 1939.

5 Humble, B, *The Cuillin of Skye*, Ernest Press, 1952.

6 Nimlin, J, 'Mountain Howffs' in *Scottish Mountaineering Club Journal* volume 24, May 1948, p. 39.

7 Traditional verse. Author unknown.

8 Plinth inscription, 2012, various authors.

Chapter 4

1 Munro, H, Munro's Tables, *Scottish Mountaineering Club*, 1891, p. 281.

2 Dawson, A, *The Murdos*, Tacit Tables, 1995, p. 17.

Chapter 5

1 Brown, H, *Walking the Song*, Sandstone Press, 2017, Foreword.

2 Ibid., 'Opening the Atlas'.

3 Reynolds, K, review of *Chasing the Dreams*, Sandstone Press, 2019.

4 Magnusson, M, review of *Highland Wilderness*, Constable, 1993.

5 Gray, M, *The First Fifty*, Mainstream, 1991, inside flap.

6 Brown, H, *The Last Hundred*, Mainstream, 1994, p. 7.

Chapter 6

1 Brown, H, *Hamish's Mountain Walk*, Victor Gollancz Ltd, 1978, p. 329. Currently published by Sandstone Press.

2 Moran, M, *The Munros in Winter*, David and Charles, 1986, p. 13. Currently published by Sandstone Press.

3 Dempster, A, *The Munro Phenomenon*, Mainstream, 1995,

p. 189.

4 In *The Great Outdoors* magazine, December 2003.

5 Cawthorne, M, *Hell of a Journey*, Mercat Press, 2000, Introduction.

6 Woods, K, online homepage comment, 2020.

7 Campbell, C, *Millennial Munros: A Postman's Round*, Ringwood, 2017, p. 8.

8 Ibid., p. 21.

9 Pyke, S, in *The Great Outdoors*, September 2010.

10 Brown, H, in *The Great Outdoors*, September 2010.

11 Ibid.

12 Pyke, S, in *The Great Outdoors*, September 2010.

13 Campbell, C, online footnote, 2010.

14 Campbell, D, online comment, 2020. See also *The Scots Magazine*, DC Thomson, December 2020

15 Ibid.

Chapter 7

1 Origin unknown.

2 Robertson, A, in *Scottish Mountaineering Club Journal* volume 7, 1902, p. 1.

3 Brown, H, *Hamish's Mountain Walk*, Victor Gollancz Ltd, 1978, *Aftermath*. Currently published by Sandstone Press.

4 *Mountain Bothies Association Handbook*. See also Allan, G, *The Scottish Bothy Bible*, Wild Things Publishing, 2017.

Chapter 8

1 Dempster, A, private log, 1988.

2 Corbett, JR, *Rucksack Club Journal*, 1911.

3 Brown, H, *The Corbetts and Other Scottish Hills*, Scottish Mountaineering Club, 1990, Introduction.

4 Docharty, W, *A Selection of Some 900 British and Irish Mountain Tops* volume 1, privately published, 1954.

5 Ibid.

6 Docharty, W, *The Supplement to a Selection of Some 900 British and Irish Tops, and a Selection of 1000 Tops under 2,500 feet*, privately published, 1962.

7   Ibid.
8   Graham, F, 'George Outram' in *The Great Outdoors*,
    November 1992.
9   Nicolson, A, in *Scottish Mountaineering Club Journal*
    volume 2, 1892.
10 Wainwright, A, Wainwright's *Favourite Lakeland
    Mountain's*, Michael Joseph, 1991, p. 103.
11 Beal, B, private letter, 1997.
12 Haswell-Smith, H, *The Scottish Islands*, Canongate, 1996,
    Preface.
13 Fallon, S, online comment, 2020.

Chapter 9

1   Origin unknown.
2   Brown, H and Gordon, A, *The Scottish Mountains*, Colin
    Baxter Photography Ltd, 2007, p. 29.
3   Firsoff, A, 'The Spirit of the Cairngorms' in Brown, H,
    Poems of the Scottish Hills, Aberdeen University Press,
    1982, p. 101.
4   Haines, M, *Fort Augustus Abbey School Newsletter*, March
    1979.
5   Burns, R, 'Tam O' Shanter', 1971.
6   Fraser, D, 'Far in the West' in Brown, H, *Poems of the
    Scottish Hills*, Aberdeen University Press, 1982, p. 103.
7   Murray, WH, *Scotland's Mountains*, Scottish Mountaineering
    Club, 1987.
8   Smythe, F, *The Mountain Vision*, Hodder and Stoughton,
    1950.
9   Pennant, T, *A Tour in Scotland*, 1772.
10 Dempster, A, private log, 1980.
11 Origin unknown.
12 Maclean, S, *The Island*, William MacLellan, 1939.

Chapter 10

1   Secretary of the National Parks Commission, 1962.
2   Stated aims of the Countryside Commission for Scotland,
    1967.

3 MacLennan, H, *Scotchman's Return*, Scribner, 1960.
4 Origin unknown.
5 Lovelock, J, *The Vanishing Face of Gaia*, Allen Lane, 2009, p. 69.
6 Povlsen, A, in the *Daily Mail*, 23 November 2020.
7 Watson, A, 1983.
8 Lister, P, in the *Daily Mail*, 24 October 2020.
9 Midgley, A, in the *Daily Mail*, 24 October 2020.
10 Muir, J, *My First Summer in the Sierra*, 1871, republished by Canongate in 1988.

Luath Press Limited

committed to publishing well written books worth reading

LUATH PRESS takes its name from Robert Burns, whose little collie Luath (*Gael.*, swift or nimble) tripped up Jean Armour at a wedding and gave him the chance to speak to the woman who was to be his wife and the abiding love of his life. Burns called one of the 'Twa Dogs' Luath after Cuchullin's hunting dog in Ossian's *Fingal*. Luath Press was established in 1981 in the heart of Burns country, and is now based a few steps up the road from Burns' first lodgings on Edinburgh's Royal Mile. Luath offers you distinctive writing with a hint of unexpected pleasures.

Most bookshops in the UK, the US, Canada, Australia, New Zealand and parts of Europe, either carry our books in stock or can order them for you. To order direct from us, please send a £sterling cheque, postal order, international money order or your credit card details (number, address of cardholder and expiry date) to us at the address below. Please add post and packing as follows: UK – £1.00 per delivery address; overseas surface mail – £2.50 per delivery address; overseas airmail – £3.50 for the first book to each delivery address, plus £1.00 for each additional book by airmail to the same address. If your order is a gift, we will happily enclose your card or message at no extra charge.

Luath Press Limited
543/2 Castlehill
The Royal Mile
Edinburgh EH1 2ND
Scotland
Telephone: +44 (0)131 225 4326 (24 hours)
Email: sales@luath.co.uk
Website: www.luath.co.uk